ADAM BUXTON

I LOVE YOU, BYEEE

ADAM BUXTON

I LOVE YOU, BYEEE

RAMBLES ON DIY TV, ROCKSTARS, KIDS AND MUMS

*For Val, Grendel, Pob, Zonuts,
Scotch Tape, Doglegs, McG, Deej, UD, CAB,
J-Corn and the Podcats*

Mudlark
HarperCollins*Publishers*
1 London Bridge Street
London SE1 9GF

www.harpercollins.co.uk

HarperCollins*Publishers*
Macken House, 39/40 Mayor Street Upper
Dublin 1, D01 C9W8, Ireland

First published by Mudlark 2025
1 3 5 7 9 10 8 6 4 2

The publisher would like to thank *Time Out* London for kind permission
to include the extract on p51, and World of Wonder for kind permission to reproduce
material in the book and clips from *The Adam and Joe Show* and *Takeover TV*
in the audio edition (full episodes available on WOW Presents Plus worldwide).

A catalogue record of this book is available
from the British Library

ISBN 978-0-00-846698-5
Waterstones ISBN 978-0-00-871542-7

Printed and bound in the UK using 100% renewable electricity
at CPI Group (UK) Ltd

CONTENTS

INTRODUCTION

Hey! How are you doing, readers? Adam Buxton here with another collection of rambles about my ludicrous life.

I'm writing this introduction in late 2024, almost five years after I finished *Ramble Book*. It's a beautiful, bright wintry day out here in the East Anglian countryside, and a little gang of pissed-looking pheasants is strutting around on the grass outside my window. They're craning their rubbery necks and looking at me as if to say, 'You're not still writing that book, are you?' Fair enough; for a book that is essentially a collection of reminiscences, it does seem to have taken a very long time to get done, but other things kept getting in the way. So, to get the pheasants off my back and to remind you of the kind of person you're dealing with here, I'm going to start this book with some excuses for why it's taken me so long to write this book.

In my professional life, I have a podcast for which I record rambling conversations with comedian friends and other interesting people. Though I take more breaks than the average podcaster, the process of researching, recording, editing and jingle-making for the podcast continues to take up most of my time. Over the last few years, I've also been gradually putting together an album of original music, which I'll tell you about later on, but that's also taken longer than it should have. In addition to all that, I do the odd live comedy show, and very occasionally I'm on TV.

The other day, for example, I was asked to appear on the celebrity version of *The Great British Bake Off* for the charity Stand Up to Cancer. Having never baked anything before, I paused my book-writing duties to do all I could to prepare for what was, for me, an unusually high-profile booking.

In case any of you have made it to this point in your life without becoming familiar with *The Great British Bake Off*, it's a televised baking contest that takes place over three rounds. Round one is the Signature Bake, in which each contestant chooses a recipe to impress the judges, currently celebrity chef Paul Hollywood and restaurateur Prue Leith. Round two is the Technical Challenge, which involves following a recipe. And finally there's the Showstopper Challenge, perhaps the most important round, in which the creativity of the bakers is put to the test.

For our Signature Bake we'd been asked to make crumpets. As a tribute to Sir Paul McCartney, a former guest on my podcast who had told me of his fondness for bagels with Marmite and hummus, I chose to make Marmite-flavoured crumpets topped with hummus made from edamame beans (I love edamame beans, and I thought it was a good bet that Macca would, too). This choice of recipe also gave me an excuse to over-prepare, which, as you'll see in this book, is something I do a lot. In this case, more book-writing time was spent recording a song in the style of 'Blackbird', in which I impersonated Sir Paul singing of his fondness for crumpets:

Paul McCartney Crumpet Song

I like crumpets
Gimme some crumpets
Stuff the doughy holes in my holey hole
Get some hummus in those holes
With Marmite, alright.
Everybody jump, it's time for crumpets
I'm a crumpet-baking strumpet
If you don't like crumpets
you can lump it
Hummus and Marmite are oozing from crumpet holes
As I stuff the crumpets in my gob
I like them light but chewy
Fluffy but gluey
Dense but airy
Tiny bit scary
Munching crumpets is my favourite job

For the Showstopper Challenge, we'd been asked to create a tribute to a favourite celebrity in the form of a pie. My first thought was to do something Bowie-related, but that seemed a bit obvious; I'm always going on about my relationship with David Bowie and his music, so I tried to think of other ways to interpret the brief.

Then, a week before the *Bake Off* recording, I was out walking with my dog friend Rosie when I was struck by one of the only flashes of inspiration I've ever had. There in the blue sky above a field of gently undulating Norfolk wheat, I clearly envisioned a cherry pie with a phallic, juice-spattered creature erupting from the centre, and I knew then that my *Bake Off* Showstopper would be a tribute to a notorious scene in one of my favourite films (*Alien*, that is, not *American Pie*).

I knew my idea would be difficult for someone with my

lack of baking skills to pull off, so in the days that followed, with guidance from Christine, a family friend and baking genius, I made several attempts at constructing a pastry baby alien that resembled the bitey little dildo creature from Ridley Scott's masterpiece. (If you're reading this book, Christine, I'm sorry your name is in the same sentence as the phrase 'bitey little dildo creature'.) Each pastry alien looked great in its uncooked form, but after a few minutes in the oven, they all fell apart. Then I hit on the idea of modelling the alien around a rigid, unripe banana stuck into an empty glass spice jar to help it stand upright in the oven.

This time, with the help of some wooden barbecue skewers, the ribbed alien sections stayed in place around the banana and baked nicely. Once the alien was drizzled with cherry juice and standing in the exploded central flaps of the pie, I marvelled at how successfully I'd been able to realise my vision. I felt sure that upon seeing the finished *Alien* pie, not only would Paul Hollywood want to shake my hand, as he does whenever a *Bake Off* contestant has impressed him, the brilliance of my creation would move him so deeply that he'd hug and kiss me too, as Noel Fielding, Prue Leith and Alison Hammond looked on and clapped, and then joined in with the hugging and kissing, though not in a way that made me feel unsafe. Once the programme was broadcast, the internet would unite in its unequivocal appreciation for me and the *Alien* pie; Ridley Scott would get in touch, begging to appear on the podcast and offering me a role in an underwhelming *Alien* franchise movie. And maybe at long last, I'd even get the call from *Taskmaster*.

All I had to do to turn this dream into reality in the *Bake Off* tent was to make the *Alien* pie in exactly the same way I'd made it in our kitchen at home.

It all started well enough. On the first day of the two-day shoot, my crumpets were decent, if a little too salty, and Alison and Noel enjoyed my Paul McCartney tribute song.

Despite a sudden bout of hay fever brought on by the exotic plants growing near the tent, I was feeling chipper and not significantly threatened in the competitive stakes by my fellow bakers, comedian Tommy Tiernan and singer Rebecca Lucy Taylor, also known by her stage name Self Esteem. Actor Meera Syal was more of a problem, as she evidently knew what she was doing and produced crumpets that everyone agreed were beautiful and delicious. Still, none of that mattered because I had an alien in my pocket.

The Technical Challenge on the afternoon of day one was to make a Lambeth cake, a three-tiered sponge construction with a filling of homemade lemon curd and buttercream icing that needed to be just the right thickness and consistency to hold the sponge and the filling in place and prevent catastrophic subsidence. How hard could it be? I just needed to follow the instructions. But after a couple of lapses in concentration, I ended up with a lopsided mound that looked like Norman Foster's London City Hall 'Snail' building plastered with yellow Polyfilla.

The thing that none of us contestants had properly appreciated was how much time during each challenge would be taken up with talking to the camera crews that roamed between the workstations. One of these followed Alison Hammond and Noel Fielding as they bantered with the bakers about what they were up to in their professional lives. At the same time, another crew, led by the *Bake Off* 'Story Producer', checked on how each contestant was progressing with the challenges. Following a recipe while chatting to a TV crew might not sound like the ultimate test of human ability, but for me, a ball of self-conscious angst at the best of times, it felt like walking a tightrope over a pit of metal spikes while being tickled with a feather duster. While making a cake.

Day two was given over to the four-hour Showstopper Challenge, and I arrived at the tent feeling confident, reminding myself not to lose perspective. We were here to help raise funds for cancer research; everything else was just a bit of fun. Oh, who was I kidding? This was an opportunity for baking immortality, and for the sake of my career and my self-respect, I couldn't afford to make any mistakes.

Not even 20 minutes into the challenge, my pastry dough was feeling weirdly sticky, and when Paul Hollywood passed my workstation, stuck his finger in the lump disdainfully and moved on without comment, I was rattled. I added flour, kneaded for a while, then stopped, worried I was overdoing it. The last thing I wanted was to be too kneady.

By the end of the first hour, I was calmer. The rest of the pie had come together as I had hoped, and I was sculpting the baby alien when the story crew returned. I waffled to them and then to Alison Hammond about my love for the first *Alien* movie, name-checking the entire cast and eulogising over the brilliance of Ridley Scott's direction and H.R. Giger's creature and set designs, before going into detail about the impact it all had on me as an impressionable 13-year-old. Alison and the crew smiled and nodded as if to say, 'None of that's making the edit.'

With pie and alien finally in the oven, I excused myself to walk briskly over to the mobile toilets outside the tent. There, I looked in the mirror as I washed my hands and was alarmed by the state of my puffy, hay-feverish eyes. However, I still felt confident that the disappointment of the Technical Challenge would soon be erased by the sight of a pastry xenomorph bursting from the centre of a beautiful cherry pie.

I was only gone a few minutes, but when I returned to the tent and saw the story crew hovering by my station, I knew all was not well. 'I think you'd better take a look in the oven, Adam,' said the story producer with an expression somewhere between amusement and concern. Bending down, I saw through the oven glass that the alien had pitched forward in its jar, and the thinly rolled pipes of dough that formed the details of the design were sagging or had fallen off, while the thicker cylindrical base section was in the process of sliding away from the banana to join the bubbling goo on the oven bottom. Had the dough been too thick? Was the oven the wrong temperature? Was the banana too ripe?

'Can you tell us what's happening, Adam? What are you going to do? Can you tell us what you're thinking?' said the story producer as the camera moved in for a close-up of my puffy face. 'Fuck' is what I was thinking as my dreams of a Hollywood handshake, Ridley Scott casting call and *Taskmaster* booking began to disintegrate. I struggled to keep my expression fun.

With time running out, the next few minutes were spent trying frantically to salvage a few parts of the alien and attach them to a new banana, but each piece of pastry crumbled, and soon all the intricate sculpting that I'd hoped would so impress the judges lay strewn around my workstation as the camera crews watched from a respectful distance. Noel sauntered over at one point, but on seeing my pained expression he ushered the crew away, saying, 'He's gone. He's in the Herzog zone. We've lost him.'

Time was up. We were told to step away from our creations. I lifted what remained of the alien carcass, by now just a baked banana with a curved pastry headpiece, and stuck it in the middle of the pie, where it stood for a moment before wilting slowly until prone. The crew filmed as I watched, apparently weeping. I explained that it was the hay fever. 'Sure it is,' said Rebecca, who came over and put a sympathetic arm around me. At that point, she represented the last of my Self Esteem.

So anyway, that was another couple of weeks when I didn't get much book writing done.

In *Ramble Book,* I wrote about growing up in the 1980s, becoming friends with Joe Cornish and Louis Theroux at school, watching a lot of 80s movies and getting into David

Bowie. I wrote about how Rosie changed my life, the challenges of being a parent and a husband, and I wrote about my dad, Nigel, aka BaaadDad, who died a few weeks before Bowie in late 2015, and the determination he grew up with to climb the social ladder and give his children every opportunity in life, even if it came at the expense of his own financial security and ultimately his marriage.

My mother never got to read *Ramble Book*, the audio version of which was released in those early lockdown days of April 2020, but I think she realised there would be a lot of stuff about Dad in there, and maybe she felt a bit sidelined or disappointed by my patriarchal bias. A month after the audiobook was released, Mum died, which seemed a bit much. If she'd wanted me to write more about her, she could have just asked.

Mum didn't die of Covid; her health was deteriorating before the pandemic took hold, but lockdown didn't help. And if it weren't for the lockdown, would I have spent so long marinating in grief as I sorted through all of Mum's belongings in isolation back in Norfolk? I even managed to extend the process by digitising and archiving not only the many boxes of photographs my parents left behind, but also the thousands of hours of video I've shot over the years, sending me on a rollercoaster of reminiscence that weaves throughout this book.

My relationship with home video started in the early 1980s when, in his capacity as travel editor of the *Sunday Telegraph*, Dad was lent a portable VCR and video camera, and as a 12-year-old TV junky, I pounced on it. To begin with, I mainly used the VCR to record my favourite comedy programmes: *The Young Ones*, *The Comic Strip Presents*, *Not the Nine O'Clock News* and *Monty Python*. Then, when I became friends with Joe Cornish, we used the camera to record ourselves imitating many of those shows and then experimenting with our own spoofs and sketches.

Joe and I filmed each other clowning around right the way through school and on into our twenties, when home video led us into an unorthodox showbiz career that blossomed in the late 1990s. That was when we made *The Adam and Joe Show*, British television's first homemade entertainment programme, though don't bother googling that claim; you'll just get a load of hits for shows about DIY.

Google might also inform you that another frequently asked question on the same topic is: 'Are Adam and Joe still friends?' Well, I hope so, although I don't know how he'll feel about some of the stuff in this book, in which I describe how two foolish 20-somethings with a fondness for taking the piss out of pop culture came to turn their friendship into a job, which, as well as happy times and wonderful opportunities, brought painful tensions that, having watched *Wayne's World*, we really ought to have seen coming.

It wasn't all competitive stress and wobbly voices, though. As you'll read, Joe and I made valuable contributions to the field of pissing about over the years, not just on television but on the radio and, before most people even knew what they were, in podcasts. I've also written about meeting and even becoming friends with some of my musical heroes, and how my mum's death and the ongoing adventure of marriage and fatherhood have encouraged me to try putting away at least some childish things in the hope of becoming a slightly less mediocre person.

Who needs self-help books when you've got Buckles? Here we go …

CHAPTER 1

HAUNTED BOXES

A couple of years ago, a listener sent me some T-shirts they'd made with some podcast-related phrases printed on them, like 'Let's Have a Ramble Chat', 'MYWIFE' and 'Shall We Go for a Walk, Rosie?' My favourite was the even more prosaic 'I'm Still in the Process of Sorting Through My Parents' Belongings'. As the T-shirt maker correctly identified, over the last decade I've probably used that phrase more than Rick Astley has said 'Never Gonna Give You Up'.

At least when my dad came to live with us we'd sorted through some of his stuff before he arrived. When Mum died in 2020, the lockdown made it harder to travel to her place and figure out what to get rid of and what to keep, so I just got everything boxed up and sent to us in Norfolk, where I could go through it all when I was ready. By that point, Dad had been dead for five years, and I still hadn't finished going through all his shit. Now I was adding another lifetime's worth of shit to the pile.

Sarah suggested I hire one of the professional house clearance companies that claim to remove the belongings of a departed loved one 'sensitively'. They set aside anything they've been specifically instructed to keep, and recycle and donate to charity where possible. As for all the non-recyclable stuff, which presumably would be the vast majority of Mum's belongings, that would be 'insensitively' shoved into bin bags, which would then be dumped in another part of the planet with all the other rubbish we don't want to think about anymore so everyone can move on with their lives.

After a parent dies, getting someone else to deal with as much of the clearance as possible is sensible advice, but as with a lot of sensible advice I've received over the years, I decided to ignore it. It wasn't that I hoped to discover valuable collector's items or priceless jewellery in among Mum's stuff, it was more that I couldn't bear the idea of letting go of something she would have wanted to pass on, something she felt would brighten our lives as it had brightened hers, something she hoped would help keep her memory alive. But mainly, I suppose, I couldn't bear the idea of letting go.

Her house in the pretty Berkshire village of Sonning on Thames was small and usually uncluttered, so I was shocked when the removal van arrived and I saw how much was inside. I guess she'd stuffed a lot of things in the attic.

Stuff

There were mountains of clothes. Dresses I remember her wearing on family holidays, the outfit she wore when I got married, the soft sweaters of her grandmother years, smart jackets for the Conservative Association all still smelling of her perfume. There were boxes and boxes of books – a more entertaining and varied selection than Pa's – and also a few dozen classical and jazz CDs, along with all the compilations I'd made Mum as Christmas presents over the years.

Then there was all the furniture. We made room for the big white Welsh dresser in the kitchen, and a couple of chests of drawers made their way to the hall despite Sarah's concerns that the house was beginning to look like an antiques shop, but there was no room for the rest. So I dragged as much as I could into the flat to join the few non-skip pieces Dad brought with him when he had moved in with us, feeling as I did so some comfort in reuniting items that I remembered being part of the family house when we lived in Earl's Court.

There was the corner cupboard that had once stood in my mum's family home in Chile before making the trip to Earl's Court, then to Clapham where, to Mum's horror, debts forced us to downsize. There, in heavy boxes, were the bound copies of early twentieth-century editions of *Punch* magazine that lived on the lower shelf of the corner cupboard. As I put them back where they belonged, I leafed through a couple for the first time since I was a toddler, when those weird cartoons and that tiny text had mystified me so thoroughly. They hadn't got funnier. I dragged in the chest of drawers that used to be in Mum's bedroom, the one I used to poke about in when Mum was out, hoping to find Christmas or birthday presents, finding instead *The Joy of Sex* wrapped in some Laura Ashley curtain material.

Box after box reminded me how much Mum had appreciated anything decorative. The brightly coloured dresses, the jazzy handbags, the flowery flip-flops, the gaudy bangles, earrings and necklaces, all of them made the trip. If anyone out there is involved with a theatrical production about flamboyant upper-middle-class women in the Seventies, get in touch. I can sort out costumes and jewellery for the entire cast.

It was important to Mum that the space she lived in looked good. I think that's where I got the urge to decorate every room I ever had and why the set of *The Adam and Joe Show* looked the way it did. Dad's interior design instincts were more practical, as was evident from the place he moved into in Newhaven after the split. His philosophy was, why spend money on furniture when you can find everything you need in a skip? Mum found that depressing. When we moved to the semi in Clapham, there was no money to get professional decorators in, so Mum did what she could herself, stripping away textured wallpaper and repainting, removing the tatty hardboard panels that ran up the sides of the stairs, then sprucing up the bannisters beneath and fixing up the old mantlepiece in the living room. But there was only so much she could do, especially with Dad so indifferent to her efforts. When she moved into her place in Sonning, she relished the freedom to make each room in the little house and every inch of the tiny garden delightful.

Several boxes were filled with the many decorative trinkets, or *objets*, that Mum had collected over the years. A good proportion of these were themselves little boxes. Silver boxes, ceramic boxes, wooden boxes and enamel boxes. A couple contained picture hooks, buttons and screws. Another contained the sixpences Mum used to put in the Christmas pudding, but most were empty. Also there, wrapped in packing paper, were several marble eggs and a bunch of marble grapes, presumably bought on holiday after a boozy lunch, because when else does a sane person think, *I simply must have those eggs made of marble! Now if only I could find some marble grapes*?

I don't mean to mock Mum's *objets*. After all, what kind of mystifyingly pointless shit will I leave behind? An inflatable *Flintstones* movie Bam Bam club. Framed *Adam and Joe* photos and magazine covers (so many that the people at the framers in Norwich started giving me looks). Broken iPods. Hundreds of every kind of USB cable. Hard drives filled with files for my YouTube videos. CDs, DVDs and cassette compilations. A framed paper plate signed by Harry Hill (with a very flattering message about one of my live shows written on it, although he only wrote the initials 'HH', so at the framers I was forced to say, 'Oh, the paper plate, yeah, it's a silly thing a comedian gave me. Do you like Harry Hill?').

Another packing box was full of pig figurines and conch shells wrapped in newspaper. Back when Mum and Dad loved each other, her pet name for him was 'Chancho', Spanish slang for 'Dirty Pig'. She would buy little pig figurines for him as love tokens. Dad's pet name for Mum was 'Conchita', from the Spanish word for 'seashell', hence the collection of conches. At Mum's memorial service, an old friend of hers, slightly pissed, asked with a lopsided grin, 'Do you know why your father called her Conchita?'

'It means shell, doesn't it?' I replied.

'Yes, but it's a conch shell, which, if you look at it, is actually rather rude!'

Great. Thanks for that. Now every time I see a conch shell, I'm going to think of my mum's fanny.

When I got around to looking through Mum's boxes of admin I felt like a burglar at first, but that gave way to a strange sense of stepping into her mind in a slightly *Being John Malkovich* way, and I spent several hours poring over the files where she'd stored her bills, bank statements, hospital appointments, minutes from meetings of her local Conservative Association, every Christmas card she ever received (thousands), letters from her mum, letters of sympathy after her sister Heather was killed in a road accident soon after Mum moved to Sonning to be near her, letters from other bereaved people thanking Mum for her condolences, filled with the set phrases everyone uses to get beyond not knowing what to say. Now and then, someone goes off-piste. 'I can't imagine ever being happy again,' says one letter.

Two large boxes were filled with stacks of embroideries that Mum had done – she took the hobby up after she and Dad separated. There wasn't much freestyle work, but they were beautiful, evidence of hundreds of hours of labour, much of it undertaken, I imagined, in front of the TV with a glass of white wine on the go. The Christmas after Mum died, Sarah had some of the embroideries made into cushion covers, which are now piled on the kitchen sofa where Rosie currently reclines in comfortable splendour. The best, most thoughtful present.

Get Back in the Moment!

The boxes that took by far the most time to sort through were those that contained photographs in the form of slides, packets of negatives and plastic shopping bags filled with prints.

There were slides from before she met Dad – a part of her life I knew nothing about. There were cake tins filled with very old photographs of relations, some dating back to the 1890s, including several of my grandfather, whom I'd never actually seen a picture of before. There were photos from our childhood that hadn't made it into the family albums that Mum put together. Some were blurry, some too dark, many featured sitting room walls with a few heads ranged along the bottom of the frame, as if Mum hadn't bothered looking through the viewfinder. She could be very artistic and always encouraged my efforts in that area, but she was not a gifted photographer.

I bought a good scanner and some professional software and started digitising in earnest, dabbing each slide and negative strip with a cotton bud dipped in cleaning fluid before loading them into the scanner in batches of 12 at a time. As the light bar clicked and groaned across the slides, I was jonesing for my next time-travel fix. Sometimes, I was presented with scenes from Mum's life before she had children, a world of beehive hairdos, groovy dresses and unfamiliar men. Other times, I'd be blasted back to weekend outings from boarding school in the early Eighties, brown cords, red sweatshirt, Brighton in the rain, melancholy picnics on the South Downs before being returned to the 'reformatory'. Then, a photo of Mum holding me, maybe a year old, outside a Winnebago on the Texas border, and I thought of her saying to me and my brother and sister after Dad died, 'When you were little, they were the happiest days of my life.'

A few weeks into my photo archiving mission, Sarah came and visited me in my Nutty Room, and seeing me hunched over the light box I'd bought, squinting at another set of negatives and looking melancholy, she asked if I might be in danger of wasting time in the present by spending so long combing through the past. I said she should tell that to historians. 'You're not a historian, though, love.'

'We're all historians,' I said. 'Whether we like it or not. The present *is all about* the past.'

Sarah blew on her tea, probably wondering how she was going to deal with the incredibly heavy slab of truth I'd just dropped on her.

'Anyway, I don't have a choice,' I said. 'These photographs are little pieces of Mum's life. I can't just throw them out without even looking at them.'

'Well, you *can*,' said Sarah, before telling me that her mum once cleared out the attic and then put most of what she found there on a bonfire, including several boxes of photographic slides that were decades old. She hadn't even looked through them. I pictured the transparencies buckling and contracting in the flames and felt a bit faint. How could someone incinerate all those captured moments and deny themselves so many opportunities to find meaning in the past, even if it did come at the expense of living in the present?

Perhaps amnesia is preferable to constantly tripping up on old times? As I searched through Mum's haunted photo boxes, I kept thinking of Doug Coughlin, the gruff Aussie bartender and mentor to Tom Cruise's character Brian Flanagan in a film that has taught me many valuable lessons: *Cocktail*. Coughlin delivers a series of no-nonsense aphorisms that he calls 'Coughlin's Laws' for his protege to live by, and his last is 'Bury the dead, they stink up the joint'.

Still, the thought of throwing out the rest of Mum's photos sight unseen felt wrong. Though some had provoked painful nostalgia, I'd also had a few moments in which I'd squinted through a magnifying glass at a sepia-toned print, and on meeting the gaze of one of Mum's relatives staring out at me from 50, 100 or even 150 years ago, I'd felt charged with a sense of connection, a feeling that we live on in each other, and that photographs are a big part of that immortality. Doug Coughlin would have scoffed, but he was a self-confessed 'logical negativist'. I'm more of a deluded hopefulist.

A Sweet Ghost

Along with the photos Mum had taken were all the pictures I'd sent her of my children over the years, including a few I hadn't seen for a while, and off I went down more memory tunnels. I stared for a long time at one of my eldest son, Frank, then aged eight, pressing the button at a pedestrian crossing in Anaheim, California. His hair was a tousled mop, and he was wearing a green Vampire Weekend hoodie, which I'd given him the previous Christmas, keen to encourage his interest after he'd said he liked a couple of their songs.

It was just after dawn on the first morning of a family trip to Disneyland. Sarah hadn't been keen on the idea of holidaying out there, but I'd pushed for it, determined to recreate memories of family trips from when I was little; Dad's travel journalism had got us to Disneyland on several deliriously happy occasions.

Jet-lagged, I'd woken at three that morning, and when I found that Frank was also up, we decided to go on a supermarket supply mission while the others were still sleeping. There was a Food 4 Less about a half-hour walk from the hotel, so we set off down one of Anaheim's soulless highways with Frank skipping ahead in the early morning gloom, pirouetting about like Michael Palin's ex-leper from *Life of Brian*.

In the vast, harshly lit supermarket, we located nappies for his baby sister, then tossed the pack between us in the empty aisle. When it hit the back of my head, Frank's gap-toothed laugh warmed up the place. By the time we got outside, it was light.

On the walk back to the hotel, we passed a Dunkin' Donuts and bought a selection. Back on the pavement, between mouthfuls of doughnut, Frank said he could recite the track listing for *Back in Black* by AC/DC, which he proceeded to do, with only a slight, shy hesitation when he got to 'Let Me Put My Love into You'. Every moment of that morning mission had been a joy.

I thought of Mum holding the photograph in her well-manicured hands and staring at it the way I was now, then tucked it back into the stack.

Exotic Mum

In more cancer-friendly times, I always tanned quickly, and in Mum's photos from our family holidays my skin is sometimes dark enough for me to pass as Mexican. 'You're brown as a berry,' Dad would say with a smile, then nodding in Mum's direction, 'It's because you've got a touch of the tar brush.' Dad was fond of the notion that Mum's Latin American heritage made her 'exotic'. I should have cancelled Dad immediately for peddling racist tropes, but as a boy, I too relished the possibility that Mum's Chilean identity made me a little more 'exotic' than most of the white, middle-class Brits I grew up around.

But if you'd ever bumped into my mum in her heyday, with her twinset and pearls and an English accent like Margo, the posh neighbour in one her favourite TV sitcoms, *The Good Life*, then you'd probably have come away thinking she was the whitest, most middle-class (sorry, Mum, *upper*-middle-class) British woman you'd ever met. You might also think she was 'glamorous' – when people sent me condolences after she died, that was the word most often used to describe her – but you probably wouldn't go for 'exotic', and not just because you wanted to avoid sounding creepy and racist.

To creepy little racist me, Mum was at her most exotic when she and her similarly glamorous older sister Heather got together, drank wine and gabbled in expressive Spanish, punctuated by peals of laughter and, in the old days, the occasional drag on a ciggie. Mum had stopped speaking to me in Spanish when I was two, after English friends suggested it would hinder her young son's development, so I never understood much of what she and Heather were saying, but that only added to the exoticism. In truth, however much Dad and I enjoyed her superficial foreignness, there had always been a big part of Mum that was more British than the average Brit.

She was born in 1939 in the Pacific coastal city of Viña del Mar, which translates as 'Vineyard of the Sea', appropriate given her lifelong fondness for wine. Several of the plotters of the 1973 Chilean *coup d'état* are said to have come from Viña, though I doubt they hung out with my mum's family, the Birrells. They were part of an exclusive community, many of whom had British parents and grandparents, and in the Birrell house, where English was spoken as much as Spanish, the kids grew up thinking of themselves as 'bi-national'.

In among Mum's boxes, I found a handful of sepia-toned photos of my grandmother, Gladys, as a young woman. In every shot, Granny wears a sad smile. She even looks a little worried in her wedding portraits, though that may have had more to do with trying to support the weight of a dress and headgear that look like a design collaboration between RuPaul and H.R. Giger.

I only have vague impressions of Granny. There were a couple of trips to Chile to visit her and my uncle Clive (no local names for the Birrell family, thank you so much), and then there were a few weeks towards the end of the 1970s when, wheelchair-bound, quiet and delicate, Granny stayed with us in London. She seems to have spent most of her time writing long letters on thin paper in a precise, only slightly spidery hand, all of which I found in rubber-banded bundles in one of Mum's boxes.

My grandfather, George (known by his middle name Adam or 'Addy'), died years before I was born. On the rare occasions that Mum talked about her family, she described Grandpa Addy as far more confident and carefree than Gladys. Studying the stiffly posed portraits of Grandpa's wealthy-looking family in the late 1800s, I can see something fun and mischievous in his expression. 'You'd have loved him,' Ma would say of her dad. 'You're very similar in many ways.'

According to Mum, Grandpa Addy made a lot of home movies with his Super 8 camera, then screened the results for the kids on his projector. I, too, am a home video enthusiast and have also forced family and friends to view the results on many occasions. Grandpa was also well known for having a great sense of humour, which I do too, and I have several awards to prove it, though admittedly I haven't been given one in a while. One of Mum's old friends also told me that Grandpa Addy had been known to amuse the kids by putting on make-up and women's clothes and pretending to be his sister. I've been asked to stop doing that.

Grandpa also loved music, which I do too, though he was a jazz nut. As a younger man in the 1920s, he and a couple of friends played in a band that would perform at local events and parties in Viña. They called themselves the Synthetic Syncopators, a self-deprecating name that acknowledged they were, in every sense, pale imitations of the contemporary artists they revered: Louis Armstrong, Sidney Bechet and Duke Ellington. I like to think that at a time when racial segregation was still the norm, Grandpa's appreciation of jazz indicated that he was more liberally inclined than many of his contemporaries. He was, after all, broad-minded and confident enough in his youngest daughter's intelligence to let Valerie drop out of school at 15 when she complained she wasn't learning anything. That doesn't seem typical of most conservative fathers in the 1950s.

As I was having this thought, I came across a photo of Grandfather Addy from 1927 posing with his bandmates at what looked like a children's party in Chile. 'Synthetic Syncopators' was painted on the bass drum, and all the band, including Grandfather, were wearing blackface. On the back of the photo, Grandma had written, 'George in his negro band'. On the news that night in June 2020, protesters were pulling down statues, and I wondered if I should burn the picture of the Synthetic Syncopators or, at the very least, write something on the back to put the photo in historical context and enable future generations to see Grandfather Addy as something more than just a terrible racist. But then what do I do with the video of me pretending to be Michael Jackson when I was 14, having darkened my skin with burnt cork as per Mum's suggestion? Don't mention it in this book, that's for sure.

So did Mum go and grab life by the throat when her racist dad let her drop out of school? Well, she was hired as a secretary in a large British tobacco company in nearby Valparaíso, which probably meant she got some free ciggies, but it was a few years before she landed the job that would change her life and lead to the beginning of mine.

At the age of 20, with help and encouragement from her sister Heather, Mum became one of the first Chilean 'stewardesses' for the state-owned British Overseas Airways Corporation, or BOAC, which later merged with British European Airways (BEA) to become British Airways. Many of Mum's flight attendant years, between 1960 and 1966, were spent in a De Havilland DH.106 Comet 4 flying the route from London Heathrow down to South America, but it was on the inaugural flight of BOAC's new Far East route in the early 1960s that she met my dad. In Tokyo, they bumped into each other at an embassy party, and Dad was smitten.

Glamour Girl

One of Mum's old friends once said that by her flight attendant years, 'Valerie had emerged as a very attractive woman despite having been a little overweight in her adolescence.' Mum's friend wasn't trying to be mean. Valerie hadn't been made to feel bad about being 'a little overweight' as a young teen; it was simply a fact that she was. But I'm sure Mum did feel bad, especially in the 1950s, when a woman's physical appearance was even more central to how they would be treated by most of society than today. Even I felt bad when I was at boarding school in 1981 and beautiful Tamsin Tucker told me I'd be quite good-looking if I slimmed down. For some people, those moments can mark the arrival of a self-consciousness that will whine like tinnitus with varying intensity for the rest of their lives. Perhaps I should sue Tamsin Tucker for historical infliction of anxiety? Or at least start a petition to get her fired? On the other hand, would I want to be sued for all the things I've said over the years that inadvertently hurt people?

Mum's life certainly wasn't ruined by her body consciousness, but it was an aspect of her personality I was aware of from a young age, and it was certainly one that I absorbed myself.

For most of the 1970s, going to the gym and talking about 'nutrition' was something only weirdos and Californians did, so Mum tried to stay slim and maintain her looks by following faddy advice from women's magazines and the *Daily Mail*. Later on, she relied on Weight Watchers, diet shakes, lunches of crisp bread and lettuce leaves and a variety of skin-toning strategies. On days when Dad was away, as he usually was, I remember Mum in the basement kitchen of our house in Earl's Court repeatedly patting the underside of her jaw and holding out her arms at right angles, describing little circles with her hands. In the evenings, as a special treat, she might watch TV with a glass of wine as a small electric current pulsed through the muscles in her tummy, thighs and underarms, delivered from pads connected to a big battery pack that she wore on a belt, like a kinky commando. These and other weight-loss gadgets were in her boxes, carefully wrapped in plastic bags should one of her children or grandchildren ever feel the need to gently electrocute themselves in the pursuit of hotness.

Luv

A stack of more recent photographs included several snaps of Mum in her seventies, out and about with a man I didn't recognise. He was around the same age as Mum, maybe a little older. I worked out that he was a widower called John, possibly a pilot she met in her flight attendant days whom she had reconnected with after moving to Sonning. Along with the photos were several Christmas cards John had sent Mum.

> *To my darling Valerie. Hope you have a lovely Christmas and hope to see you again before too long. I luv you. John*

Mum never mentioned she had a boyfriend. Perhaps she was too embarrassed? She was religious, a regular churchgoer to the end, and she and Dad never got officially divorced, so maybe she felt it wasn't appropriate to be romantically involved again, though my brother, sister and I wouldn't have minded. We would have been happy that she was happy. Maybe she thought we wouldn't like him because he spelt 'love' 'luv', which wasn't the spelling generally favoured by the upper middle classes. I don't know. She never talked about her life in Sonning. Maybe we never asked.

With each Christmas card John's handwriting got more spidery, and then, beneath another sheaf of pictures, I found his obituary notice from June 2017. Thinking back, this was around the time Mum started to go downhill physically and mentally.

Oh God, More Photos

I left Ma's boxes alone for a few months, but one weekend, when we had friends coming to visit, Sarah said she needed a couple of extra bedside lamps and wondered if we might find any in the boxes from Mum's house that still sat in the shed waiting to be unpacked. In we went and discovered more books, china, glassware and around 300 DVDs of classic movies that had been given away free with the *Daily Mail*, but no lamps.

Instead, I came across a couple of plastic shopping bags stuffed with more old photographs. My heart sank. I knew I wouldn't be able to resist looking through them all, and I knew I'd pay for it.

Half an hour later, in my office, I was staring at a couple of snaps taken on board the *QE2* in 1970, when I was about nine months old, and Mum and Dad were still enjoying the novelty of having their first child.

In one photo that Mum must have taken, Dad had me propped up on his knees as he reclined on a deck chair, and she'd caught him looking uncharacteristically happy and carefree. Another photo, taken by Dad this time, showed baby Buckles being held by Mum on her lap and grinning. I stared at it hard, convinced I knew how Dad felt about us at that moment: his son in the red sailor hat, his glamorous wife in her towelling robe and white turban. He didn't know yet that his little boy would not be going to Oxford or getting a proper job, and would instead earn a living from making fart jokes and pretending to be a dog on a podcast.

I was sure I knew too what was going on in my nine-month-old head. I would have been feeling that Mum and Dad were the absolute shit. Just the most fun, interesting, great-looking people in the world. And now they're gone. Not just a few hundred miles away, but removed from the whole universe.

So why am I not more grateful for photos, where at least images of them live on? Because photos are violence.

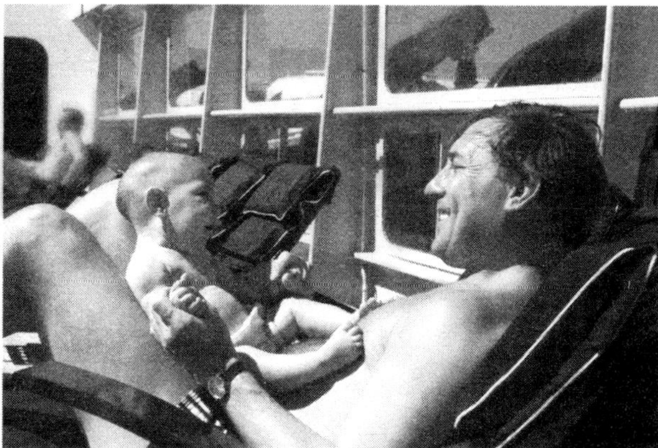

TOO CLEVER
ADAM BUXTON

CHAPTER 2

THE PATH TO MEGASTARDOM

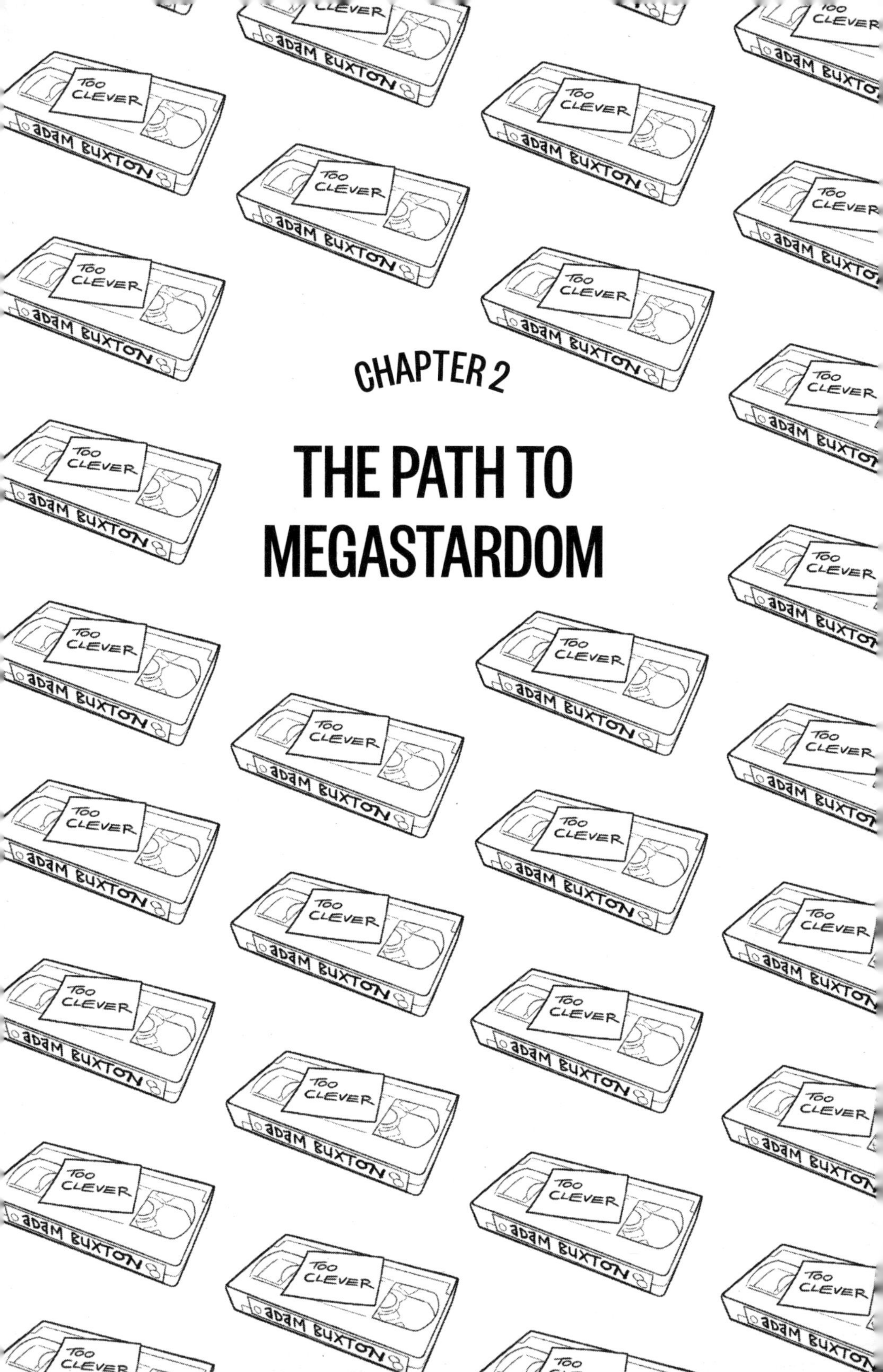

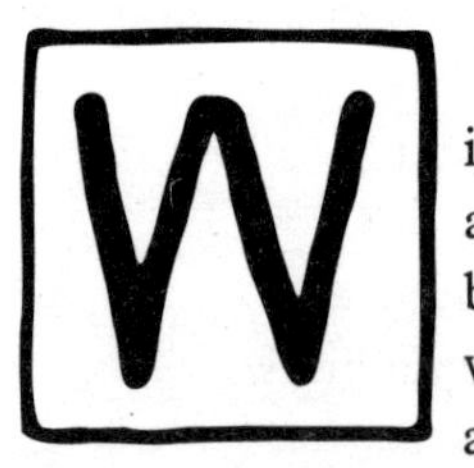

ith hindsight, it seems obvious that I should have applied to art school when I was doing my A levels, but my tutors at Westminster made it clear that I was unlikely to get into the Slade and that studying art anywhere else would be tantamount to taking a dump on the costly conveyor-belt of excellence my parents had sacrificed so much to place me onto. So, after retaking some A levels, I scraped in to Warwick University to study English and American literature, hoping vaguely that I might follow in Dad's footsteps and somehow earn a living from writing. But I left Warwick before the end of the first term due to poor finances, creative differences with my tutor and a dose of psychedelic mushrooms that disconnected me from my reflection and made my willy shrink to the size of an acorn (see *Ramble Book*, Chapter 20).

Back in London, I divided my time between bartending jobs in the West End, watching a lot of late-night TV and making daft videos with Joe on his weekend visits from Bournemouth, where he was at film school. Who knows how long I would have drifted aimlessly if it hadn't been for Miriam, a restaurant co-worker I'd been seeing for a few months before I went to Warwick. She'd been spooked when I started bandying around the 'L' word ('Love', not 'Lesbianism'), but our relationship got a boost when Miriam, who was a few years older than me, resolved to curtail her own drifting and devote her life to art. For a while, we became a couple of crazy art-loving kids scampering between life-drawing classes and exhibitions of pretentious bollox by day, guzzling wine, smoking cigarettes and waffling about land art, kinetic sculpture and postmodernism by night. After just a few months, we felt ready to take the next step and apply to art school.

The honeymoon ended when Miriam got into her first choice of course, which was also my first choice of course, but I didn't get in. Of course. I got onto a different course, and though my relationship with Miriam disintegrated soon afterwards, thanks to her I was finally on a path that would eventually lead to me revolutionising the worlds of DIY TV comedy *and* podcasting (OK, yes, that is a stretch, but I think that's the sort of thing you're supposed to say in books like this).

Who Arted?

After completing a one-year art foundation in East London, I got a place at Cheltenham College of Higher Education for a three-year degree course in sculpture, which, I was told, didn't really mean 'sculpture' in the traditional sense. On this course, you could carve blocks of stone if you really wanted to, but you could also paint your genitals blue while singing Kate Bush songs, and as long as you could cobble together some art jargon to explain what your piece was 'dealing with', it would count towards your degree.

After a few terms, I decided my work 'dealt with' television. It felt good to think the thousands of hours I'd accumulated staring at the boob tube were finally being put to use as I produced a series of pieces that combined my familiarity and affection for TV with the doom-laden contempt for the medium I'd absorbed from Dad. My work included a wooden effigy of a newsreader containing a tape recording of me reciting invented news reports that it was later pointed out to me sounded like the satirical radio programme *On the Hour* but not as good. I built a padded cylindrical cell, the ceiling of which was a back-projected image of hypnotically revolving video-feedback patterns I'd made by pointing the camera at a television screen while the screen was displaying what the camera was shooting. I constructed a giant kaleidoscope attached to a TV screen to create the illusion of a huge video ball suspended in a black space displaying a fast-cut mash-up of footage from gameshows, the news, adverts, porn, Disney movies and Richard and Judy. All of this was dealing with the deterritorialisation of visual and emotional aesthetics in the modern mediasphere. I wouldn't expect you to understand it, but trust me, it was some deep, very subtle shit.

As knottily intellectual as my work could be, it also included humour from time to time, but I quickly got the sense that in the fine art world, making people laugh was considered a cop-out. The prejudice seemed to be that art was deep and humour was superficial, so I shouldn't try to mix the two. I suspected it was the more vacuous parts of the art world that were sending these signals because they didn't want to be laughed at, or maybe they were right, and I was just a bad artist. Whatever, as far as I was concerned, the self-important and wilfully obscure fine art exhibitions that our tutors encouraged us to visit usually contained only a fraction of the craftsmanship and the interesting, subversive ideas on display in an episode of *The Simpsons* or *The Larry Sanders Show*, which were then just a few years old. I came to realise that American TV shows like these, as well as *The Monkees*, *The Kelly Monteith Show* and *Moonlighting* before them, also contained examples of a concept that kept coming up in our lectures: postmodernism.

Hyperreality Bites

Trying to decipher what exactly postmodernism meant via critics and philosophers like Jacques Derrida, Roland Barthes, Umberto Eco and Jean Baudrillard invariably left me feeling sleepy and stupid (though that may also have been related to my excessive consumption of Crunchy Nut Cornflakes around that time). As far as I could tell, an important part of what lay between the 'simulacra', the 'mimesis' and the 'sliding signifiers' boiled down to moments in which a piece of art in whatever medium stepped outside of itself and went 'metatextual', thereby incorporating and acknowledging its own artificiality. On TV, that would happen when the 'fourth wall' was broken and characters addressed viewers directly. I found that exciting because it felt like being invited into a VIP area of heightened reality beyond the velvet rope of theatrical bullshit.

The other aspect of postmodernism I liked was the sense that anything could be art, depending on how it was 'framed'. Traditional ideas of what constituted 'high' or 'low' culture were for old farts, and now there was as much meaning and beauty to be found in garish commercial imagery and cheap product packaging as there was in a Bach concerto or a Van Gogh sunflower. 'Nonsense,' scoffed Dad at our next family get-together. 'If you get rid of good and bad, then nothing means anything, and you're left with chaos.' He opened another bottle of wine.

'It's empowering!' I protested.

'It's nihilism,' he shot back, filling his glass.

'Nihilism!' chuckled Mum darkly and rolled her eyes. 'I think it sounds fun, Adam.'

Whatever Mum and Dad thought about my artistic and philosophical direction, I put my money where my mouth was and used my earnings from bartending and DJing at the Rock Island Diner, a Fifties-themed restaurant in Piccadilly

Circus, to buy a second-hand camcorder, VCR and 4-track tape machine with which I would turn myself into a one-man postmodern media hub.

Projecting

The holy grail of my art-school-era AV purchases was a video projector, which I felt sure would take my installations to a level of weightiness worthy of Bill Viola or Nam June Paik, and I knew it would also come in handy for trippy visuals at parties and watching movies on the wall of my bedroom, a barely conceivable level of indulgence in those days. But video projectors in the early Nineties were not common, and it took me a while to establish whether a domestic version even existed.

On one occasion, around 1990, a shop assistant in a Tottenham Court Road electronics store responded to my enquiry by snorting derisively, 'You can't *project* video, mate. It's not like film. Light doesn't pass through videotape, does it?' I slunk out of the shop feeling like a moron, but a couple of years later I was back-projecting video feedback with my Sharp XV-C1E LCD Projector, and I wished I could find that condescending shop assistant and say, 'Turns out light *does* pass through videotape, after all. So who's the moron now, *mate*?'

Randy Tartt

As I couldn't play any instruments, my first musical experiments with the 4-track involved me singing over music made by other people. For one of these, I used an instrumental version of 'Guess I'm Falling in Love' by the Velvet Underground, over which I sang a song about being a performance artist I called Randy Tartt. Then I spent a few weeks making a music video for the track in which I wore a tight black T-shirt, cycling shorts and Dr. Martens, and filmed myself lip-syncing to lyrics that included:

> *I've read extensively from Derrida to Eco.*
> *My favourite artists are Rolf Harris and El Greco.*
> *I like the opera: Placido and Winfrey.*
> *High art or low art it's all the same to me.*

For one shot, I risked electrocution by wedging a little black and white TV into the bowl of the toilet in my flat and filming

'Randy Tartt', 1993

as it played back some of the lip-syncing footage. I was pleased with the results, and that night I celebrated with a Chinese takeaway and a screening of the Sean Connery sci-fi film *Outland* on the projector before nodding off to the Beach Boys *Smile* sessions from the newly released *Good Vibrations* box set.

When my finished Randy Tartt video was shown in our end-of-year exhibition, people I'd never spoken to before came up and told me how much they liked it. I may have been cocking a snook at the art world, but it was a lovingly crafted snook from a not entirely cynical cock. Nevertheless, one tutor suggested disapprovingly that I appeared to be using the course as a stepping stone to a career in television.

'The Zikestone Cowboy'

In truth, it never crossed my mind that I might one day be on TV. What seemed more of a realistic possibility was a job in radio. Towards the end of 1992, I'd seen that a new local station was opening up in Cheltenham, and I sent in a demo tape containing some of my fake news reports, spoof adverts and radio parodies. One day, a letter arrived emblazoned with the logo of the new station, CD603. To my amazement, rather than a polite rejection, the letter was an invitation to 'come in for a chat' with the boss of CD603, Paul Boon.

On a cold, bright morning the following week, I cycled out to an industrial estate on the outskirts of Cheltenham, and in a chaotic office above a small, newly fitted out radio studio, Paul, a dead ringer for moustachioed Super Mario brother Luigi in a brown leather blouson, told me he'd enjoyed my demo. 'Most of the tapes people send are just a voice on a stick,' he grinned. 'They're all trying to sound smooth, so yours stood out. What shall we do with you, then?'

Unbelievably, what Paul did was give me my own three-hour show to fill however I wanted. It was a graveyard slot on a Sunday night that was unlikely ever to be listened to by more than a handful of people, but that didn't matter. With a wave of his local antenna, Paul had transformed me from a diffident chancer into an actual broadcaster, though what *kind* of broadcaster remained to be established.

Having pegged me for a wacky sort, Paul declared that I was to be the travel correspondent on the breakfast show, with the twist that I would deliver my regular reports via walkie-talkie while riding around in Cheltenham's rush-hour traffic on a battery-powered bicycle – the Sinclair Zike – wearing a gold lamé shirt and a cowboy hat. Paul pictured me becoming a well-loved local figure, the Zikestone Cowboy, to whom cheery Cheltenham commuters would impart nuggets of up-to-the-minute travel info, but neither of us had reckoned with the wave of acute self-consciousness that swamped me on the morning of the station's launch.

I didn't mind dressing up like a tit and clowning around for customers in the DJ booth at the Rock Island Diner because there I was surrounded by friendly restaurant staff, but out on the mean streets of Cheltenham, I was just some rando dressed as a disco cowboy on an electric bike. When it came to asking strangers how traffic was moving on roads I didn't know the names of, let alone doing travel bants with Glynn, the breakfast show host back in the studio, the best I could come up with was mildly surreal nonsense.

I quickly developed a routine of cycling out from the office with a portable radio, hiding behind a nearby hedge, and then writing down the travel reports from Danny Baker's breakfast show on BBC Radio 5 before delivering a slightly reworded version for my bulletin. If Glynn asked about the roads in Cheltenham, I'd say, 'Yup, they're still there!' He'd give a chuckle, then put on some Wet Wet Wet.

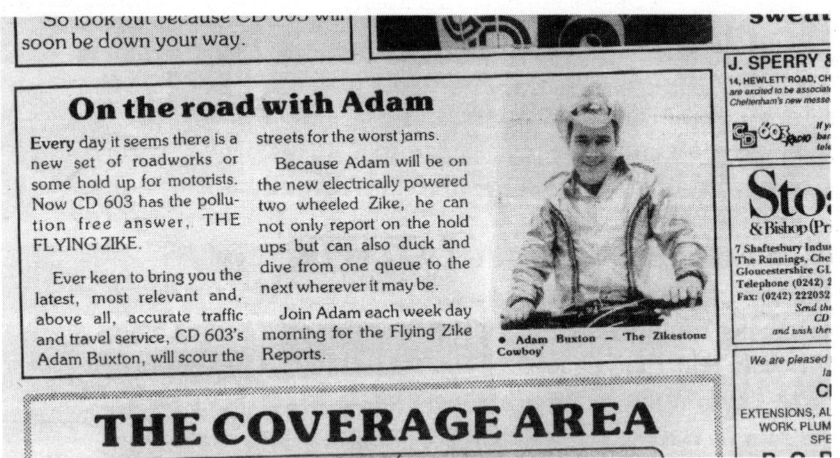

soon be down your way.

On the road with Adam

Every day it seems there is a new set of roadworks or some hold up for motorists. Now CD 603 has the pollution free answer, THE FLYING ZIKE.

Ever keen to bring you the latest, most relevant and, above all, accurate traffic and travel service, CD 603's Adam Buxton, will scour the streets for the worst jams.

Because Adam will be on the new electrically powered two wheeled Zike, he can not only report on the hold ups but can also duck and dive from one queue to the next wherever it may be.

Join Adam each week day morning for the Flying Zike Reports.

• Adam Buxton – 'The Zikestone Cowboy'

THE COVERAGE AREA

CD603's launch newspaper, March 1993

It was a relief when Paul decided to jazz down the travel reports a few weeks later, and I was able to hang up my gold shirt and cowboy hat. Instead, for the next few months, I spent hours every week writing and recording more made-up news reports, parodies and jingles for my Sunday night show.

On one occasion, Joe and our old school friend Zac Sandler joined me in the CD603 studio and, swathed in clouds of doobie smoke, we improvised a spoof arts programme with Joe and Zac as musical guests, Tarquin and Tony. The high point was their rendition of one of Zac's numbers, 'Football' (later renamed 'The Footie Song').

The low point was the long, rambling apology I felt obliged to make after Joe, both in and out of character, said 'fuck' several times on air. To my relief, the incident was never mentioned by Paul Boon or anyone at CD603 thereafter, almost as if no one was actually listening.

'Too Clever'

One afternoon in spring 1994, during my last term at Cheltenham, I was working on my second bowl of Crunchy Nut Cornflakes when I saw an ad in the *NME* asking for 'funny, weird and original home videos' for a new Channel 4 show called *Box Pops*. After worrying for about 15 seconds that I might be using my sculpture degree as a stepping stone to a career in television, I made a VHS tape of a few of my sillier art college pieces, including *Randy Tartt*, and sent it off.

Fenton Bailey, British co-owner of the production company World of Wonder, which was producing *Box Pops* (soon to be renamed *Takeover TV*), was in an edit suite in Soho putting together a reel of submissions for Channel 4, and he was feeling despondent. Fenton had hoped to find the kinds of entertainingly eccentric clips that had featured on another World of Wonder production from 1991, *Manhattan Cable*. Presented by sassy US journalist Laurie Pike, whose response to anything especially spicy was a cool 'Hello!', *Manhattan Cable* was filled with weird, titillating and hilarious clips from New York's three public access stations. When I would tune in after a bartending shift, *Manhattan Cable*'s cast of colourful attention seekers, weirdos and artists (future *Drag Race* superstar RuPaul appeared in the first episode) seemed to a sheltered Brit like me, brilliantly crazy.

Three years after *Manhattan Cable*, Fenton was wading through submissions for *Takeover TV* that tended to be less outrageous and more like short lectures on veganism, local council inefficiency and crochet. Then he came across a VHS tape on which a researcher had stuck a Post-It note that said simply, 'Too clever'. Fenton had spent most of the 80s immersed in New York's arty and hedonistic club scene with his American partner and World of Wonder co-founder Randy Barbato, and to him, 'Too clever' meant

'Interesting'. He slid the tape into the VCR, and up popped *Randy Tartt*.

Back living with my parents in Clapham after graduating, I returned from a restaurant shift one day to find a note from Dad saying a producer from a TV company had called about a tape I'd sent in. Reading that note produced a jolt of uncomplicated excitement seldom matched since.

I cycled over to World of Wonder's office opposite Brixton tube, and there Fenton told me how much he had loved *Randy Tartt*, not least he said because he and his boyfriend Randy had a band called The Fabulous Pop Tarts. 'It's a sign!' hooted Fenton. He said he'd like to include *Randy Tartt* in *Takeover TV* and suggested I might present a couple of episodes, too. Of course, I said, before realising I should try to take advantage of Fenton's enthusiasm and wangle myself a more regular position at World of Wonder. So, in the autumn of 1994, I started as a part-time researcher on *Takeover TV*. Now it was my turn to watch submissions and scribble judgements on Post-It notes, sitting a few feet away from the researcher who had delivered the 'Too clever' verdict that led to my tape getting noticed (so fuck you, but also thanks very much, Dan).

RAMBLE

PUBLIC ACCESS TV

Public access had begun in America during the early 1970s as part of an effort to democratise television and give non-showbiz types the means to create and broadcast their own content on local cable channels. Most of the time it was pretty turgid stuff which reminded viewers that production values and articulate presenters were not the worst things in the world, but occasionally something weird and wonderful slipped through that would never have made it past the gatekeepers of conventional broadcast TV.

Some public access programmes became legendary, like New Jersey's *The Uncle Floyd Show*, which aired from the mid-1970s to the early 1990s. A chaotic, semi-improvised mix of comedy characters, puppetry and music in the style of a kids' programme, *Uncle Floyd* picked up celebrity fans like John Lennon, Iggy Pop and David Bowie, directly influenced *Pee-wee's Playhouse* in the 1980s, and helped inspire the 'zoo format' style of Howard Stern and countless TV talk-show hosts that followed.

Elsewhere, musicians like Public Enemy, Nirvana and the Butthole Surfers made appearances on public access before the mainstream came knocking. Comedians Tom Green, Louis C.K., Fred Armisen, Chris Gethard and talk-show legend David Letterman all honed their skills on public access while exploring half-baked ideas and generally pissing about in a way they couldn't have done on network TV.

In the UK, there were a few experiments with local community cable TV projects in the 1970s and 80s, but nothing compared to the US. When Channel 4 launched in 1982, it was committed to including programmes you wouldn't find on BBC One, BBC Two and ITV, the only other channels available at the time. Though there were a few late-night programmes on Channel 4 that certainly had the *feel* of public access (and not always in a good way), that was as close as Britain got to the kind of thing you'd find in America.

By the early 1990s, with camcorders becoming more affordable, the BBC reached out to ordinary people from a variety of backgrounds in an effort to include a wider diversity of voices on broadcast TV. Though BBC shows like *Video Diaries* and *Video Nation* were undoubtedly worthwhile, they weren't always that much *fun*. If you wanted to see amateur footage that was more entertaining, the only alternative at the start of the Nineties was *You've Been Framed*, presented by Jeremy Beadle from *Game for a Laugh*.

As a boy watching TV on a Saturday evening in the early 1980s, too young to appreciate the joys of *Blankety Blank* on BBC1 and *The Old Grey Whistle Test* on BBC2, ITV's *Game for a Laugh* provided my first exposure to hidden camera stunts involving unsuspecting members of the public. These segments were presented by Beadle, *Game for a Laugh*'s prankster-in-chief (mis-chief, more like!!), who, in his uniform of suit, beard and cheeky smirk, looked like the annoying office joker.

On *You've Been Framed*, Beadle introduced compilations of 'camcorder cock-ups' from a candy-coloured front room set in which every object stood at a weird angle, like a toddler version of *The Cabinet of Dr. Caligari*. Joe and I referred to it as Beadle's Wonky House.

Sub-Ramble

Around 2000, I went to see American indie rock legends Guided by Voices play in London, with comedy writer Graham Linehan, who adored the band. Before the show, we met at Joe's flat in Clerkenwell's Exmouth Market, and Graham brought along his writing partner Arthur Mathews and comedian Dylan Moran, who was starring in Graham and Arthur's new Channel 4 sitcom *Black Books*. We had pre-show drinks and watched a *You've Been Framed* 'Best Of' compilation that happened to be on that evening. It was all the usual stuff – kids being knocked over by pets, people embarrassing themselves at wedding receptions, show-offs face-planting satisfyingly on holiday – but for some reason, it hit the spot so precisely that by the end of the episode each of us was hyperventilating with mirth and Graham said it was the funniest thing he'd ever seen on TV. Guided By Voices were good, but they couldn't compete with *You've Been Framed*.

What Jeremy Beadle was not serving up at the Wonky House were clips that were *intentionally* funny or more creative than the average camcorder cock-up. *Takeover TV* was the first show in the UK to do that, though, of course, not everyone agreed on what qualified as funny or creative.

'Turnover TV'

The first series of *Takeover TV* went out in spring 1995 with eight half-hour episodes hosted by a selection of the show's amateur contributors, which, as well as A. Buckles, included a pair of singing hairdressers, some feminist witches who were also strippers, and the future Xfm and Absolute Radio DJ Eddy Temple-Morris, or to be precise Eddy's bare bottom, which he called Norman Sphincter.

To become Norman, Eddy would lie on his side with his arse cheeks crudely decorated to resemble the faces of celebrities; Chris Evans, Loyd Grossman and presenter of *The Word* Terry Christian, for example. With all but his bum framed out by the camera, Eddy would reach down to wobble his arse crack while doing an impression of whichever celebrity his cheeks were decorated as. The publicity pieces wrote themselves, especially when the *News of the World* discovered Eddy's father was a Conservative MP and published a story intended to embarrass the Temple-Morris family. Eddy and his father hadn't always seen eye to eye, but his dad laughed it off, perhaps adding that as a Tory MP, he was pleased to see his son was also making a living by talking out of his arse. (Come on, *Have I Got News for You,* surely it's time to get me back on?)

The excitement of appearing on TV for the first time was only slightly diminished by the awkwardness of friends and family members who had tuned in to *Takeover TV* and then struggled to find anything positive to say about it when they next saw me. By and large, the press concurred, though the *Evening Standard*'s normally acerbic TV reviewer Victor Lewis-Smith was a fan, congratulating World of Wonder for 'striking gold by ignoring the conventional comedy formulae'. Indeed, as well as the stuff that didn't work on *Takeover TV,* there were many great clips from contributors that included nascent directors Edgar Wright and Garth Jennings, performance artist David Hoyle, aka the Divine David, comedian Leigh Francis, aka Keith Lemon, and a young comedian called Graham Norton.

However, the reviewers of *Time Out* magazine, which at school had been our cultural bible, were unimpressed. Over *Takeover TV*'s eight-week run, *Time Out* gave every single episode an effervescent pummelling. Here's a tiny selection:

> *Of course, in theory, public access TV is a highly laudable pursuit, but in practice, if this mess is anything to go by, what we end up with is a load of crap – quite literally. If you like poo-poo and wee-wee jokes, this could be for you. But I reckon they'll soon be calling this Turnover TV. If modern television isn't bad enough, camcorders are the nails that forever fasten the coffin lid of taste.*
>
> *While the proletariat may have seized the means of TV production in the shape of the camcorder, the means of distribution are still in the control of the petty bourgeoisie, resulting in this mess.*
>
> *The slogan is Takeover TV: because the medium needs a massage … A massage with a sledgehammer.*
>
> *Not so much irreverent as irrelevant. Link man Adam Baxter does a nice job of tying things together though.*

Mum was pleased by the positive mention of her son, albeit with my name misspelt, but not even she and certainly not Dad could work up much enthusiasm for *Takeover TV* itself, despite me being the show's poster boy. As well as presenting the first and last episodes, mine was the voice on the trailers, and the image from my *Randy Tartt* video of my face on the TV in the toilet accompanied much of the press for the show. I also came up with the publicity phrases 'Take the tedium out of the medium' and 'The medium needs a massage', a Marshall McLuhan reference that I was more smug about than I ought to have been.

Grimbo

The man responsible for *Takeover TV* at Channel 4 was Peter Grimsdale, who had only recently started as the commissioning editor for religion, history and features. Shows from that department were not usually expected to set the world on fire, so Peter was left to do more or less what he wanted, unbothered by ratings or reviews. He commissioned what he thought would be interesting or fun and loved Fenton Bailey and World of Wonder's pop-punk attitude to programme making. While *Time Out* was still fulminating about the awfulness of *Takeover TV*, Peter decided he wanted more and commissioned a one-off sci-fi special with me presenting, to be broadcast as part of a Channel 4 Science Fiction week in August 1995.

The only problem was that there weren't quite enough sci-fi-themed clips in the *Takeover TV* contributor bin to fill a whole programme, so Fenton asked if I'd be up for making a few new ones as long as I wasn't on camera, to avoid the show becoming too Buxton-heavy. Realising I was going to need some help, I called Joe, who at that point was working as a production assistant and office boy in a film company when he wasn't busy writing scripts, watching movies and smoking joints. He said he was up for it and came over to my parents' place in Clapham to talk about ideas.

Mum was pleased to see Joe. It was a reminder of happier times for her, when her children were all at home and money worries hadn't yet soured relations with Dad. 'Hello, Valerie,' said Joe, and I cringed. We were 26, but I still wasn't used to anyone but oldsters using my parents' first names. It just seemed cheeky, the kind of thing my dad found impertinent, but in those days Cornballs was in bumptious 'cheek' mode more or less permanently. Anyway, Mum didn't mind. 'I draw the line at "Val",' she would say.

'Now, Valerie, do you think you might have any of Adam's old childhood toys lying around somewhere?' asked Joe.

Mum said she'd look, and she disappeared for a few minutes before calling us up to the top landing. There, we found her peering down from the loft where she had, almost literally, hit the motherlode.

The two big boxes Mum passed down to us contained my old *Star Wars* toys, which she'd stashed when, as a young teen, I'd pulled focus from action figures to Bowie, booze and heartbreak. There in the boxes were the Landspeeder, the X-wing, the Troop Transporter, the Millennium Falcon, the Droid Factory, the Creature Cantina and the Death Star playset, all dusty but in decent shape. There, too, was my collecting case bulging with the figurines that had meant so much to me in the years it took to accumulate them. They were smaller than I remembered but the scuffs, the chewed lightsabres and the soles of the little feet with my initials scratched in by compass point were all as familiar as the marks and scars on my own limbs.

Childish Things

Much as I loved seeing my *Star Wars* toys again, I was initially sceptical about Joe's suggestion that we use them to film a piece for *Takeover TV*. When *Toy Story* was released in the UK the following year, the comedic potential of childhood toys (as distinct from puppets) suddenly became blindingly obvious, but in late summer 1995 my only reference for anything similar were kids' shows of my youth, like *Thunderbirds* or *Michael Bentine's Potty Time*. We hadn't yet seen American director Todd Haynes' 1987 student film *Superstar*, in which he used Barbie dolls to dramatise the tragic story of Karen Carpenter, but my instinct was to use the *Star Wars* toys in a similarly adult way and stage mini-domestic dramas with them. I imagined a married Stormtrooper couple arguing about money at the dinner table the way Mum and Dad did. Luckily, Joe, who, in his youth, had spent many hours recreating James Bond films with his Playpeople, convinced me we should try something less dreary and more childish.

The premise for the first toy sketch we filmed was that peace had broken out in the *Star Wars* galaxy, and Darth Vader had built a new space station called the Disco Star that looked like a big mirror ball. Bored one Friday night, Luke and Han go to check it out and have to get past a couple of Tusken Raider bouncers who keep saying 'Sound' in a Cockney accent, as in, 'Yeah, *sahnd*, mate, saaahnd' (cos they're '*Sand* People'!). Once inside, they join assorted alien ravers in the Trash Compactor while DJ Vader spins the tunes.

As soon as we'd suspended Luke and Han's Landspeeder with thread from Mum's sewing kit and filmed it flying over an undulating duvet desert lit by table lamps, my reservations began to evaporate, and Joe and I spent a happy afternoon filled with the sort of low-stakes goofing we might have been indulging in 10 years earlier. At one point, Mum poked her head into my bedroom, and I saw her get misty with nostalgia. Or maybe she was wondering when her 26-year-old son was going to stop playing with toys and become a productive member of society.

Later, at World of Wonder's Brixton office, *Takeover TV* editor Jon Willis showed me how to use the edit suite to cut our footage together, and he chuckled away gratifyingly at what we'd recorded. The finished Disco Star clip ended up at the top of the Sci-Fi Special, credited to 'The Totties', and it felt pleasingly novel at a time when *Star Wars* nostalgia and meme culture had yet to achieve their fully crazy cultural dominance.

Far more likely to be spoofed in those days was *Star Trek*, another sci-fi mega-franchise that I'd never much cared about until 1992 when, one evening in my mouldy room in Cheltenham, I watched an episode of *Star Trek: The Next Generation*. It was the first of a two-parter called 'The Best of Both Worlds', in which Captain Jean-Luc Picard is abducted by the Borg, a race of cybernetic beings who roam the galaxy, assimilating all those they encounter and turning them into robot zombie members of a collective that looks like a leather fetish party in a Berlin techno club. From then on, I was hooked, hungrily consuming all seven seasons of *TNG* and falling in love with the crew of the *Enterprise*-D, especially the paternal Picard, the brave but emotionally inarticulate Klingon Lieutenant

Takeover TV *Sci-Fi Special, August 1995 – Louise in Worf uniform (with Disco Star hanging behind).*

Worf, and Data, the android who wishes he could have human feelings. When the final episode of *TNG* aired in 1994, I cried because I knew something great had ended.

I channelled this slightly obsessional relationship with *TNG* into another clip for the *Takeover TV* Sci-Fi Special, in which I sang a song about *Star Trek* as a male character called Louise, the kind of socially awkward superfan whose appreciation for their favourite TV shows sometimes borders on the unhealthy (the typically female name for the male character was meant to emphasise the awkwardness). As a tribute to Lieutenant Worf, I made Louise a yellow *Star Trek* uniform, tin foil badge and sash, then, with a straggly old black wig that Mum actually used to wear before she had children and some brown plasticine that I moulded into rising furrows, I constructed a Klingon headpiece and Worf goatee. No one could have accused me of phoning it in, although the cultural appropriation was off the charts.

STAR TREK: THE NEXT GENERATION SONG

Star Trek: The Next Generation
You're loved throughout the nation
You're my favourite show
(I've seen every episode)
You're lucky, you don't have to wait for buses
You just step into the transporter
And off you boldly go
Mr Worf's my favourite person
Because he's very strong and large
Jean-Luc Picard is fair but hard
He has to be, cos he's in charge
When I found out that it was ending
I wrote them a letter
To say they had to die

(They sent policemen round to see me)
Now, my whole life is rather empty
Because you've gone and left me
Where did you boldly go?

Still More Takeover TV

Peter Grimsdale was delighted with the Sci-Fi Special, and when he commissioned a second series of *Takeover TV* towards the end of 1995, I was given the job of presenting all eight episodes, with Joe joining me as co-writer/director.

The Takeover TV *II set with art-school feedback patterns on the TVs.*

Though it quickly became clear that this particular presenting gig was not going to make me rich, World of Wonder at least subsidised the rent for a flat in Brixton Hill on the understanding that it would double as a set where I could shoot my links using a Hi-8 camera and three little ARRI lights. So I packed up my postmodern bedroom media hub in Clapham, and Mum drove me over to Brixton. There, I got to work building a set in the living room with stacks of VHS tapes and second-hand televisions bought from flea markets, piled one on top of another, many of them displaying the video-feedback patterns I'd made at art school.

Dawn of Ken

The links for *Takeover TV* II were a combination of straightforward pieces to camera, which I'd often shoot on my own late at night, and more elaborate parodies and sketch items, which I tended to make with Joe. We shot more bits featuring superfan Louise, got my dad to play me as an old man for one link, and Joe had an idea for another character I could play who was the editor of a video-hobbyist magazine Joe had made up called *Can I Camcorder Now Can I?* 'He's called Ken Korda,' said Joe. 'He gives tips and hints from his video workshop. I thought you could wear this wig I found in my mum's cupboard.' I put on the cropped, straw-coloured wig, then turned it backwards, and that made us laugh. So, with the look nailed down, the next thing was to decide on a voice. I ran through all my usual favourites: cheesy TV presenter guy, brash Australian bloke, boring nerd man and then a strangled muppet voice that owed a lot to Vic and Bob and Harry Enfield, and that seemed to do the trick (though Ken Korda's voice continued to change throughout the series and indeed ever since).

Ken eventually became a polymorphous pretentious media twat/entrepreneur in *The Adam and Joe Show*, but in *Takeover TV* II he was just a strange man with a weird voice and some odd ideas about filmmaking. 'Want to know how to get an expensive-looking filter effect on a budget? *I'll tell you!*' shouted Ken before smearing strawberry jam on a camcorder lens. 'Want to know how to make a blue movie but don't know anyone willing to have sex on camera? *I'll tell you!*' shouted Ken before showing a close-up of a frankfurter being pushed into a wine bottle while milk was poured over it. 'Want to know how to be taken seriously as a director? *I'll tell you!*' shouted Ken before cutting to a shot of himself wearing a fake fur coat and a baseball cap, filming his sister Kerry (played by Joe in lipstick and a long orange wig) reading a letter that began 'Dear Mr Fitzgibbons' while Ken shouted, 'Action!' and 'Cut!' at random intervals, in between turning to smile proudly at the camera. And at the end of each segment, Ken would say, 'I'm going now, byeee!'

My Toyfriend's Back

Recalling how much everyone had enjoyed the Disco Star sketch in the Sci-Fi Special, Joe suggested making a toy tribute to one of the year's biggest movies, *Apollo 13*, starring a future guest on my podcast, Tom Hanks (or, to give him his full name, which several of my listeners used after I failed to get the best out of him, 'What Happened with Tom Hanks?').

This time, instead of the *Star Wars* figures, we used a Humpty Dumpty knitted by my granny, which was joined in the space capsule we'd made out of a grey plastic bin by a couple of pleasingly insane-looking refugees from the Cornish toy box. *Appallo 13* was the only toy parody we made for *Takeover TV* II, and it featured a queasy mix of childish puns and attempts at more edgy material (what would Granny have made of the joke in which Humpty confesses to having once 'slept with underage kids'?), but it helped add some visual variety to a show that was otherwise dominated by grainy footage of nerdy blokes.

When it was broadcast in July 1996, the second series of *Takeover TV* was met with far more enthusiasm from viewers and critics than the first. A particular thrill was having DJ John Peel, hero of all the hard lads back at school, calling me 'droll' in a positive mention of the show for his *Radio Times* column. *The Telegraph* didn't agree and thought I was annoying, but I didn't mind because somehow we'd won over the reviewers at *Time Out*. Yes, they still found some parts of *Takeover TV* 'appalling', but they also said it was 'compelling', 'very funny' and 'addictive'.

Fenton said that Peter Grimsdale wanted to know if we had any other ideas for programmes, and, not for the last time, Louis Theroux came to our aid. Louis was living in New York at the time, and he sent us a tape of a show called *Squirt TV*, originally broadcast on public access and made by 14-year-old Jake Fogelnest in his bedroom. The show, which contained pop-culture-themed reports and sketches, had recently been picked up by MTV, and it encouraged us to think that a whole show about pop culture, in which everything was made by Joe and me, might work in the same sort of way.

The only thing that had crossed my mind, albeit fleetingly, was how working with Joe on a more full-time basis might be a bit strange. Ever since we'd become friends at school ten years earlier, I'd tended to think of Cornballs as the senior partner in our relationship – at least creatively. So, when we were working on *Takeover TV*, it felt odd to have that dynamic shift. I knew Joe was aware of it too. When I first invited him to get more involved, he said, 'I'll work with you, but I'm not going to work *for* you.' The truth was, despite our friendship, we were both, in our own ways, insecure and competitive. We just didn't realise how much yet.

YES
NO
AB
GHI
NOPQ
STU
Z
12
67890
GOODBYE

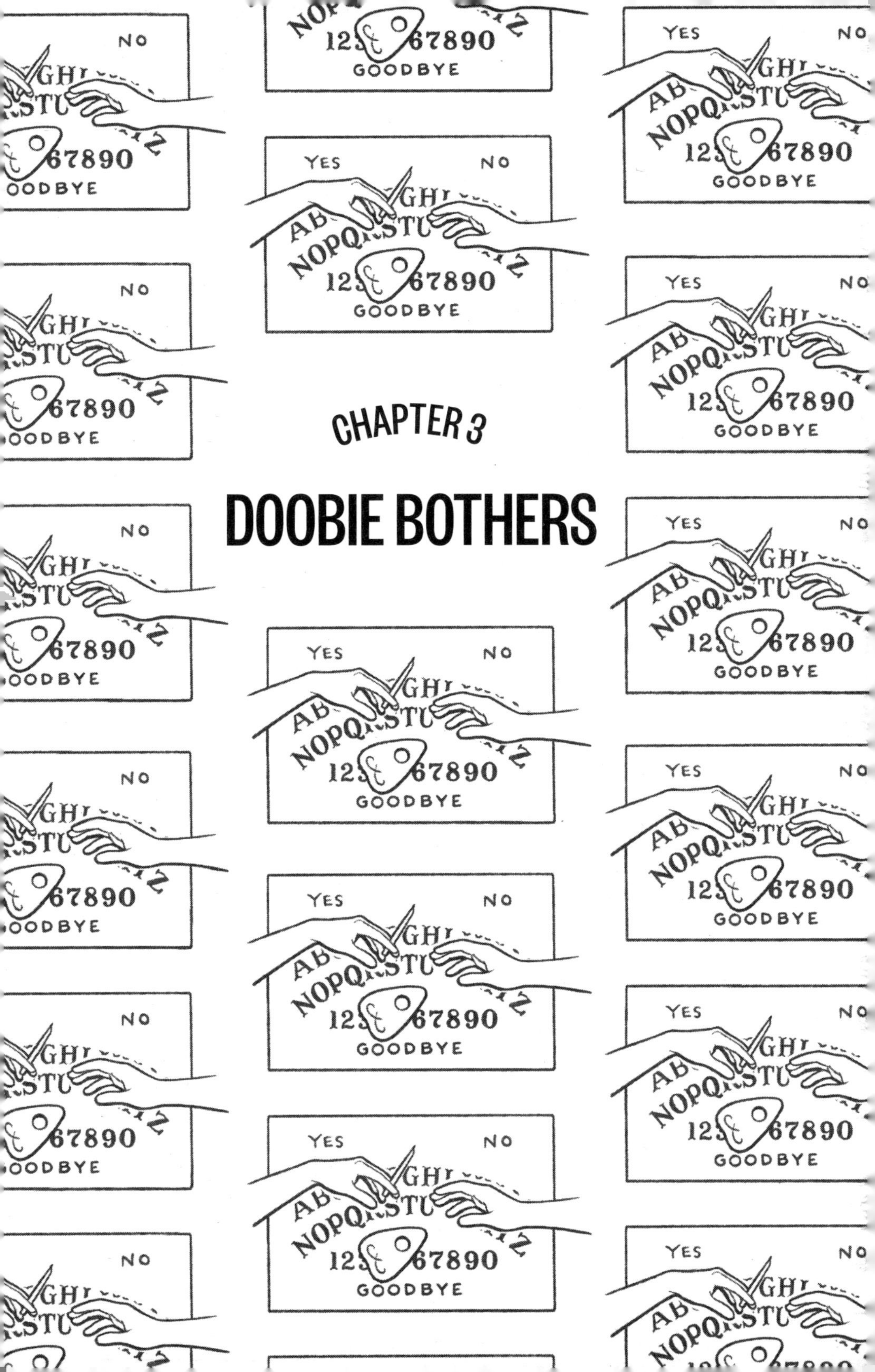

CHAPTER 3

DOOBIE BOTHERS

The two things Mum warned me against most emphatically when I was little were Drugs and Witchcraft.

When I was sent to boarding school aged nine, it was the Witchcraft she worried about more than the drugs. I think Mum imagined that some night after a midnight feast in the dormitory, someone might produce a Ouija board, and her little boy would end up being groomed by an evil spirit. If she had other worries about sending her child away at such a young age, I didn't hear about them. It was the Ouija board danger she really hammered home.

For those of you squares who haven't tried to contact the dead, a Ouija board (also known as a talking board or witch board) is a flat piece of wood with letters, numbers, and the words YES and NO painted on it. People wishing to chat with the departed sit around the board, and each one places a finger on a moveable indicator known as a planchette that, in theory, can be controlled by spirits to spell out messages from beyond the grave.

This wasn't the sort of thing I had expected my otherwise sensible mother to warn me about, and when she did, I asked, 'Do you think ghosts are real, then, Mummy?'

'I don't know if they're real or not,' she replied. 'No one *really* knows. But if there *is* another place and evil spirits are trying to cross into our world from there, why take the chance of opening up a portal by using a Ouija board?'

Mum's warning stayed with me, but one evening at

boarding school when I was 14, I went to visit my friend Patrick in the common room of his house, where I found him and some pals in a state of jittery excitement. Sure enough, one of them had got hold of a Ouija board and was proposing a séance. Keen, as ever, to be accepted by the group, I pushed Mum's words to one side and apprehensively joined in. Within minutes of dimming the lights and asking the spirit world if anyone wanted a chat with some post-pubescent public school boys, the planchette twitched. There followed a round of passionate denials that anyone had moved it themselves, after which we stared wide-eyed at one another, suddenly sombre. This was serious. We had a spirit on the line.

'What is your name, spirit?' asked Mayilone Arumugasamy. My heart pounded as the planchette lay still for a long while; then it stirred again, travelling smoothly over the board to a series of letters: B-Z-L-A-L-A-S-Z-S. Mayilone looked up. 'How do you think you pronounce that?'

'Maybe "Blallaz"?' said Patrick Dickie.

'Oh, shit. That sounds *ancient*,' said Nick Burton.

Images of reanimated mummified corpses flooded my head as, tremulously, I asked Bzlalaszs, 'Are you ... an *evil* spirit?' This time, there was no hesitation. The planchette shot directly to 'YES'.

We screamed and ran out of the room, laughing but a bit freaked out. At least, I was freaked out, and for the next few days I worried that I'd ruined my life by inviting an evil spirit into it. I think that was the reason for Mum's Ouija board warnings; if you're extremely intelligent, highly imaginative and unusually sensitive (tick – tick – tick), then dabbling in the supernatural can easily scramble your head. I'm glad to say that so far, I haven't been aware of any problems being caused directly by evil spirits (unless our Wi-Fi issues here at Castle Buckles have something to do with Bzlalaszs), but since that one Ouija board session, I've stayed away from active involvement with Witchcraft.

As for Drugs, I did stay away longer than some of my friends, but I eventually managed to develop one of the more pathetic Class B dependencies the entertainment world has ever seen.

As a young teenager, Mum's warnings and the government's 'Heroin Screws You Up' campaign, which ran on TV and in cinemas during the second half of the 1980s, frightened me off experimenting with any illegal drug that might make me vomit, go crazy or die (still three of my least favourite things). But by the time I'd turned 20 in 1989, a decade of desperation not to miss out had led to me trying marijuana, magic mushrooms and Ecstasy. I found all of them alarming to varying degrees and always much preferred booze. Drinking made me feel more confident and enjoyably different, and, unlike marijuana, alcohol didn't trap me in a state of fearful paranoia that might last hours or induce an incapacitating

attack of faintness which, due to the sufferer's pallid complexion, was known as a 'whitey'.

The worst that would happen with booze was that when I went to bed and closed my eyes after drinking too much, the room would spin (I called this Falling off the Edge of the World syndrome), a problem that could be dealt with by heading to the toilet and sticking a couple of fingers down my throat to induce vomiting. It wasn't pleasant, and I knew it couldn't be good for me (the first time I made myself sick, the force of the puking burst a load of blood vessels in my face, and I emerged from the toilet looking like I had measles), but it was the price that sometimes had to be paid for the fun that came before: the fun of taking a holiday from myself.

Me, my brother David, Joe Cornish and Louis Theroux posing as 'Champagne Charlies' for my mum on Christmas Eve, c. 1995

For my school friends and me, alcohol had been the drug of choice throughout sixth form, but by the time people started heading off to further education a year or two later, I was one of the few in my social set who hadn't yet transferred their allegiances to marijuana.

In the early Nineties, I worked as a bartender in several West End restaurants, and I loved the social aspect of alcohol. Going out to bars after work, drinking cocktails and meeting new people from different backgrounds was, to me, far superior to sitting around beneath Indian wall hangings purchased on gap-year trips (or in the souks of Notting Hill), listening to noodly music that went on for ages and laughing helplessly for reasons that were infuriatingly obscure to anyone who wasn't stoned, spaced, mashed, baked, bombed or boxed.

In those days, everything about the routines and habits of the drug smokers irritated me, from the infantile lexicon ('Giggles', 'Munchies', 'Blims', 'Blowbacks', 'Bongs', 'Bumsucks' and, of course, 'Doobies') to the unfunny movies that were supposed to be *so hilarious* if you were sufficiently wasted (have you ever tried to sit through a whole Cheech and Chong film *without* being heavily medicated? It's bleak). One of the things that wound me up most was the tone of moral superiority when I would say I preferred a cocktail to a joint. 'No one ever got addicted to marijuana, man,' I was told. 'And it's so much better for you than alcohol. Doobie doesn't ruin lives the way that alcohol does, but because it's not addictive, the government can't make as much money off it, so they make it illegal. You should really listen to Bill Hicks; he's got it all sussed.'

I knew some of that was probably true, but other parts were definite bollox, and I couldn't deal with the smug, eyes-closed, blissed-out expressions of the stoners that seemed to say, 'I'm connected to the universe in a way you could never be with your yobbish beer, *maaan*.' It seemed the only time it was acceptable to get excited about beer was when there was a big football game on, and if there was one thing I hated more than doobie, it was football.

RAMBLE

WHAT DO YOU DO WITH A BALL?

At art school, I'd watched the Noam Chomsky documentary *Manufacturing Consent*, and if friends were foolish enough to ask, 'Ads, man, what's your problem with football anyway?' I'd reply, 'Football is a way of building up irrational attitudes of submission to authority and group cohesion behind leadership elements. It's training in irrational jingoism, man.' Though this kind of talk never actually got me slapped, it did provoke some very slappy expressions. As ever, there was a part of me that wished I could join the footie set, but I didn't have the skills and, more importantly, I just couldn't work up any enthusiasm for the game itself. All I could see were shouty, occasionally violent men getting very stressed, while not very much happened.

In mid-Nineties Britain, that attitude to football was what would now be termed 'problematic', because football was everywhere, a central feature of a newly prosperous and confident British society in which celebrity footballers hung out with comedians, musicians, actors, writers and TV presenters, all of whom loved football with religious fervour.

But the more we were all supposed to be excited about the Game of Two Halves, the more I resented it.

My football-loathing ally was Joe Cornish. If we were round at our friend Mark's house while he was trying to watch a game, Joe and I would amuse each other by providing our own stupid commentary. *'And here's Jenkins ... it would make him so happy if the ball went inside the goal, and he's moving it over there with his feet, but Sancho wants to make the ball go somewhere different, and he's using his lovely legs to go very close to Jenkins and jiggle about ... it's confusing Jenkins.'*

The acme of stupid football commentary was Alan Partridge on *The Day Today*, but whereas Partridgisms like 'Liquid football!' and 'Eat my goal!' appeared to come from a place of affection for the game and familiarity with the language of the professional commentators, Adam and Joe commentaries were more, well, annoying.

It wasn't long before we were banned from Mark's place whenever there was a game on, but by that time we had *The Adam and Joe Show* to provide an outlet for our footie contrarianism. In 1996, the song 'Three Lions' by Baddiel, Skinner and the Lightning Seeds had caught the cultural mood of enthusiasm around football, so for the first show of our second series in 1997, Joe and I made a video for a song written by our friend Zac, an outsider sport anthem called 'The Footie Song'. The lyrics were some of Zac and Joe's strongest:

Ball, ball, ball.
Footie, footie, footie.
Ball, ball, ball,
Football.
When I go see United, I get over-excited.
When I go see Tottenham, I know there'll be no stoppin'em.
When I go see Millwall, I know I'll see a good game of football.
When I go see Spurs
If it's cold and Debbie's got a hat, I'll borrow hers.
Football.

On World AIDS Day in 1998, Joe and I were asked to take part in Stephen Fry's *Live from the Lighthouse*, a televised fundraising event in aid of the Terrence Higgins Trust that featured star turns from Elton John, Ali G, Victoria Wood, Noel Gallagher, Alan Partridge and All Saints.

We were there to join a group of actors, musicians and comedians who were filmed taking donations by phone. At the party afterwards; we stood around awkwardly among the likes of Alan Davies, East 17, Ulrika Jonsson, Simon Le Bon, Martine McCutcheon, Anne Robinson and Lulu. One of the only celebrities who spoke to us was Matt Lucas, who was best known in those days as George Dawes, the romper-suited drummer and keeper of the scores on one of my favourite TV shows, Vic and Bob's *Shooting Stars*.

It was a thrill to meet Matt for the first time and exciting to discover that he and his comedy partner David

Walliams had watched *The Adam and Joe Show*. But, said Matt, they'd found 'The Footie Song' a bit annoying. Not because they didn't like it, but because they'd also written an outsider sports anthem called 'Sporting Nuts', which they'd wanted to record with Chas & Dave. 'But then I saw "Ball, Ball, Ball, Footie, Footie, Footie" and I thought, *Oh no! Inconsequential sport song! It's been done …*' said Matt.

As a passionate football supporter, Matt was able to move on from inconsequential sport bants, but for Joe and me, who still harboured an unhealthy level of disrespect for the beautiful game, it wasn't so easy. During one of our Xfm podcast recording sessions in 2006, nearly ten years after 'The Footie Song', we celebrated the World Cup by coming up with some new, improvised football chants:

You can kick that ball
You can kick that ball
You can kick that ball
Into the goal with your foot

Penalty
Menalty
Fennel tea
Mint tea
Lovely tea
Have some tea
Penal-tea

Your team is no good
Your team is not good today
You are not playing well
Your team is no good
Ooh oh!

What do you do with a ball?
(Kick it in the goal! Kick it in the goal!)
What do you do with a ball?
Kick in the goal if you can
(Fuck off)

Now that I have children who love sport (despite Castle Buckles' mandatory screenings of *Manufacturing Consent*), I've come to appreciate football a little more than I did in my twenties. As far as my prejudice around 'doobie' is concerned, I had overcome that by the mid-Nineties, and if a joint was being passed around, I might condescend to take a drag. More often than not, I was reminded why I didn't like the stuff, but on a couple of occasions, once the whitey was over and the paranoia had subsided, I got a glimpse of what all the fuss was about.

In my thirties, I realised that if I was careful, I could get stoned just enough to get the joke when the dreaded giggles took hold of the other smokers and, most wonderfully of all, enjoy the same semi-religious experience when listening to music that I'd seen my weed-smoker friends having in our twenties. Over the years, my occasional stoned musical epiphanies included listening to the newly released stereo mix of the Beach Boys' *Pet Sounds* in my London flat in 1997, feeling I was on stage with Thom Yorke as he sat at the piano and played 'Videotape' during a Radiohead concert at Nîmes amphitheatre in southern France one summery night in 2012, and a couple of years later, skipping about beneath the stars in Norfolk while listening to 'Desire Lines' by Deerhunter, 'Pyramids' by Frank Ocean and 'Another Park, Another Sunday' by (yes) the Doobie Brothers. Each time, I felt I'd been released from my dreary hang-ups and transported inside the magical intricacies of the music.

When my dad moved in with us in 2015, I decided that it was finally time to quit my occasional doobie sessions. So, for the next few years, I made it a daily routine.

During those last months of caring for Dad, my night-time unwinding ritual involved listening to a podcast and smoking a joint when everyone had turned in, so that by the time I was ready for bed, I would drift swiftly off to sleep before too many unwelcome thoughts formed in my head. When she realised what I was up to every night, Sarah challenged me, saying, 'It's bad for your brain, let alone your poor lungs.' I didn't like seeing her disappointed in me, but at that point I still valued too many things about the routine to forgo it entirely. Anyway, I told myself, the joints were only small and not strong, and if it meant I no longer smoked cigarettes, that was a good thing, wasn't it? For a few more years, My Pathetic Drug Hell dragged on.

RAMBLE

WHITEY PRIVILEGE

One of the last times I saw the comedian Sean Lock was when I appeared as a guest on the TV panel show *8 Out of 10 Cats Does Countdown*. *What We Do in the Shadows* star Tash Demetriou was also a guest that day, and when the taping was finally over, we bundled into a taxi that took us from the TV studio in Salford to the hotel we were staying at in central Manchester, where we would head to the bar in the lobby to compare notes on panel-show pain.

At that point, I was still in the habit of smoking a joint after doing a show like this as a kind of celebratory anaesthetic to help blot out painful recollections of the studio audience staring blankly when one of my bits missed its mark. I guess I tended to roll them too strongly, and this fact, coupled with my long-term propensity for fainting, led to a few embarrassing moments on my trips to Manchester.

Tash and I were sitting outside the front of the hotel bar, and I was finishing my post-show doobie when Sean Lock arrived and sauntered over to say hello. 'I've seen you near cannabis before,' he said to me, referencing the story I'd told him the previous time I was on the show.

On that occasion, I'd had my doobie and was standing in the hotel bar talking to the comedian Dara Ó Briain, when suddenly I began to feel the blood drain out of me as my legs started to buckle. I was too embarrassed to admit to Dara that I, a 45-year-old father of three, was having a massive whitey, so, doing my best to appear nonchalant, I perched on the arm of a sofa behind me, then when Dara went to the bar I decided that leaving without saying goodbye and having him think me rude was preferable to passing out right there in front of him and assorted comedy peers. So, with the edges of my vision darkening, I shuffled over to the lifts, hoping I could make it back to my hotel room before losing consciousness.

But when the lift doors opened on my floor, I found the corridor leading to my room was, for some reason, pitch black. I reasoned that perhaps as an energy-saving measure, a motion sensor activated the lights, so I began waving my arms about, but the windowless corridor remained completely dark. I knew it was also possible that I was just so close to fainting that I had temporarily lost the power of sight, and I held out my hands and shuffled hopefully in the direction of my room, occasionally bumping into things. I imagined the security staff watching me on CCTV and shaking their heads.

At one point, I reached what I thought was a corner, only to find when I tried to walk around it that it was, in fact, still a wall. Rather than immediately changing direction, I spent a good few seconds stubbornly shuffling against it like a wind-up robot toy.

Eventually, unbelievably, I arrived at my room, collapsed gratefully on my bed and tried not to consider what this evening said about me.

The following day, I got the train back to London, and Sean came and sat opposite me. I told him what had happened the previous night, which made him laugh, and a couple of years later, back outside the front of the hotel with Tash Demetriou, Sean encouraged me to tell the story again. I would have been happy to do so, but for one thing: I was in the process of having yet another massive whitey.

I started saying, 'Actually, the funny thing is I obviously haven't learned my lesson because I think I'm about to pass out right now ...' Then I passed out.

I came around with my head resting on Sean's lap, and he was looking down at me with an amused smile. He went to get me a glass of water and spent the next hour or so chatting, being funny and generally making me feel like this happens to a lot of people after TV panel show tapings, and there was no need to be worried or mortifyingly embarrassed. Whether or not that was true, I learned my lesson, and Sean Lock remains the last and best person I've passed out on after smoking a doobie.

Towards the end of the pandemic, I noticed, with not-insignificant pangs of grief, that the fun was going out of my doobie ritual. Less and less it took me to a place of transcendent musical joy, and more and more it left me feeling a bit ill and unable to remember what I was thinking about 30 seconds earlier. Still, the thought of forsaking the routine entirely made me anxious, which was worrying in itself. Just how weak-willed was I, anyway? And how could I hope for my children to avoid unhealthy habits with such a hypocrite for a father?

Then, one day, I just stopped and never started again. For a few nights, it was a bit weird going to bed without smoking anything, but thinking about how pleased I'd feel in the morning usually got me off to sleep before too long. There are still a few stressful days or fun nights when I miss wrapping up proceedings with a doobie-fuelled mission to another musical dimension, but now the attraction of feeling physically and mentally together is more powerful than the desire to escape.

A while back, I did a live show in which I mentioned that I'd stopped smoking, and afterwards I saw a couple of older women who had been at the show sitting outside a nearby pub having a cigarette. They said they liked the show except for the giving up smoking part. Perhaps they felt I was virtue signalling or maybe they felt judged, but I tend not to judge other people's habits unless they include murder, Nazism or football. Everyone's trying to figure out a system that gets them through their days, and if you've found one that brings you some pleasure, then good for you, perhaps even if, in the long run, it's not good for you.

It always used to cheer me up to see interviews with artists like David Lynch, Maggi Hambling and David Hockney, who were still productive in their seventies and eighties and still puffed away on ciggies. *They're winning!* I would think, but it depends on how you define winning. Maggi Hambling had a massive heart attack in 2022, and David Lynch got emphysema and died in January 2025. The outlier is Hockney, 87 as I write, still making beautiful pictures and still refusing to give up his beloved cigs. 'I'm 100 per cent sure I'm going to die of a smoking-related illness or a non-smoking-related illness,' he reasons.

People tell me about the joys of getting high without smoking by micro-dosing mushrooms, sucking on cannabis gummies, or gargling with MDMA-infused Solero Balls (though I don't think those currently exist). So far, I've been able to resist, though I do miss that feeling of otherworldly connection that doobie sometimes provided. But if it's otherworldly connection I'm hankering for, perhaps now that more friends and family members are dying, I should give the Ouija board another go.

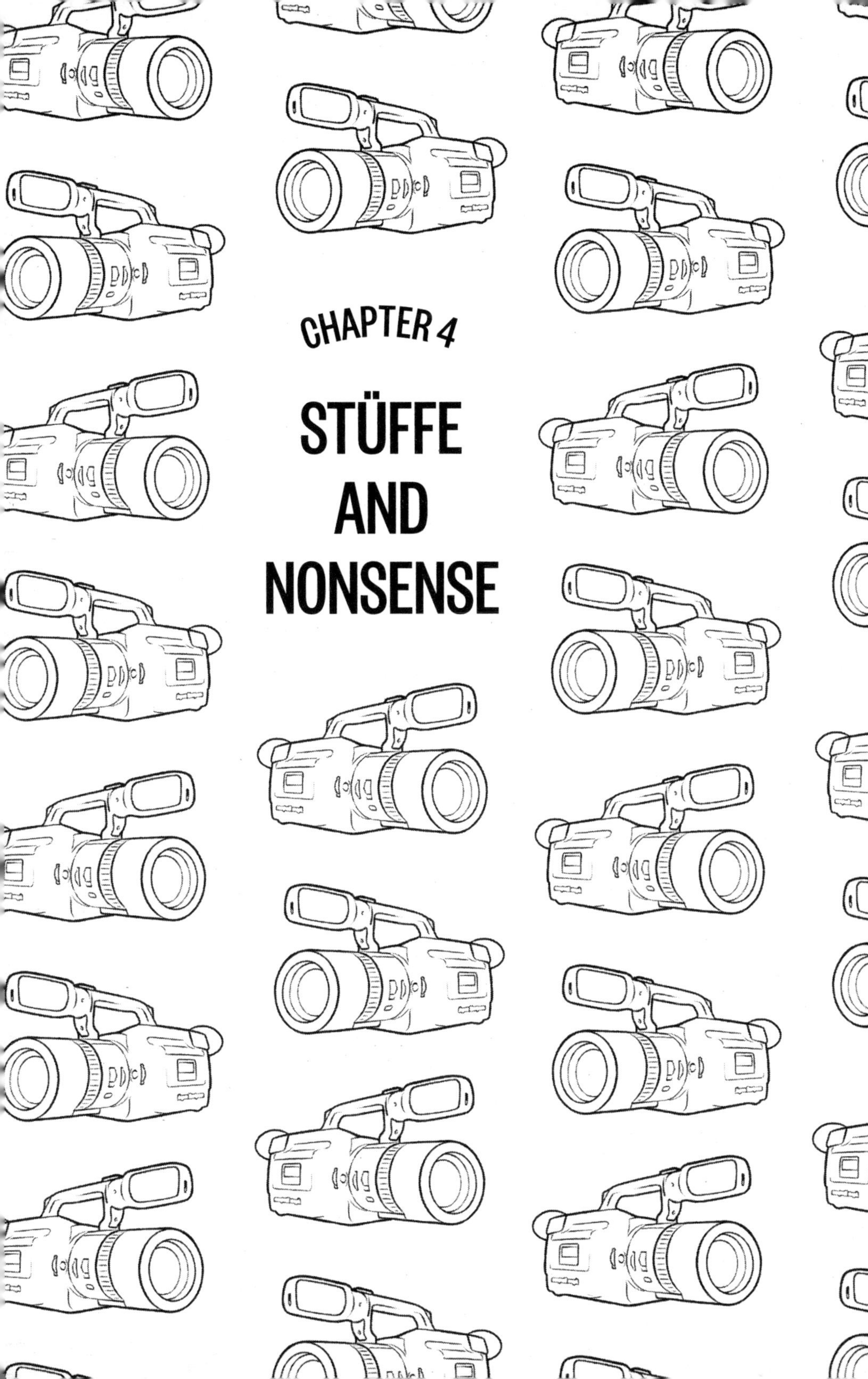

CHAPTER 4

STÜFFE AND NONSENSE

ost people watching the first episode of *The Adam and Joe Show* when it went out on Channel 4 at ten past midnight on Friday, 6 December 1996 would have assumed it had been thrown together in a couple of weeks. In fact, it had been a year and a half since Peter Grimsdale, *Takeover TV*'s commissioner at Channel 4, had asked Joe and me if we had any other ideas for shows. During that time, as well as working on the second series of *Takeover TV*, it felt to us that we had explored every conceivable permutation of what our own homemade low-budget late-night TV programme might look like, and in the process we had occasionally got on each other's tits in a way we never had before.

We had started with the idea of making a TV version of a homemade, photocopied, hand-stapled 'zine, offering our take on modern life and pop culture in the style of contemporary American zines like *Ben Is Dead* and the Beastie Boys' *Grand Royal*, combined with the less brash, more British tone of our friends at *The Idler* magazine.

Our working title was *Stüffe* (pronounced 'Shtoof'). Why? 'Because it's about Stuff but with a strong homemade accent' proclaimed the first of the many development documents we produced every few weeks in the hope of convincing Peter Grimsdale to commission a pilot. These development documents tended to be light on specific ideas and heavy on waffly

bollox that veered between a caffeinated media-studies manifesto and a Club 18–30 recruiting poster:

> *Stüffe is an anti-structure TV show that does away with studios, audiences, constant teases, recurring departments and traditional presenting styles. Stüffe is for anyone who wants to fight back at the constant bombardment of advertisers, promoters and manufactured lifestyles. Stüffe is for anyone who wants to know what's new, what's really worth checking out and what isn't. Stüffe is for anyone who likes to be stimulated and have a laugh.*

Summer 1995 was spent with similarly nebulous documents being faxed between me, Joe, Fenton and Randy at World of Wonder, and sometimes Louis Theroux. Louis was out in New York, having recently made a name for himself on Michael Moore's political prank show *TV Nation*, but he was always keen to do what he could to help us get our show off the ground.

Privately, I felt we needed all the help we could get. Coming up with links and the occasional skit for *Takeover TV* was one thing, but I was far less confident when it came to convincing Channel 4 we had a strong enough idea for a show, and from time to time, self-doubt would get the better of me. In these moments I would bug Fenton, alternating between self-deprecating and pushy as I angled for reassurance. After sitting in on one of these calls, Joe sent me a fax:

> Ad. Here's some golden showbiz rules that I know you know already, but I want to say for the hell of it.
>
> Never do yourself down – there's no shortage of people who'll do that for you.
>
> Confidence breeds confidence. If we worry, they'll worry.
>
> Finally, in the words of the Jackson Five on 'Maybe Tomorrow', 'My beautiful bird, you have flown away, I held you too tight, I can see'. For 'beautiful bird' read 'TV show'. Be easygoing at all times – that's why they chose us in the first place. The bottom line is this: to come up with the goods with minimum fuss and maximum quality. That's all we have to worry about.
>
> I say all this only because Fenton sounded a bit like, 'What are they calling me for?' today. We should know exactly what we want to ask and put it succinctly when we call them. After all, who knows how busy and pissed off with other things they might be when we call.
>
> Now I'm off to teach my Granny to suck eggs
>
> love Joe

This was all fine advice, which I tried to take in the right spirit, but for someone like me it wasn't easy to put into practice. And when it came to never doing ourselves down, well, neither of us stuck to that one. Later, we would frequently joke in the show and during interviews about how 'crap' we were, partly because it seemed preferable to being blowhards but mainly from a defensive impulse to flag our shortcomings before anyone else did.

Attempted Development

Our confidence received a boost when Fenton was able to get some development money out of Channel 4. As soon as we'd finished our contributions for the *Takeover TV* Sci-Fi Special, we spent August 1995 being paid £250 a week (which came in the nick of time, as I was broke and borrowing money from my girlfriend) to make a *Stüffe* development reel. At last, we would show what our vision of an *anti-structural, non-traditional cultural fightback* would look like.

According to the VHS reel we turned in a month later, that vision entailed Joe and me sitting in my poster-covered bedroom in my parents' house in Clapham, talking about our most embarrassing records, noting the fascist overtones in clips of Michael Jackson's *Dangerous* Tour, analysing the deadly virus film *Outbreak* with a 'Goodness Graph' to illustrate the peaks and troughs, and being rude about David Bowie's new album *Outside*.

When I dug out the *Stüffe* development reel recently, the parts that made me cringe less were the skits in which Joe and I dressed up and lip-synced, first to a scene from *Grange Hill* and then a Clean and Clear face-wash advert. Also smile-inducing, mainly because it reminded me of the fun we'd had making it, was a sepia-toned music video for our (sort of) pastiche of decadent 1930s bright young things, 'The Jazz Queens' (the bulk of which was written with our friend Zac).

We'll motor up to Oxford and hire out a punt
And you'll admire how my trousers are sticking out in front
My darling love, I love you
Lend us five bob
We're the Jazz Queens, boop boop be doop
We're the Jazz Queens, boop boop be doop

We're the Jazz Queens, boop boop be doop
Ooh. Get off. You bitch.

The item that had aged least well on the *Stüffe* development tape was a sketch in which I pretended to interview David Koresh, the messianic leader of the so-called Branch Davidian cult in Waco, Texas, which had been raided by the FBI and the ATF in 1993, leading to a siege that ended with the deaths of Koresh and 75 other cult members. But in 1996, I hadn't yet grasped how appalling the events at Waco actually were. All I knew was that Louis Theroux, who back then had shaggy hair and specs, looked a lot like Koresh, and Joe and I thought it would be funny to get him to play the cult leader for our development reel. Louis, who knew far more about the Waco siege than we did, was adamant that this was a bad idea but relented when we started accusing him of getting too big for his boots now that he was a TV star.

So, during Louis's next visit to the UK, we filmed him performing messianic miracles like producing bread from his mouth and receiving a can of Coke that fell into his hands from the heavens, which we intercut with actual footage from the Waco siege. I suppose it was an attempt at being edgy, but it was horribly unfunny stuff, and Louis said he hoped it wouldn't come back to bite him in the arse one day. 'Get over yourself,' I said, 'No one will ever know. It's not as if I'm going to put it in my memoirs.'

In his glass-panelled office on the first floor of the flamboyantly modern Richard Rogers-designed Channel 4 building, Peter Grimsdale tapped his fingers on the *Stüffe* label I'd glued to the VHS of our development reel. Like a kind parent who's been enthusiastically presented with a bad drawing from one of their children, he complimented us on the good bits, didn't mention the bad bits and encouraged us to keep going. 'Focus on the minutiae,' he said. 'That's what'll make the show special. Recognisable minutiae and *layers*.'

What did he mean? Before we could ask, Peter was telling us that on our way out, we should pause to look down from the balcony over the entrance to the Channel 4 building, where we would see that the two circular glass covers of the revolving doors and the walkway beyond made the shape of a big cock and balls. 'Apparently, Richard Rogers always puts one somewhere on his buildings,' said Peter. It was nice to think there were people in the adult world who were even more juvenile than we were.

RAMBLE

When Richard Rogers gave a talk to Channel 4 staff in 2015, Cathy Newman of *Channel 4 News* asked him about the entrance cock. Rogers seemed genuinely surprised by the suggestion that he would be so puerile and dismissed the notion as an urban myth. But I don't buy it. You don't spend all that time designing and *erecting* a building without someone pointing out that there's a big knob in the middle of it.

Babymen

Ever since we'd become friends as 14-year-olds at school, I'd looked up to Joe, and not only because he was nearly a foot taller than I was. Teenage Joe was chipper and self-assured to the point of arrogance, unfazed by authority and unimpressed by the notion that being 'grown up' was something to aspire to. It was an outlook I was happy to be on board with. There were things in the adult world that did impress us, and even as we took the piss out of the celebrities in magazines like *SKY*, *The Face* and the *Daily Mail*'s *YOU*, we pored over the lifestyles of rich and famous young Americans and coveted them hard.

Speaking for myself, what I didn't covet were the kinds of concepts my dad was big on: responsibility, reliability, accountability, self-discipline-ability ... Boring! We were in our mid-twenties by the time we were working on *Stüffe*, but if anything I was less of an adult than I had been in my teens. And now I was making a living from being childish.

The person who bore the brunt of that childishness was my girlfriend, Karen. She was one of the people I'd met in my art school days when I would work weekend and holiday shifts at the Rock Island Diner in Piccadilly Circus. There, Karen wore rollerskates and glided gracefully between tables with trays of burgers, fries and apple pies. She was sweet but didn't suffer fools gladly. She made an exception for me, though, and would laugh when I imitated her lovely Bristolian accent and the lingo she'd inherited from her Scottish parents. 'You're a *daftie*,' she would tell me. Karen laughed a lot as she and I drank with workmates, hung out with my old school friends, went to the movies and ate Chinese food. Also, in those *Takeover TV* and *Stüffe* years, she drove me to DJ gigs, encouraged me to be a *little* more healthy (I had never eaten broccoli before I met Karen) and lent me money when I was turning myself into a postmodern media hub. We had many happy times, Karen and I, except when creative angst and insecurity got the better of me. Then I was way less fun.

Cleared for Takeoff

When the first episode of *Takeover TV* II aired on Friday, 12 July 1996, Joe and I had a party round at Mum and Dad's place in Clapham. Many of our closest pals were there, along with Joe's parents, Fenton, the production team at World of Wonder and even Peter Grimsdale. Dad got some sparkling wine in, Mum made smoked salmon blinis, and I brought over my TV so we could have one in the kitchen as well as the living room. That way, everyone would get a good view of the fruits of our labours when the show went out at 10 past 11.

Ma said she enjoyed the show except for the sketch in which Dad had appeared playing me in the future, which she said was 'embarrassing'. Luckily, Pa was busy pitching programme ideas to Peter Grimsdale and didn't hear, so for the rest of the evening the sparkling wine flowed and everyone was on their best behaviour. That was a good night.

A few weeks later, Peter called us into Channel 4 to give us the news that he was giving us a green light not just for a *Stüffe* pilot, but for what he called a 'pilot series', four episodes of just under half an hour to be broadcast on Channel 4 towards the end of the year. In the Entertainment department, commissioning a comedy series without a script or a conventional pilot was unheard of, but things worked differently in the Religion, History and Features department. Peter told me years later that when he had asked Channel 4's director of programmes about making a *Stüffe* pilot, the reply had come, 'If you've got the budget, why not do four?'

Joe and I would be paid £600 a week for the duration of the five-month production, enough money for me to pay Karen back as long as I carried on doing the occasional DJ shift at weddings and bar mitzvahs. Although the challenge of filling four shows instead of just one pilot led to several attacks of barely restrained panic in the following months, I tried to remind myself that the very thing I had idly fantasised about since I started staring at the boob tube as a child had become a reality – my best friend and I had our own TV show. Now, we just had to make it … and, if possible, make it not shit.

We started with the things that had worked best in *Takeover TV*. The *Star Wars* toys came out again. This time, we used them for a homage to Cilla Black's dating game show *Blind Date*. In our version, *Blind Data*, Luke, Han and C-3PO were the potential suitors behind the curtain hoping to be chosen by Princess Leia, while the Cilla Black role was played by Jedi love master Yoda, who declared, 'A lorra lorra fun will we have, Chuck.' The first time Joe did his Yoda voice, I thought, *OK, maybe this show will be good.*

We also built a multicoloured cardboard Wonky House for another *Star Wars* toy clip, *Chew've Been Framed*, in which Chewbacca was the Beadle-style host of his own camcorder cockup show. Luke and Yoda tuned in from their front room in the Dagobah swamp, and when Chewie failed to show the clip Luke had sent in, Yoda encouraged the young Jedi to destroy the Wonky House remotely using the Force. This we did by igniting half a firework under the model that, of course, set off the smoke alarms at World of Wonder's Brixton office during one of our late-night beer, doobie, Marvin Gaye and Haircut 100-fuelled filming sessions.

Louis had suggested that my dad could review gangster-rap records for *Stüffe*, under the moniker BaaadDad (a reference to Channel 4's *Baadasss TV*, in which presenter Andi Oliver and the rapper Ice-T took a 'fly and funky' look at 'the idiosyncrasies of black culture'). We got hold of the videos for 'Natural Born Killaz' by Dr Dre and Ice Cube, and, for the sake of variety, 'Higher State of Consciousness' by Josh Wink and 'Men in Black' by Frank Black, then we headed over to my parents' place in Clapham. In the living room that Mum had worked hard to make cosy and pretty, we set up our lights and filmed Dad watching the videos and then holding forth about them between sips from a glass of sparkling wine.

As we had hoped he would be, Dad was amusingly pompous and opinionated, but when the expressions of mystification and contempt started to get repetitive, we coached him to find something positive to say about one of the videos. Knowing I was a fan, he chose the Frank Black track and said that he could imagine dancing a jig to it, but only if he'd had enough to drink. It wasn't exactly earth-shattering stuff, but in 1996 it was still a novelty to see a posh-sounding 72-year-old talking about indie rock, club techno and gangster rap, and by the time we'd finished filming we agreed it should make a good piece. Good old Dad. He usually came through when you needed him to. Unless you were married to him, I suppose.

Choose Toys

Everyone agreed we should make more cuddly toy parodies, or 'toy movies' as we started calling them. We did versions of Paul Verhoeven's deranged, hi-camp sex-romp *Showgirls*, Larry Clark's chilling tale of teen immorality *Kids*, and David Fincher's grisly thriller *Seven*. But the first toy movie we made for *Stüffe* was in the form of a trailer for another of 1996's most talked about films, Danny Boyle's junkie opera *Trainspotting*. With its heavy reliance on swearing, violence, drug taking and toilet swimming, Joe was certain that a cuddly toy version of *Trainspotting* would be funny, but I had lingering doubts about the toy movies. I worried that, unless we were careful, they would end up looking childish in a bad way.

The first thing we shot was the opening scene of Ewan McGregor's character Renton running down the street. We filmed outside the tiny artist's studio flat I'd recently moved into behind Kensington High Street, and to play Renton we used a small stuffed pig that we called Runton. We positioned the pig in front of the lens with one end of a coat hanger stuck up its bum and the other end taped to the camera. Then we ran backwards with the camera as low to the pavement as possible while we sang 'Lust for Life'. It was *sort of* funny but not the most beautiful shot.

Back in my flat, we thought about how to film the scene in which Renton dives into a filthy betting shop toilet to retrieve some bum drugs. Joe said all we needed was a white loo roll for a toilet and a couple of bits of cardboard to make the toilet stall, and we'd be ready to film, but I was worried that would look too rubbish. This wasn't *Takeover TV* anymore. We needed to raise our game, I said, and a slightly wobbly voiced conversation ensued. I wondered if Joe thought I was only being difficult because the toy movies had originally been his idea. But I held my ground, and we spent the rest of the afternoon constructing a tiny toilet with a little cardboard seat, cistern and walls for the cubicle that were covered with drips of mud and obscene graffiti about Power Rangers and Barbie. I printed out a sign for the door of the cubicle that said TOYLET. Joe lit the set with some blue backlight and a warm key light on Runton, and we were ready to roll.

It only took five minutes to get the shots we needed, but they looked better than anything we'd made up to that point, and Joe conceded the extra work had been worth it. A few days later, we filmed the scene in the drug den where a floppy toy lamb (knitted by my granny) injects 'Sherbert' into its arm with a toy syringe then collapses in a woolly stupor. By then, I was beginning to think we might finally be on the right track.

In early September 1996 we returned to the Channel 4 Big Cock building to share our progress with Peter Grimsdale. 'You've really been busy!' he said as we watched the tape together. *Toytrainspotting* looked good, and the BaaadDad review worked well, but I was less confident about some of the other items that were more like sketches crossed with magazine articles and looked offputtingly amateurish.

But, to our amazement, Peter asked if we were going to be available in the new year to make another series. 'What if nobody likes the first one?' I said. 'I don't care,' replied Peter, 'but I think they will.' Giddily, we tottered out of Channel 4, and after a day or so of feeling pleased with ourselves, we got back to worrying about how the hell we were going to generate enough material to fill four half-hour programmes in the next twelve weeks, let alone make a whole new series after that.

'Oh, Fuck'

Fenton instructed our producer, Debbie, and assistant producer, Rob, to ensure that items from the ideas list were always being worked on to give us the best chance of making our December deadline.

We filmed for a day at a child model agency, thinking this strange world might yield a piece that was funny and non-creepy. Wrong on both counts. We did a snarky review of three less well-known UK theme parks, filming ourselves apparently asleep on all the rides, although anyone watching the final piece would also be rendered unconscious by how boring and pointless it was. We tried to film an item about the practicalities of having sexual intercourse in zero gravity, for which we shot garishly lit interviews with members of the newly formed Association of Autonomous Astronauts and with a university professor specialising in human sexuality who got grumpy when he realised he wasn't dealing with serious people. Sex in Space had been on our ideas list since the dawn of *Stüffe*, and we'd always been so certain it would make a spicy piece. Wrong again.

Another idea that seemed fun in written form was When

Will Pop Music Run Out? We had wanted the piece to be a slick presentation with CG graphs and stats like a sketch from Chris Morris and Armando Iannucci's news parody *The Day Today*. But we didn't have the budget for the slick approach. Instead, we shot interviews with a couple of musicologists and, more excitingly for me, with musician Stephen Jones, aka Babybird, hoping as we did so that we'd figure out how to make the piece work. But again, noooo.

RAMBLE

BABYBIRD AND SHOOBY

I was excited to meet Stephen Jones because I'd been enjoying the series of Babybird EPs he'd released in 1995. But when I said how much I appreciated the eccentric, homemade feel of his music (which journalists had dubbed 'lo-fi'), he tensed up, saying he was tired of being thought of as the lo-fi guy. Then, thinking he might feel some kinship with another brilliantly eccentric artist, I played him a clip of cult American scat singer Shooby Taylor.

I was introduced to Shooby's music by Louis after he'd met a New York DJ, Irwin Chusid, whose radio show featured tracks that wobbled along the fine line between fascinatingly unconventional and entertainingly awful. In the late 1970s and early 80s, Shooby had taken the scat genre's lexicon of 'Doo-bee-doo's and 'Skee-bah-dooby's and pushed it, unironically, into joyfully absurdist territory on tapes in which he would sing over recordings by other artists, using phrases like 'Shwee-dah-rah', 'Shabba-do-splah', 'Rah-sah-ha, siddly doh-be' and 'Pah-pee-pah-pee-pah-pee-pah-pee-tah-pee-tah-pee-tah-pee'.

Stephen Jones didn't appreciate the comparison. He was a proper musician, not some weird outsider artist, and he said the new Babybird single would prove it. He was right. When it was released the following month, 'You're Gorgeous' was a big hit, but I still preferred the stuff where he sounded like an outsider artist weirdo, whether that's the way he thought of himself or not.

Our next progress check with Peter Grimsdale at Channel 4 was more subdued. Peter told me years later that when we'd showed him the reel with the unfinished versions of Child Model Agency, UK Theme Park Reviews, Sex in Space, and When Will Pop Music Run Out?, he'd thought, *Oh, fuck.*

We plodded on.

'Ello, 'Ello, 'Ello

One of the items Fenton and Randy always liked in our *Stüffe* development reel was Vinyl Justice, in which Joe and I took turns to defend our most uncool musical purchases. For the pilot series, Joe suggested raiding the record collections of pop stars as if we were officers from the Vinyl Justice squad. I had fantasies of looking through David Bowie's records and duetting with him on 'The Laughing Gnome' or improvising ambient music on a toy keyboard with Brian Eno. Our researchers nodded patiently and said they'd make some calls, but it turned out fewer music legends were eager to invite us into their homes to clown around on the pilot of a low-budget homemade TV show than you'd think.

In the end, our first guest was the future 6 Music and Radio 4 DJ Cerys Matthews, then on the brink of pop stardom with her band Catatonia. We got VINYL JUSTICE T-shirts printed, and the day before we travelled to Cardiff to film with Cerys at her house, I bought a couple of plastic British Bobby policeman helmets and attached records to the top. That was the extent of our preparation for Vinyl Justice. It was a stressful shoot, with Joe, our researcher, Matt, and me trying to figure out how the piece was going to work, while Cerys, who couldn't have been nicer, sat patiently on the couch in her woolly beanie hat, drinking a can of beer and stroking her cat.

Watching the footage from the shoot the next day, I was disappointed with how technically rough it looked and how flimsy our comedy copper shtick had been, but our editor, Jon, was able to carve something mildly fun out of it. Meanwhile, the schedule demanded to be fed, and before we knew it we were filming more Vinyl Justice segments with Neil Hannon of the Divine Comedy, a couple of members of another Welsh band I was obsessed with at the time, Gorky's Zygotic Mynci, and, to our intense excitement, the frontman of Haircut 100, Nick Heyward, who was especially fun and quite nutty.

During each of these shoots, I regretted the ''Ello, 'ello' comedy copper voices Joe and I had instinctively settled on during the shoot with Cerys. I just wanted to talk about music, but instead we were locked into holding up any vaguely unfashionable record and saying, 'Now, what have we here? This looks problematic!', followed by trying to force the embarrassed guest to dance to a track from the offending record, which they nearly always refused to do.

Get Set

By November 1996, we'd shot a good proportion of what would end up in the pilot series. With just over a month to go before our first episode was due to be broadcast, Peter

Grimsdale dropped a bombshell: he wanted us to change the title. He thought *Stüffe* was pretentious and people wouldn't know how to pronounce it. I was livid, convinced as I was that the name of a TV show, like the name of a band, is a crucial part of what makes it not just good but great. Anyway, we'd tried changing the title before. We'd switched to *TV Zine* early on, but that was too boring. For a short period we called it *The Freaky Shit Machine*, but then we sobered up. We always came back to *Stüffe* because *the show was about stuff but with a strong homemade accent!* And '*Stüffe*' would look good on T-shirts.

We discovered that Peter had hated the title all along and had just been waiting for the right moment to make his move. He wanted us to call it *The Adam and Joe Show*. I thought that made it sound like a crappy kids' programme, not a cool, subversive cultural fightback. We compromised on *Adam and Joe's TV Show*, which at least was a bit more meta. That's why in the opening and closing title sequence in which Joe and I construct then deconstruct the bedroom set, there's a 'T' with the words '*Adam & Joe's*' on the back of my T-shirt, and a 'V' with the word '*Show*' on the back of Joe's T-shirt. After we'd shot the titles, word came back from Channel 4 that they preferred *The Adam and Joe Show*. 'Now we're going to have to get new T-shirts printed and film the titles all over again!' I bleated, before it was pointed out to me that no one cared.

We'd known from the beginning that the set was going to look the way our bedrooms at home had looked since we were teenagers: covered with posters, drawings, souvenirs and childhood toys in a personalised pop-culture patchwork. I put a few of my art-college pieces on the set as well: a giant wall hanging of newsreader Moira Stuart, a red wooden cog with a heart-shaped hole in the centre, and a couple of old TVs from the *Takeover TV* II set displaying my swirling video-feedback patterns. Whereas the sets of most TV entertainment shows tend to include brightly coloured couches and desks in front of fake cityscapes or abstract designs, we delivered our links from a bed with a *Star Trek TNG* duvet on it.

The idea of wearing black T-shirts with our names printed on the front in white Helvetica bold was something we decided on fairly late, when we realised having a uniform would save time when it came to wardrobe choices for the links. Joe would say in interviews that the T-shirts were a nod to *The Goodies*, a British sitcom we both loved in the Seventies, but searching the internet, I have never been able to find any pictures of the Goodies wearing T-shirts with their names on the front. To me, the T-shirts were a shortcut to becoming friendly with the viewers and helping them remember who we were. As someone who struggles to remember names in everyday life, I wish more people wore T-shirts with their names on them in big white letters.

I also wore a sailors' cap I'd picked up at a seaside tourist shop in Corfu a few years earlier. Having admired a photo of Bowie wearing something similar in the late Seventies, I imagined it might give me a touch of the same style. In fact, the combination of the cap, shorts and Dr. Martens boots with white socks folded over the top merely led many people to assume I was gay, which, again, like Bowie, I was happy to encourage. I even found myself being interviewed for the gay lifestyle magazine *Attitude* and, in a bid to endear myself to readers, tried a bit too hard to play up my potential for gayness.

Meet the Press

Suddenly, it was time to publicise the show. World of Wonder sent out VHS tapes of items that included *Toytrainspotting* and *Chew've Been Framed*, one of BaaadDad's video reviews and a link we'd shot about our favourite ways to fiddle with candles during restaurant meals. To our relief and delight, interview requests started to trickle in.

Doing interviews with Joe in those early days was a lark, an opportunity for us to witter about movies and TV and make each other laugh, which often led journalists to write about how close we seemed and how we finished each other's sentences. I always liked reading that. Occasional backstage friction notwithstanding, I did feel close to Joe and was proud of our friendship. In later years, we'd occasionally get ratty after interviews about which one of us had talked too much, who had claimed credit for an item that wasn't theirs, and who had deliberately made the other one look stupid for the sake of a laugh. But at first, the only thing we feared from interviews was being outed as public-school boys.

Channel 4's head of publicity at the time said to us in passing that if we were asked directly whether we'd met at Westminster, an expensive fee-paying school, we shouldn't deny it, but it was probably best not to volunteer the information. I was indignant because the implication was that we were rich boys who had been handed a show without working for it, and I didn't think that was the case. On the other hand, we certainly weren't poor, and who knew how many doors had opened for us because of how we looked and how we spoke? Peter Grimsdale, who had been educated at both state and private schools, thought the conversation about our social background was less important than whether or not the show was any good. Other than the 'Oh, fuck' moment, he never wavered from his conviction that it was. Of course, there were those who disagreed.

The *Daily Telegraph* called our first episode 'very offensive, so perhaps a box of tricks better left unopened, but this mutant child of *Wayne's World*, *Toy Story*, and *Viz* comic has the odd sprinkling of wit as it skims across the surface of popular culture.' Despite this grudging encouragement, the review concluded: 'Even this time slot may not be late enough.'

But, writing for *Time Out*, Peter Paphides gave us our first rave review under the headline 'Talentspotting':

Even if the rest of 'The Adam & Joe Show' glides clean over your head, the first episode contains at least one moment of clear-cut, fuck-off, instant-immortality, genius that guarantees Adam Buxton and Joe Cornish at least an ashtray in the comedy Hall of Fame. Prepare yourselves for 'Toytrainspotting', wherein Britain's most successful ever cult movie is rendered by our hosts' collection of teddy bears ...

With mass acclaim just around the corner, it's just a matter of time before Adam and Joe get to sample the accoutrements of '90s comedy greatness: award ceremonies; guest slots on 'Shooting Stars'; free entry to the Groucho. Adam and Joe, are you ready for the big time?

Transmission Accomplished

There wasn't much time to celebrate, as we were still finishing off the other three programmes. But on Friday, 6 December, a small group of friends joined Joe and me at my flat to watch the first episode being broadcast. For the last five months, we'd worked so intensively that hearing the announcer trail *The Adam and Joe Show* in the closing credits of *TFI Friday* felt surreal, as did the advertisements and a trailer for my favourite show, *ER*. Then came the swooping primary-coloured blocks that resolved into the iconic Channel 4 logo, followed by the announcement: 'Warning! *The Adam and Joe Show* is a high-density programme. Start taping now.' All our friends cheered.

It was a huge relief to have delivered the show and it turn out to be something that, on the whole, felt exactly the way I hoped it might: like a homemade gift from an arty and only slightly annoying friend. More importantly, my friendship with Joe had survived intact despite a few choppy moments.

Console Wars

A few months earlier, in the World of Wonder office after everyone else had gone home, we'd had an unusually bitter argument. It was about gaming consoles. Joe had an idea for a link based on the observation that after you've had a marathon gaming session, you keep seeing the game playing every time you close your eyes. The argument was about which console we should use to illustrate this observation. Joe had lobbied for the N64, on which he'd been playing a lot of *Mario Kart*. 'No way!' I said, and insisted that a PlayStation game like *Tekken 2*, *Wipeout* or *Tomb Raider* would be far more relatable. Joe thought I was being overbearing and offensively dismissive of Mario and his karts and it all kicked off.

It doesn't take a genius in Nerd Psychology to realise that there were other factors at play in this mind-blowingly trivial confrontation. I was too often on the lookout for ways to act like an 'alpha' because, deep down, I felt like a 'beta', and maybe Joe felt his contributions weren't being properly appreciated. However, discussing any of those things directly would have been too appalling – hence Lara Croft vs Mario.

We eventually shot the gaming link for the second series, and when Joe closes his eyes, you see a shot of the game he's still playing in his mind superimposed onto his forehead. It's *Mario Kart*. To this day, I refuse to play it.

Here We Go Again

After a few weeks of decompression in early 1997, the reality of having committed to a second series of the show started to sink in. It sank all the way in when World of Wonder faxed over a provisional production schedule for six new episodes to be transmitted in November. By March, Joe and I were working on the first two toy movies, though we were doing so separately. Joe was shooting his stuffed toy version of *The English Patient* (*The Toy Patient*) at the office in Brixton, while I was working on a toy recreation of *ER* (*Emergency Play Room*) in my Kensington flat. We told ourselves we'd get more done if we worked separately, but the fact was, after the previous year, we also relished having some time apart. Still, it bothered me. The competitive tensions persisted, and this way of working wasn't going to help resolve them.

A&J in the USA

An opportunity to properly enjoy each other's company again came in April 1997, when, hoping to give our second series a touch of transatlantic glamour, World of Wonder arranged for us to travel to Los Angeles to shoot some items, take some meetings and indulge our Stateside fantasies.

We stayed with Fenton and Randy at their house, which was built on one of the steep hills of Hollywood Heights above the famous Magic Castle. From the road, the house appeared to be a bungalow, but once inside we found ourselves looking down from a balcony over a huge open-plan living room lined with bookshelves filled with variously transgressive art books. On the wall behind the sofa was a giant sign that said 'TV' surrounded by light bulbs. *If I ever live in a big house*, I thought, *I want it to look like this.* Fenton told us the place had been designed by Wilfred Buckland, often cited as Hollywood's first art director, who worked with director Cecil B. DeMille in the 1910s. One of the cinematic innovations for which Buckland was celebrated was the art of miniature stage building. 'Like you and Joe!' said Fenton.

Stepping through the tall French doors onto the wooden terrace outside, we looked out over LA, breathed in the warm air, and savoured the peculiar scent of the surrounding hillside – delicate notes of marijuana and cat wee. It was the first time I'd visited America without my dad paying for the flight, and the idea that my friendship with Joe and our silly pissing about had got me there felt thrilling.

Rough Justice

One of the main justifications for the trip was to secure some big-name guests for Vinyl Justice, which, despite my reservations, Fenton and Randy continued to insist was a great segment. Perhaps they felt it was a good way to inject some celebrity glamour into the otherwise dorky proceedings. The week before we arrived in the US, a researcher at World of Wonder's LA office faxed us an impressive list of celebrities that were 'looking promising'. It included Lemmy from Motörhead, Beck, Snoop Doggy Dogg, Rivers Cuomo of Weezer, Sheryl Crow, Pat Boone (?!) and, most extraordinary of all for me as a Beach Boys obsessive, Brian Wilson. I couldn't believe Joe and I were going to dress up like berks and clown around in the home of one of the all-time great geniuses of modern music. And I was right not to believe it – because it didn't happen. In the end, the only names that didn't dematerialise from the guest list were Frank Zappa's children – Moon Unit, Dweezil and Ahmet – and guitarist Dave Navarro of Jane's Addiction and the Red Hot Chili Peppers.

One whole wall of Dave Navarro's apartment was decorated with a giant black and white reproduction of *Saigon Execution*, the famous photo showing a Viet Cong prisoner being shot in the head. On another wall was an original painting of a forest landscape featuring the cartoon figures of Disney's Seven Dwarfs. It was by the serial killer and sex offender John Wayne Gacy.

Dave was elfin and faintly vampiric in sweatpants and an open kimono that revealed his hot bod. He was polite, but when he saw us in the full policeman outfits we'd hired, with records on our helmets and new badges I'd made featuring the face of Nick Berry from the heartwarming Sixties-set cop show *Heartbeat*, he seemed unsure about what he'd let himself in for. At one point, he called a halt to our buffoonery and said, 'Guys, this isn't cool!' Not in the modern sense of something not being appropriate, but rather as if someone had assured him that in England, Joe and I were considered 'cool', and he was only just realising he'd been misled.

We didn't do that much better with the Zappa children. Moon Unit was warm and instantly likeable but had only a small collection of CDs at her apartment, none of which were in any way 'embarrassing' or otherwise remarkable. We met her brothers Dweezil and Ahmet at the Zappa family home in Laurel Canyon, where Frank had recorded so much of his music up until his death in 1993 and where his widow Gail still lived. It was exciting to walk through the dimly lit interiors where Frank himself would once have stalked and to peer at master tapes, photos and original artwork that would be familiar to any Frankophile.

When it came to filming the piece, Dweezil, like Dave Navarro, seemed worried by our lack of coolness. Having kept us waiting for half an hour, he told us we only had 20 minutes rather than the hour he'd agreed to, during which the phone never stopped ringing and he never stopped looking bored. Ahmet was more enthusiastic, if slightly deranged. However, none of that mattered because most of the footage, which had been filmed by a World of Wonder intern who had claimed to be an experienced videographer, was so dark and badly shot that it was completely unusable.

We didn't bother rescheduling with Dweezil, but Ahmet was kind enough to make another date for us to record at his apartment. It ended up being the only Zappa piece we used.

The fact that the highlight was an improvised routine with Ahmet in which we took turns popping up from behind a sofa while singing along with 'Mahna Mahna' by the Muppets gives you an idea of the general standard of material we were getting.

Back in the UK, we shot further Vinyl Justice segments with amiable up-and-comers Symposium, Tim Gane and Lætitia Sadier of avant-pop wizards Stereolab, and two of my long-time musical heroes: Edwyn Collins of Orange Juice and Gary Numan of synthesisers. We had fun afternoons with every one of these guests, but as a music fan it never stopped bothering me that Vinyl Justice was never much about the music. Stereolab's Tim and Lætitia had a huge, eclectic collection of fascinating records in their reassuringly studenty south London home, but in-depth examination of their musical treasures wasn't an option because the finished segments were only three minutes and our daft policeman shtick precluded anything but stupid conversation. I wouldn't have minded so much if we were coming up with Chuckle Gold, but too often it was only Comedy Copper.

Breaking Baaad

BaaadDad's music-video reviews had been one of the more popular parts of the pilot series (I found out later that John Peel and even David Bowie had enjoyed Pa's pop grumbles). So, for the second series, we returned to Clapham, primed Pa with sparkling wine and stoked his antipathy for some of 1997's biggest chart hits. There was 'Song 2' by Blur:

> *I really hate this video. It seems to be a celebration of violence, a celebration of ugliness. It is mindless to announce that your head's been almost shaved by a jumbo jet and that, as a consequence, you're feeling a bit heavy metal. The whole amusement, as far*

> *as he's concerned, is that it's very daring to come near to being decapitated by a jumbo jet which is flying where it ought not to be. But so what?*

Unsurprisingly, he also took against the anarcho pop collective Chumbawamba and their global smash 'Tubthumping':

> *This is the most unpleasant performance that one has ever seen. I get knocked down occasionally, and like everybody else, I get up again because I have to. I certainly don't go around shouting about it in the sort of obscene way that these amazingly ugly performers do.*

The biggest-selling single of 1997 was Elton John's 'Candle in the Wind', reissued as 'Goodbye England's Rose' in a charity tribute to Princess Diana, who died in August of that year. For Dad, the single and Elton John's performance of it at Diana's funeral summed up everything that was wrong with the tidal wave of public anguish following the Princess's death.

As usual, the finished review was made up of commentary chunks that we'd directed Dad to repeat in a more concise form, having filmed an initial, looser response to the video he'd just watched. With 'Candle in the Wind', there was a chunk in the free-form first take that I wish we could have used, but it was too long and the more naturalistic tone of his delivery didn't fit with the rest of the review. This was what he said about Diana's death and Elton's single:

> *The popular reaction to it was an undignified, unrestrained gut reaction to something which stirred emotions. Not to say it didn't stir them profoundly, but the expressions of sorrow, the expressions of regret, were not expressed with any dignity, with any profundity, but were expressed with monumental superficiality, as witness, the high priest of pop, John Elton [sic], in Westminster Abbey.*

It was all part of a Pop whole. And ironically, a whole which was stage-managed, produced by the very forces which we're told contributed to the tragedy itself, which is to say the tabloid press, and with the tabloid press, all those who then react to the tabloid press, the commentators, the television presenters, the producers of the television programmes, and the whole thing snowballs. The whole thing becomes a cascade of cheap sentiment.

In a bid to introduce some variety into BaaadDad's segments, if not his general outlook, we alternated his video reviews with reports from three music festivals that took place that year. Dad treated each one as if it were a visit to the Glyndebourne opera festival and came equipped with a picnic blanket and a cool box of wine and cheese.

At the Tribal Gathering dance-music festival, Dad found a spot on the grass outside one of the big rave tents, and while he was uncorking a bottle of wine, Joe convinced a young Australian woman to come and chat. She said she was tripping on acid, and when Dad said he'd never tried drugs, she rolled him a joint, which he appeared to take a drag on before telling her she was very beautiful.

Mum hated that bit when she saw it. She wasn't worried about the drugs as much as Dad being lecherous. I thought Mum was making too much of it at the time – he was BaaadDad, after all – but looking back, she was right. Dad thought he was being charming, and sometimes he was, but other times he was definitely on the sleazy spectrum. Meanwhile, he was always ready to pontificate about the degeneracy of the youth. 'It's a sort of chaos,' he said, picking his way through the bodies and the litter while Skunk Anansie played at what turned out to be the last Phoenix festival. 'And this is what is sincerely troubling to someone of my generation. That we may actually be returning in a large circle to an age of barbarism.'

'I'm Here to See Mike Crichton'

We retired my superfan character Louise for series two and, instead, brought back *Takeover TV*'s Ken Korda. This time Ken was in a slightly more naturalistic guise as a cocky and opinionated filmmaker hoping to surf the wave of success in the British film industry that followed Nineties hits like *Four Weddings and a Funeral*, *Secrets & Lies*, *Trainspotting* and *The Full Monty*. So, Ken presented a six-part guide to Making It in the Movies, demonstrating the key stages of getting an edgy independent film made, with emphasis on the importance of shooting, shouting, swearing, drugs and jungle music.

The first episode of Ken's guide showed him calling LA-based production companies from a payphone on Sunset Boulevard and delivering pitches for a series of projects with titles like *Soho Smackboys*, *High in Crazy City* and *Pickers, Nickers and Shit Kickers*. Whereas directors like Quentin Tarantino would make references to obscure martial arts movies and cool American Seventies pop culture, Ken's influences were more current, more British and less likely to be understood by Americans. Regular touchstones were British TV shows like *Birds of a Feather* and the children's programmes *Playbus* and *Bodger and Badger*, and British TV personalities like Carol Vorderman, Ainsley Harriott, Toyah Willcox, Dale Winton, and Ken's favourites PJ & Duncan. What Ken didn't seem to understand was that PJ & Duncan weren't real people, but characters in the teen drama *Byker Grove*, played by future British TV entertainment behemoths 'Ant' McPartlin and 'Dec' Donnelly. 'PJ's on board with *Smack Me Up Gunbitch*,' Ken would explain to the baffled American film company employees. 'But he wasn't so sure about Duncan. He thought maybe Duncan would be frightened by the guns and the slapping.'

I didn't mind doing the stupid phone pitches as Ken. Harvey Weinstein's assistant threatened to call the police if I didn't stop leaving messages about PJ & Duncan, but I wasn't too worried about that. What made me sick with nerves was driving with Joe to Warner Bros. Studios in Burbank and trying to blag my way onto the set of the medical drama *ER* while wearing a hidden camera.

I adored *ER*. It was one of the things that bonded Sarah and me during the early stages of our relationship, and I thought it was one of the most consistently exciting, well-acted and well-made shows on TV at the time. Despite my nerves as I approached the entrance to Warner Bros., I was also exhilarated just to be near where the third season of *ER* was being made. Joe had suggested that, in order to get past security, I should pretend to have an appointment with the creator of *ER*, Michael Crichton. So, with Joe waiting in the car nearby, I strode over to the security cabin and, as the guard emerged, I said confidently, 'Hello. Just here to see Mike Crichton. It's Ken Korda.'

I was dressed in shorts, a T-shirt with a devil patch on the front and a USA baseball cap on top of Ken's obviously fake hair, a straw-coloured wig. The tiny camera, which was attached to a recorder in my backpack, was taped to the inside of my T-shirt behind a little hole in the devil patch. I prepared myself for the guard to take one look at my wig and tell me to get lost, but to my amazement he nodded and waved me through. Perhaps he was impressed by the British accent? Whatever, I was in.

I knew it wouldn't be long before I was busted and escorted out, but as I walked down the sunny street between the neat hedges in the shadow of the big Warner Bros. water tower looming ahead of me, nobody gave me a second glance. I stopped someone to ask for directions to the *ER* studio, which, in a very friendly way, they gave me. The further I got, the sicker yet more excited I started to feel, and when I saw a group of people standing around outside the giant hangar of Stage 11 and realised that several of them were dressed in the County General medical scrubs of *ER*, I nearly fainted.

There, also in costume among the actors beginning to file back onto the set after a filming break, was one of my favourite *ER* cast members. No, not George Clooney, I was never that fussed about him. And no, not Julianna Margulies either, though I loved her. It was Eriq La Salle, who played the fiercely talented, ambitious and often intense *ER* surgical resident Dr Peter Benton. As I got closer, I saw Eriq was talking to Laura Innes, who played the pragmatic, strong-willed and occasionally polarising administrator and physician Dr Kerry Weaver.

On the show, their characters were stern and serious, so it was strange to see them drinking coffee and laughing. Remembering that I was filming, I walked straight up to Eriq and said, 'Hello, I'm looking for Mike Crichton. I'm here to talk about the *Bodger and Badger* project. Do you know where I can find him?' I could see Eriq taking me in and thinking that I looked weird, but there are a lot of weird-looking creative types in Hollywood, so he wasn't going to be rude in case I really did know Michael Crichton. 'I don't think he's here today,' he replied. 'But you could ask on set.'

He called over to a production assistant, and moments later I was being led through a side door into Stage 11 and then directly onto the hospital corridor set that I recognised from *ER*, bustling with actors and crew preparing to start filming again. 'Wait just one second,' said the production assistant, who went over to a bearded man talking to a big bloke with a camera on his shoulder. With my heart pounding, I did my best to look bored as I turned one way, then the other, so my tiny camera would take in as much as possible of my iconic surroundings.

The bearded man walked over to me and said, 'Michael isn't here today. Were you supposed to have a meeting?'

'Yes, he wanted to talk to me about a couple of projects that he's interested in, namely *Smack Me Up Gunbitch*, but also the *Bodger and Badger* movie, which I've heard both PJ and Duncan are very excited about. I'm assuming he's told you about *Bodger and Badger*?'

Like Eriq La Salle, the bearded man, who I think was the director, was aware that there was something strange about the sandy-haired British man with the loud shirt, the backpack and the odd voice. But he, too, assumed I wouldn't have been allowed onto the set if I was a nutter. He said he hadn't heard about the *Bodger and Badger* project, but if he saw Michael Crichton he would be sure to mention that I'd come by. I took that as my cue to get out while I was ahead. I could have made more of a nuisance of myself, but I just couldn't bear it, especially when every single person had been so kind to Ken. As it was, I had to stop myself from saying, 'By the way, I think what you all do here is wonderful. This is one of the greatest TV shows ever made. Seriously, it's up there with *Playbus*.'

I waved a cheery farewell to Dr Benton, Kerry Weaver and everyone I'd spoken to at Warner Bros. and drifted back in a daze. Feeling like a bank robber with a bag full of cash, I got into the car saying, 'Let's go! Let's go!', and we made our getaway. I didn't want to tell Joe what had happened. I wanted to show him, so when he pulled over I got the recorder out of the backpack, flipped out the screen, rewound the tape and pressed play.

The footage of my arrival at the security cabin was grainy, and the top corner of the image was slightly obscured by the edge of the hole in the patch, but it was good enough. I pressed visual fast-forward to get to the bit with Dr Benton, but as I did so the picture went black. I rewound the tape and played it again without fast-forwarding. Again, it went black soon after the security guard had waved me through. The queasy, nervous feeling I'd had walking towards the sound stages returned, but this time there was no excitement. Just deep dread. I scrolled through the rest of the tape. It was all black. The connection to the camera must have come loose soon after I'd arrived at Warner Bros. Joe tried to console me. 'Don't worry, man. We probably couldn't have used it anyway. It's cool that you got in there.' At that moment, and whenever I thought about my *ER* adventure for months afterwards, I felt too sick and miserable to acknowledge it, but it was cool. And even though it's not on video, it happened.

Well Out of Order

When the second series of *The Adam and Joe Show* was broadcast in November 1997, Channel 4 showed only the first four episodes of the six-episode series, then waited until March of the following year to show the last two. Peter Grimsdale was apologetic. Scheduling was mysterious, he said, and this was one of the times we suffered from being in the Religion department rather than Entertainment, but there was good news. After the last two episodes of our new series went out in March, the channel would air the pilot series again before repeating the rest of series two.

The decision to show the second series out of order like this initially seemed insane and slightly insulting. It made a mockery of Ken Korda's carefully constructed six-part guide to making an edgy indie movie, for a start. On the plus side, it meant there'd be an episode of *The Adam and Joe Show* going out on Channel 4 every Friday night for ten weeks in early 1998. What was more, we were part of a post-watershed lineup that began with *Ellen* at 9, *Father Ted* at 9.30, *Frasier* at 10, *King of the Hill* at 10.30, and *The Adam and Joe Show* at 11.05, right before a repeat of *TFI Friday* from earlier in the evening. Millions of people munched into that Mike Judge and Chris Evans sandwich, and enough of them liked the Adam and Joe filling for word to spread. We stood teetering on the vertiginous verge of minor celebrity.

RAMBLE

EVANSGATE

It's possible that one of the people who wasn't so enthusiastic about *The Adam and Joe Show* around that time was Chris Evans himself. Was it just a coincidence that Channel 4 mysteriously dropped episode four from our repeat run when that was the show that featured my *Star Wars* figurine parody of *TFI Friday*? Could it have been that Chris, who was a powerful presence with a reputation for getting his own way, suggested to the Channel 4 schedulers that it might be better *not* to run a programme that took the piss out of their tentpole show right before it was repeated?

OK, it's more likely that Channel 4 themselves chose not to air that episode in deference to one of their biggest stars, or for some other entirely unrelated reason, but I like the idea of myself as a brave satirist being silenced by a powerful ginger despot (even though I met Chris Evans years later when he presented us with a Gold Sony Award for our 6 Music radio show and he was charming and complimentary). Look, I'm just asking questions ...

CHAPTER 5

ALL I WANT TO DO IS ROCK

The man in black Speedos and the boy with ginger hair paddled their lilo towards me through the warm Jamaican sea. As a seven-year-old boy on holiday, the most exciting person I could encounter was another seven-year-old boy, and I was thrilled to discover this one was the best kind: an American. The Buxtons were living in Wales at the time, where Dad had moved us from London a couple of years before, hoping to find a more salubrious country life. At the local village school, the other children told me I had a posh accent and Chinese eyes, neither of which they considered desirable. But as I paddled with my new friends, the man in black Speedos told me he liked my accent, his son agreed that it was 'neat', and no reference was made to the nationality of my eyes. We shot the breeze about my favourite TV shows (anything to do with robots and spaceships) and my hobbies (watching TV, drawing robots and spaceships), and I luxuriated in the cadences of their cool American voices.

Back on the beach, I told Mum I'd made some new friends, and when they came out of the sea, I beckoned them over. The man in black Speedos shook Mum's hand and asked about England. He enthused about Chile when she told him that's where she was from originally, and he told her how much he loved visiting Jamaica and that her son was a very polite young man.

After they left, Mum said, 'Do you know who that was?'

'He said he was called John,' I answered.

'Yes, he's called Johnny Cash,' said Mum. 'He's a famous musician.'

I was pleased to have met someone famous. I wished it had been a celebrity I'd heard of, but back in 1976 that was a very select group that consisted mainly of Kermit the Frog, Mickey Mouse, kids' TV presenters Floella Benjamin and Johnny Morris, and Steve Austin (the Bionic Man).

Ten years after my holiday hang with Johnny Cash and John Jr, music had replaced robots and spaceships as my primary enthusiasm, and never again would I be so blasé about encountering a famous musician. Perhaps it's the power that musicians have to connect with an audience more directly (and in much less time) than the average writer, director, painter or playwright, but meeting someone who's recorded a song that's become a welcome part of my life always feels to me like encountering a superhero with magical abilities.

Weller, Weller, Weller ...

Of course, as the Marvel universe has taught us, even superheroes can turn out to be surprisingly tedious and dull sometimes. How was it, for example, that a musician as accomplished as Paul Weller was unable to realise how funny it was when I asked him, live on BBC Radio 2, 'Does anyone ever say to you, "Paul Weller, Weller, Weller, Ooh! Tell me more! Tell me more!"?'

Liza Tarbuck and I were covering for Jonathan Ross for a couple of weekends in 2010, and the night before we were due to interview the Modfather, I was having some wine and thinking of things to ask him. If I were doing the interview now, I'd limit my questions to music and not try to engineer any funny moments, but in those days there was still a part of me that treated every celebrity encounter as an opportunity for mild mischief. Anyway, I told myself after my third glass of wine, someone who'd produced as much great art as Paul Weller would surely laugh and laugh at hearing his name so artfully incorporated into a line from the *Grease* song 'Summer Nights'.

Twelve hours later, Paul Weller was glaring at me with his angry Mod eyes for what seemed an eternity before muttering, 'Was that supposed to be funny?' At this, my co-presenter, the Radio 2 producers, and everyone in Paul Weller's entourage watching through the glass panel from the room next door looked away or shook their heads while the previously fun atmosphere was sucked out of our studio like the collapsing newborn Xenomorph at the end of *Alien: Resurrection*. For weeks afterwards, people who'd been listening to the encounter on Radio 2 told me how excruciating they had found it. I told them not to be too hard on Paul. An artist who operates on such a primal emotional level can't always be expected to discern the discreet amplitudes of finely wrought comedy craftsmanship like mine. Altogether now, 'Paul Weller, Weller, Weller, Ooh!'

But as well as the more tricky musical geniuses, I've met a few with whom I've spent some of my favourite times, and my introduction to several of them came as the result of a photoshoot that Joe and I did to promote the third series of *The Adam and Joe Show* in 1999. That day, our make-up was applied by a young German woman called Nora, who I discovered was a fan of the comedy show *Big Train*. I told Nora that Joe and I had contributed a couple of embryonic ideas to *Big Train* that the writers Graham Linehan and Arthur Mathews and a cast that included Julia Davis, Simon Pegg, Mark Heap, Kevin Eldon and Amelia Bullmore had turned into memorable sketches.

Joe's idea was to have the Eighties musical duo Daryl Hall and John Oates being sent by British police to tackle problems on a crime-ridden housing estate. My idea was turned into a sketch about a group of workers who are outraged when they're told they need to stop wanking in the office. Nora was impressed by our *Big Train* credentials and said she looked forward to telling her boyfriend, Fran, who was also a *Big Train* enthusiast. Nora said Fran was in a band called Travis.

I knew about Travis. I'd listened to their first album, *Good Feeling*, and I loved a song on there called 'All I Want to Do Is Rock', a swaggering, anthemic blast of guitar joy that I'd included on a compilation CD I'd recently made. In fact, I'd put 'All I Want to Do Is Rock' in the opening Timeless Banger section of the compilation, in between 'Abstract Plain' by Frank Black and 'Lord Only Knows' by Beck. I didn't mention the CD to Nora because I know how overexcited people get when men mention their music compilations, and I didn't want to blow her mind while she was applying my make-up.

RAMBLE

THE LOST ART OF THE HOMEMADE MUSIC COMPILATION

Before the Streaming Age, I spent literally thousands of hours assembling my favourite music onto compilations (or 'compies').

The first albums I owned were all on cassette, and with the money I made from working in a pizza restaurant at the end of the 1980s, I bought a Technics RS-T130 Double Cassette Deck so that I could compile my favourite tracks onto tapes that I'd listen to on my personal cassette player while walking to the tube to meet Joe or while wandering aimlessly through London's West End on my own, imagining myself as the star of a movie about a deep young man wandering around the West End on his own.

C30, C60, C90 GO

I soon realised that with compies (as with films and the theatre), 90 minutes was the optimum length for a satisfying experience. True, I did go through a short phase of thinking I could reduce the number of tapes I carried around in my backpack by making a collection of Mega Compies on C120 tapes, which ran for two hours, but I soon found that this longer length stretched not just my early music collection to its limits but the magnetic tape itself, which was thinner and prone to snapping.

After the hours it took to complete a compilation, there was no way I was going to discard one if the tape snapped, and over the years I became adept at repairing broken cassettes with the skill of a master surgeon.

Sub-Ramble

KEEPING TABS ON KERMIT

My first lesson in cassette-tape anatomy came during a long car journey when I was eight and boredom induced me to stuff bits of chewed-up paper into the two little square holes on the top of our *Muppet Show* cassette. I forgot what I'd done until the next time I went to listen to the Muppets on Dad's

Dictaphone, and along with 'Play' I inadvertently pressed down the red 'Record' button, then spent a few seconds wondering why I wasn't hearing *The Muppet Show* theme tune. It wasn't supposed to be possible to record over a store-bought album, but by filling the holes on the top of the cassette, I had unwittingly circumvented the tape's record-protection mechanism.

Was I exhilarated by the discovery that I could hack the preset world this way? Did I amuse myself by recording specially placed fart sounds over my dad's Wagner cassettes from then on? No. I was horrified by what I'd done. It was 1978, and that *Muppet Show* cassette represented the only way I could have Kermit fun whenever I wanted. Now, after he sang, 'To introduce this record, that's what I'm here to do', there was a big, breathy slice of my boring life. From then on, I would fast-forward past the theme so as not to be reminded of my accidental frog erasure.

MIND THE GAP

In the late 1980s, the arrival of the auto-reverse function for personal cassette players finally eliminated the agony of having to remove a cassette, flip it around and reinsert it at the end of a side. At last, a nearly seamless playback experience was possible, so filling every second of space on a compilation tape became more important than ever. But what to do with those awkward spaces at the end of a side that weren't long enough for a 'regular' song? These were some of my favourite end-of-side fillers:

'Allison' by Pixies (1.17)

Everything you could possibly want from a song in 77 seconds.

'Another Green World' by Brian Eno (1.41)

aka the theme from the TV documentary show Arena, *a perfect looping miniature mood bath.*

'Jump' by Derek and Clive (1.20)

Oh, the transgressive ecstasy of borrowing my friend Patrick's Derek and Clive album at age 13 and sticking this F-bomb-heavy Dudley Moore number on my next compy!

'Penis Song (Not the Noel Coward Song)' by Monty Python (0.42)

More excellent naughtiness for 13-year-old Buckles, even sweeter for being delivered in the style of one of Dad's favourite humorists, who, in those days, I absolutely did not see the point of.

'Oil on Canvas' by Japan (1.25)

A beautiful, piano-heavy ambient palette cleanser that leaves listeners in no doubt that the compiler is next-level sophisticated.

'Outdoor Miner' (short version) by Wire (1.45)

At 1.45 in length, this is practically prog compared to my other short selections, but it's still 15 seconds shy of the indefensibly indulgent 2-minute mark.

'Boat of Car' by They Might Be Giants (1.15)

75 seconds of Dada-esque oddness from my favourite 'too clever' American art-rock duo that even samples my Jamaican swimming buddy Johnny Cash.

'Irate Tile Man' the Jerky Boys (0.52)

Our friend Zac got hold of a tape of phone pranks by New Yorkers the Jerky Boys in 1992, and for several years thereafter our conversations were liberally peppered with phrases like 'assneck', 'liver lips' and 'sizzle chest'.

THE CD ERA

In 1997, with money from making *The Adam and Joe Show*, I bought my first desktop computer (an Apple G3), and my brother Dave, the Buxton family's tech savant, showed me how to use the CD-ROM drive to 'rip' songs from my CDs, arrange them into playlists and 'burn' them onto a 74-minute blank disk. The process was laborious. If a CD was scratched, the songs would take ages to rip or fail to do so. Then, when the time came to burn the compilation onto a blank CD, I'd sit hopefully watching the progress bar creep to completion, only for it to freeze frequently, whereupon a dialogue box would pop up to inform me that the job had been aborted.

After the second series of *The Adam and Joe Show*, the BBC got in touch to ask if Joe and I wanted to make a pilot for a comedy programme on Radio 1. Yes, we said, but I insisted that to maintain our homemade aesthetic, we needed to do everything ourselves rather than work with BBC producers, so to put the pilot together, we were given a copy of the audio editing software Pro Tools.

If I'd spent a little more time working on the Radio 1 pilot, it might have been commissioned, but on the plus side, after a month or two, my compies had taken a quantum leap forward as I started creating elaborate seamless mixes on Pro Tools with artwork I created in Photoshop, then painstakingly printed, cut out and folded to fit into CD jewel cases.

Then the streaming age happened, and as people got used to listening to music on their devices, my compilation empire crumbled. Oh well, I suppose it was good that I had more time to concentrate on relationships with humans – until I started spending hours organising MP3s into playlists on iTunes, of course. I'm trying to keep this chapter upbeat, so I won't tell you about the dark days of the early 2010s when an iTunes upgrade wiped out my entire MP3 playlist library. There's only so much pain I can dredge up for one book.

The last CD compilations I made at the end of the 2010s were for my mum, who, by then, was the only person I knew who still listened to music on CD. Every Christmas for the previous couple of decades, I'd made her a new compy filled with a mix of tracks she'd requested from favourites like Ella Fitzgerald, Barbara Streisand, Bing Crosby and Roberta Flack, as well as songs I thought she might like from artists that were new to her like Shuggie Otis, Spoon, Laura Marling, Pavement, Ariel Pink and Travis. The finishing touch would be a recent picture of her grandchildren on the front. Now That's What I Call A Granny Compy!

When we'd get together for our festive family celebrations, I'd make sure the CD was the first thing Mum opened so we could listen to it while everyone unwrapped their presents, and Mum would sing along or say, 'I don't know this one!' or sometimes 'I'm not sure I like this one, Adam.' Making the CD and listening to it with Mum and my family was one of my favourite parts of Christmas.

Let's Do Launch

Nora told me Travis had a new album coming out, which they'd recorded with Radiohead's producer Nigel Godrich. It was my turn to be impressed. She said the new album was called *The Man Who*. 'The man who what?' I asked. 'Just *The Man Who*,' said Nora. I told her we were having a party in a couple of weeks to celebrate the transmission of *The Adam and Joe Show* series three, and that she and Fran should come along.

The launch party took place at the Tardis, a collection of cluttered workshops, artists' studios and function rooms tucked away below street level in an old London Transport parcel depot by Farringdon tube. Our friends at *The Idler* magazine often held events at the Tardis, and memories of nights there feature a jaded Alex James of Blur sipping absinthe, actor Keith Allen putting his arm around loudly pissed poet Jock Scot, journalist Miranda Sawyer looking cool and interesting, and John Moore from the band Black Box Recorder playing the saw. Every time I went to the Tardis, I smoked about a hundred cigarettes and woke up the next day feeling as though I'd been in a car accident.

The evening of our party, Fran turned up without Nora but with his friend Dougie, who played bass in Travis. They were two of several musicians there that night, some of whom had appeared on the Vinyl Justice segment of our show in which Joe and I dressed as policemen and searched music collections for 'criminal records'. As well as Fran and Dougie, we played host to Mark from the Bluetones, Robin and John from the Beta Band, and most of that month's lineup of the Fall, including, to my great surprise, lead singer Mark E. Smith.

We'd invited M.E.S. as a courtesy, but assumed he'd be a no-show, as he was too legendary and cantankerous. However, the day before, our producer Debbie said Mark had called and had asked if he could bring some of his bandmates.

Adam with Mark E. Smith of the Fall, 1998

IS EVERYTHING OK, MR SMITH?

Our Vinyl Justice segment with Mark E. Smith had been filmed a few months before the Tardis party. Mark didn't want to do it at his real home in Salford, so instead, we shot in the basement flat I'd recently moved into in Clerkenwell. With Mark's reputation for irascibility in mind, we'd hired riot police uniforms with big helmets and truncheons and, on the advice of his record label, we'd stocked up on booze.

We started by filming an intro sequence in which Joe and

I pretended to forcibly enter the premises, and as we came through the door, Mark playfully slapped, punched and kicked us a little more forcefully than we were expecting. Then we got down to business and started looking through the bag of records he'd brought along. We picked out the *Miami Vice Theme* by Jan Hammer, an album of trucking songs and a single called *Blind Man's Penis* by John Trubee & The Geeks. Though he seemed to relish the opportunity to talk about these kinds of records rather than more obvious Fall influences like Captain Beefheart, Can, The Monks and R. Dean Taylor, Mark was reluctant to use conventional sentences and instead responded to our questions with a mixture of shouts, rants and weird sobs.

Then, when we were halfway through filming, and Mark was halfway through a bottle of vodka, he suddenly stopped talking completely. It was as if he'd just realised he was involved in something he might regret.

'Is everything OK, Mr Smith?' I asked in my policeman voice, to which Mark replied, 'How much am I being paid for this?' I explained that our budget didn't generally stretch to paying anyone for these segments but asked how much he thought was reasonable. 'Two hundred pounds,' came the reply. Still in my riot police uniform, I ran across the street to the nearest cashpoint and withdrew £200 from my current account. Back at the flat, I handed the notes to Mr Smith, and he perked up, perhaps a little chastened that he'd held us to ransom and we'd given in so timorously.

We filmed for a while longer, with Mark playful and amused one minute, sarcastic and menacing the next. At one point, the landline rang (I don't think I even had a mobile phone back then), and I let it go to the answering machine, but everyone stopped and listened. After the beep, the room suddenly filled with the RP tones of my friend Lucretia (she wasn't called Lucretia, but she may as well have been). 'Hi, Adam. I hear you've got a new place in Clerkenwell? So cool.

When are you going to invite me over? OK, give me a call. Bye.'

Mark immediately launched into an impression of Lucretia as if she were a ditzy flirt. '*Oh, Adaaam, so coool! When can I come ooover, Adaaaam? Call mee! Byeee!*' Looking back at the footage of this moment during the Great Archiving Session of 2020, it seemed to me that Mark was, in his own way, being friendly and having fun that day, but at the time I very much felt that I was being bullied for being posh by one of my musical heroes.

A few minutes after the phone call, Mark told Joe he had a head 'like a fucking egg', called him a cunt, then put a plastic bag over his head, sat on top of him and punched him repeatedly, albeit fairly feebly, in the arm and head.

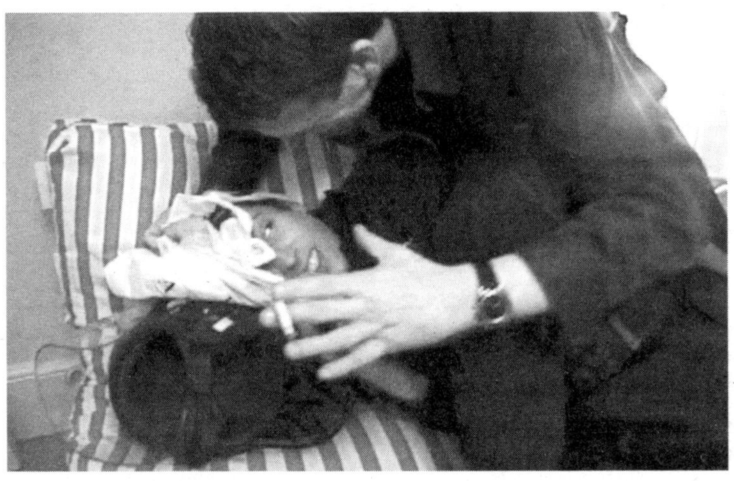

Unsafe space – Joe being sat on and punched by M.E.S.

There was no doubt in my mind that Mark E. Smith was one of music's great unhinged originals, and when I saw him coming down the Tardis steps for our launch party a few months after we'd shot our Vinyl Justice segment, I was amazed.

And slightly terrified. Many of my closest friends and family were also at the Tardis that night, and I wondered how they would respond if Mr Smith launched into mocking impressions of them once he'd had a few free beers.

At one point, I was talking to Lucretia when Mark E. Smith sauntered over and put his hand on my shoulder. 'I liked the Richard and Judy thing with the toys,' he slurred, referring to our *Star Wars* figurine parody of the TV magazine show *This Morning,* which had been in the episode of the new series we'd all just watched as it was broadcast. 'Hey, thanks, Mark!' I said, then, feeling it would be rude not to make introductions: 'Uhm, this is my friend Lucretia.'

'Oh, hello. And what do you do?' said Lucretia, like the Queen meeting a subject.

'Musician!' barked Mark with a wonky grin before wobbling across the room to shout at a bartender. I think he had a fun night.

Travis Fun

Meanwhile, Fran and Doug were chatting in a corner with Joe. I went over to join them, and we spent a while discussing whether *Antz* was better than *A Bug's Life*. I thought, *Yes, it was,* because the main title theme for *Antz* is so good and I liked seeing an explicitly anti-war message in a mainstream kid's film. Doug and Fran weren't so keen on *Antz,* because of Woody Allen, who was entering his divisive-figure era.

A few days after the party, I was in HMV on Oxford Street and the DJ played 'Driftwood' from the new Travis album, which I hadn't heard yet. It was definitely pretty, but I missed the gusto of 'All I Want to Do Is Rock'. *That's a shame,* I thought to myself. *They were such nice guys. It would have been great if their new album did well, but it sounds a bit too, I dunno,* nice, *and everyone knows what happens to nice guys, especially in the music industry* (they get bad reviews).

Fran and Doug invited me to see Travis play at the Forum in Kentish Town, so my brother Dave and I went along. The show was excellent; the band was tight, Fran was a warm and engaging frontman, and the songs no longer sounded simply 'nice' but bursting with memorably lovely tunefulness. In the bar afterwards, Dougie introduced me to Nigel Godrich, who said he liked *The Adam and Joe Show* and patiently answered my fanboy questions about recording with Beck, Pavement and Radiohead. At the end of the night, we all exchanged numbers, and over the following months we hung out a few times, bonding over Bowie, art school, films and comedy. Fran suggested I join Travis on tour in Germany with my video camera to shoot some behind-the-scenes footage for a possible documentary. 'Yes, please,' I said.

I loved being on tour. The camaraderie, the catering, the hotels, the music chats, the internal politics, the booze (back when I could still drink too much without being incapacitated for several days afterwards), the boredom alleviated by cigarette smoking, the soundchecks, during which I'd wander between band members with my video camera while they played 'All I Want to Do Is Rock', but perhaps most of all, I loved the AAA laminate and the tour bus. I've always been a fan of accessing areas, but suddenly, with my AAA laminate, I could access ALL the areas, and it made me feel important (one of my favourite feelings). As for the tour bus, it was a glorious haven of childlike masculinity at a time when, as I entered my thirties, I was just beginning to realise that I might be getting a bit old for childlike masculinity.

At the end of a show, we'd climb onto the bus, and while the crew packed up the band's gear, a night of drinking, smoking and waffling got underway in the cramped rear lounge. Then we'd set off for the next city, choogling down the autobahn to the sounds of David Bowie, Joni Mitchell, the Clash,

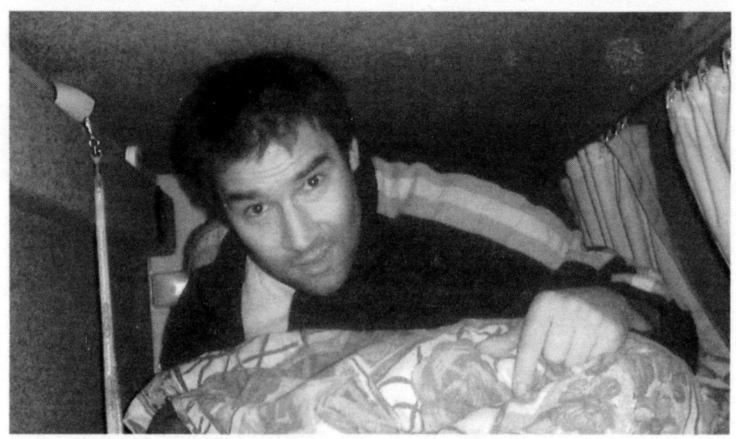

In my Travis tour bus bunk, December 1999

the Pogues, Madness, XTC, Pixies, Queen and Kraftwerk ('Autobahn', obvs). The music and the booze meant the conversation only got heavy when we wanted it to, and when we started to flag, it would be hugs goodnight, followed by staggering out of the lounge and rolling into my bunk. Here in my cocoon, I was lulled to sleep in minutes by the soft roar of the air-con and the comforting rumble of the engine, like a baby in a buggy. The next day, we'd do it all again!

Picking Up Something Good

When Joe and I were making the second series of *The Adam and Joe Show* in 1997, I would sometimes unwind after a hard day in the chuckle mine by smoking a doobie, putting on my headphones and disappearing into the widescreen angst of 'Subterranean Homesick Alien', 'Let Down' and 'Paranoid Android' from Radiohead's album *OK Computer*. Those songs, along with Cornershop's 'Brimful of Asha', the Verve's 'Bittersweet Symphony', *ER*, honey mustard pretzels, New

Labour and the death of Princess Diana, powerfully evoke for me the beginning of my relationship with Sarah, and though our union eventually achieved joyful perfection four years later when we got married, our courtship was weird. When we started hanging out (platonically), she was sort of seeing someone else and hadn't quite decided if I was a better option, a fact that caused us both a fair amount of heartache. Well, it did for me. I'll just check if it did for her.

> *God, I don't want to do this at all – you wouldn't ask me to do this if it was on the podcast because you would be too embarrassed about my voice being too plummy (and I bet you take that last sentence out of the book, too). To be honest, my memory is so bad now that I can't really remember much about that time – but I think you are completely overegging the heartache. There were probably only a couple of weeks where I was a bit noncommittal – although I suppose there was definitely a moment when I realised that hanging out with the other bloke was not half as much fun or as nice as being with you. And then we got married – is that enough?*

Anyway, the point is I adored Radiohead, and I relied on their music to lift my anxieties into a shimmering realm of exquisite emotional turmoil during a time that was incredibly intense for me (though not apparently for Sarah). The following year, Grant Gee's excellent Radiohead documentary *Meeting People Is Easy* painted a portrait of a band frazzled by touring and unsure of how best to process the hyperbole that had been heaped upon *OK Computer*. Lead singer Thom Yorke seemed especially uncomfortable with being told that he lifted people into a shimmering realm of exquisite emotional turmoil, and for the next few years the band became increasingly elusive and mysterious. But for fans like me, becoming elusive and mysterious just deepened the fascination, and as my friendship with Travis and Nigel Godrich grew, I couldn't help getting over-amped whenever I grazed the Radiohead orbit.

In October 2000, I visited Travis in Los Angeles, ostensibly to do more videoing as they worked with Nigel on their album *The Invisible Band*, the follow-up to *The Man Who.* The afternoon of my arrival, a taxi took me from LAX straight to Ocean Way Studios, where the band was recording in the mid-sized Studio B. They had transformed the live room, as well as the adjoining control room in which Nigel sat with his feet up on a vast mixing desk, into a creative cocoon festooned with coloured fairy lights that glowed welcomingly amid rugs, sofas, musical instruments and ashtrays; the sort of place where you could imagine a teenage Santa getting stoned with the elves.

There, I found Fran, Dougie, Andy, Neil and touring keyboard player Jeremy recording a track called 'Afterglow' that sounded the way the studio looked: warm and twinkling. Over the next ten days, I watched another few album tracks coming together, including a song that would turn out to be one of Travis's biggest hits. Next time you hear 'Sing' on the radio, listen very closely and you might be able to hear a grinning Buckles wandering between the band members with a video camera, watching the backing track being recorded in a series of ensemble takes.

Perhaps most fascinating for me, as an award-winning songsmith in my own right, was watching Fran finish song lyrics, which he scribbled down on a yellow legal pad between vocal takes and drags on his cigarette. He told me that a previous producer had heard an early version of 'Sing' and hated the original opening line: 'Baby, you've been going so crazy. Lazy, I've been driving Miss Daisy'. Fran had been annoyed but later changed the line to 'Baby, you've been going so crazy. Lately, nothing seems to be going right'.

Trying to write a song lyric that isn't supposed to be funny is embarrassing. How much of yourself should you share? Can you get poetic without being pretentious? Have you made it too easy for the listener to see how your mind works? It's a negotiation with vulnerability that most people would prefer to keep private. I admired the fact that Fran was able to write while I was filming him. For a sensitive man, he could be surprisingly tough.

Nigel and the band were staying at the Chateau Marmont in West Hollywood, where they were holed up in the hotel's little complex of cottages and poolside bungalows nestled in the foothills overlooking Sunset Boulevard. My room was in the main 'chateau' building, where vaulted ceilings, stone flooring, arched doorways and wrought-iron detailing made the place look like Dracula's French holiday home. It made sense that this was one of the drinking haunts frequented in the early 1970s by a gang of wayward musicians that included John Lennon, Alice Cooper, Keith Moon, Ringo Starr, Micky Dolenz and Harry Nilsson, known collectively as the Hollywood Vampires, whose stated mission for a night out was to drink until no one could stand up.

Travis gave the Vampires a run for their money on a couple of occasions at the Bar Marmont next to the hotel, but were perhaps slightly better behaved. Still, there was a lot of steam to let off. *The Man Who* had been phenomenally successful, and the band were under pressure to follow it up with something equally huge. Though Joe and I had never had the same weight of expectation on us, I recognised the strain it put on Fran and Dougie's friendship from time to time. What prevented the train from coming off the tracks was their ability to be emotionally engaged without ever taking themselves too seriously. It was a quality shared by the whole band that infuriated the kind of music critics who think an artist needs to be tortured to be 'authentic', but it protected Travis in the long run.

Chasing Rainbows

A couple of days after I arrived in LA, Radiohead came through town to play the last show of their *Kid A* tour at the Greek Theatre. They were also staying at the Chateau Marmont, and on the afternoon of the show I came down to the lobby to find Thom Yorke and Radiohead drummer Phil Selway waiting for their bandmates before being taken to the Greek for their soundcheck. Thom was chatting with Nigel, so I sidled up to the more approachable-looking Phil and introduced myself before hitting him with a barrage of fan blather: 'Do you get nervous before a show? Is it hard to see what you're doing with the flashing lights on stage? Are you playing "Subterranean Homesick Alien" tonight?' Phil smiled sweetly and answered all my questions ('Yes. Sometimes. No.') before being called away to join his bandmates in the car, while I, giddy from having invaded the space of one-fifth of the mighty 'Head, glided across the tiled lobby to meet Fran and Dougie.

Six hours later, I was again just a few feet away from Thom, but now he was on stage at the Greek Theatre, wobbling his head around and chanting, 'Ice age coming, ice age coming!' I cradled my cup of strawberry margarita and nodded approvingly while thinking, *Which is it? The Ice Age or global warming? I think the messaging needs to be clearer.*

By the time we got to the aftershow party at some not especially nearby Los Angeles bar, I'd put away another few strawberry margaritas, and the combination of booze and over-excitement was bringing out my worst celebrity vampire tendencies. After getting separated from the Travis posse, I spent a while making aimless circuits of the noisy, dimly lit bar until I spotted Thom sitting with Brad Pitt and Jennifer Aniston at a table in the corner. I then spent several more minutes hovering nearby just in case one of them beckoned me over to say how much they'd enjoyed the Adam and Joe toy versions of *Friends* or *Seven* or the 'No Surprises' video (which I'd parodied in our 1998 video for 'Sweet Johnny' by Gorky's Zygotic Mynci), though I wasn't getting my hopes up. I knew that if Thom did spot me, he'd be more likely to think, *What the hell is* he *doing here? He doesn't belong here …* (because his thoughts are like the lyrics of 'Creep').

In the years that followed, I continued to see a lot of Nigel and crossed paths with various Radiohead members from time to time, particularly bassist Colin Greenwood and guitarist Ed O'Brien, with whom I shared a love of Eighties acts like the Police, XTC, Junior, Imagination and Haircut 100. When I got to know Colin's brother, Jonny Greenwood, better, I discovered that he was the band's chief comedy nerd, and he turned out to be a fellow Jerky Boys fan. During the recording sessions for Radiohead's first album at Oxford's Courtyard Studio in 1992, their American producers Sean Slade and Paul Q. Kolderie played the band some Jerky Boys material from a DAT tape on which was written 'Pablo Honey and other classics'. The tape, or parts of it at least – some of the more extreme moments made Thom uncomfortable – was enough of a hit with Radiohead for them to call their debut album *Pablo Honey*.

In late 2007, the music-video director Garth Jennings and I had lunch with Ed O'Brien and Nigel Godrich, and they asked if we'd be up for travelling to Radiohead's studio outside Oxford to help put together a three-hour live webcast called *Thumbs Down* to celebrate the completion of their album *In Rainbows*. It was an unusual moment for the band, who, finding themselves out of contract with their label EMI, had decided to release the new album independently, using a tip jar system whereby fans could download *In Rainbows* for free or pay whatever they felt was fair. At a time when the music industry was struggling to adjust to a culture of online music sharing (or piracy), this was seen as a bold and controversial move. From Radiohead's perspective, though, it was pure expediency, a fleeting opportunity to circumvent the lumbering machine of record releasing and promotion that all successful bands inevitably become a part of. The webcast was to be made in a similarly rough and ready DIY spirit, which was why Garth and I had got the call.

Nigel, whose talents include electronics wizardry, had essentially transformed the band's workspace into a TV studio using vintage cameras and vision mixing equipment from eBay. Here, the band would perform tracks from *In Rainbows* as well as a few covers for the webcast, but as with a regular TV music show, there would also be a few links which Nigel suggested I could help present, as well as odd clips the band had put together and some new no-budget music videos for other *In Rainbows* tracks that Garth and I would be responsible for.

RAMBLE

GARTH JENNINGS

One of my favourite clips from the first series of *Takeover TV* was a music video called 'Polish Plums' that featured a shot of a plum with a human face singing a song about being a plum. It was the work of Garth Jennings, whose friend Dominic Leung was the face of the plum. Along with their art school pal Nick Goldsmith, Dom and Garth formed the production company Hammer & Tongs, which went on to make some of the most ingenious and striking music videos of the late 90s and early 2000s. Just a few of the multi-coloured blasts from the Hammer & Tongs cannon were the milk carton promo for Blur's 'Coffee & TV', the video showing the evolution of man from a single-celled organism to a burger-munching city dweller for Fatboy Slim's 'Right Here, Right Now', and the stretchy-limbed Muppet video for 'Pumping on Your Stereo' by Supergrass.

When we were thinking about what we should do for the fourth series of *The Adam and Joe Show*, Fenton Bailey, who never forgot 'Polish Plums', suggested we meet Garth to see if he might contribute some new ideas. Happily, Garth was a fan of our show and agreed to direct a couple of items for us (a *Robot Wars* spoof xaaain which souped-up toasters jammed forks into each other, and a homage to the Stu-Stu-*Studio Line* hair-gel advert that Joe and I had loved in the Eighties).

Garth became a close friend, and many of the home videos I digitised during the 2020 archiving session feature him, his wife Louise and all our kids larking about on weekend visits and holidays. There are videos of Easter egg hunts in toddler times, galloping on the spot to 'Gangnam Style' as preteens and video game benders (usually featuring Super Smash Bros.) on time off from GCSE and A-level revision. Meanwhile, Garth moved from directing music videos to feature films: *The Hitchhiker's Guide to the Galaxy*, *Son of Rambow* and then the globe-conquering animated *Sing* films.

Nigel Godrich, Jonny Greenwood, Garth Jennings, Thom Yorke, Radiohead's studio, 2007

One of Garth's contemporaries at St Martins art school was Joe Wright, who went on to direct films including *Pride and Prejudice* and *Atonement*. His response to a characteristically cheery hello from Garth one morning at St Martins was to call him a 'Chirpy cunt'. However it was intended, it was an observation that captured something about Garth that I continue to value highly: an energetic positivity coupled with a sense of curiosity and playfulness that endures through personal and professional ups and downs and makes you feel better about everything. The world needs more chirpy cunts.

At lunchtime on Thursday, 8 November 2007, I was eating butternut squash soup at the big wooden kitchen table in Radiohead's studio outside Oxford, and I was thinking, *I'm sitting in Radiohead's kitchen!*

All around me were bits of musical equipment and artwork that I recognised or was curious about, but I had to focus on the matter at hand: what were we going to shoot in the next 30 hours that could be used to supplement the live elements in the *Thumbs Down* webcast? Stanley Donwood (who creates Radiohead's artwork) had already been working with Thom, Nigel and the rest of the band on little bits and pieces, but they needed more.

When the soup was finished and the small talk had concluded, Thom straightened up and looked over at Garth and me. 'So, what have you got?' he said, and suddenly it felt as though we were in work mode, pitching to the CEOs of Radiohead plc, a highly esteemed organisation that, despite an appreciation of comedy, had so far conspicuously avoided the kind of silliness that Garth and I had built careers on.

Rather than share every half-formed idea we'd come up with at this early stage, Garth started with something straightforward and non-silly to get us settled in. He suggested taking Thom and Jonny out to a field somewhere to shoot a performance of a track he particularly liked from the new album called 'Faust Arp'. Within the hour, the four of us were squeezed into Thom's small car, driving briskly to Wittenham Clumps, a hill overlooking Didcot Power Station where, Ed later told me, the band used to hang out in their younger days and smoke joints.

Thom wondered if he'd remember all the lyrics for 'Faust Arp', so as he drove I put my headphones over his head and played him the song from my MiniDisc copy of *In Rainbows*, and he sang along as Garth and Jonny banged their heads in the back seat, *Wayne's World* style.

By the time we got to the top of the hill at Wittenham

Thom and Jonny about to sing 'Faust Arp' (my podcast mics in the foreground), Wittenham Clumps, November 2007

Clumps, it was cold and windy, and we were losing the light. Nigel was busy back in the studio, so it had been left up to me to figure out how best to record the sound of Jonny on guitar and Thom singing. I used a couple of little Rode NT5 mics (which I now use to record my podcast interviews) clamped to a tripod and plugged directly into my camera's 2 XLR inputs. But the mic covers I had back then were no match for the wind, and listening through my headphones as Thom and Jonny started their first performance of 'Faust Arp', I could hear every other line being buried beneath noisy gusts. When Thom called, 'Cut,' saying he'd fucked up, I was relieved that we were going to get another go and hoped the wind would die down. I was working with world-class musicians at the peak of their powers, and that was my plan: hoping the wind would die down. But it was all in the DIY spirit of the webcast and the release of the *In Rainbows* album in general.

The second take was better, but Thom fluffed a line and Jonny was too far from the mic. By take three, the sun had set, and the image in my viewfinder was grainy in the gloaming, but the performance was lovely, and although there were a couple of gusty rumbles, they added to the mood. When Thom sang, 'You've got a head full of feathers. You're going to melt into butter,' I felt, with my headphones on, that he was singing directly into my ear. If Thom had known how elated I was at that moment, he'd probably have shuffled a few steps away from me, perhaps to around Didcot Power Station.

Falling into Place

The next morning, Ed mentioned that Thom was off being interviewed for *Wired* magazine by David Byrne, and when they'd finished, Thom brought him up to the control room. I was surprised by how white Byrne's hair had become, but it looked good, a tousled quiff somewhere between David Lynch and Samuel Beckett. I was still star-struck by Radiohead, but to find myself face to face with David Byrne, whose music, both solo and with Talking Heads and Brian Eno, had soundtracked so many moments in my life, was more than trippy. It was a big deal for the band, too, who were all big Talking Heads fans; Radiohead took their name from a track on one of the less celebrated Talking Heads albums, but one that I always loved nonetheless: *True Stories*.

A few minutes before Thom and David arrived, Garth and I had finished editing the video for 'Jigsaw Falling into Place', which we'd shot the evening before using five 'helmet cams' I'd made for the band. These consisted of little security cameras (the GoPro was still a few years away) attached to poles that were stuck into bicycle helmets that I'd sprayed silver. The helmets fixed the face of each band member at the centre of the frame while the background slid around behind them whenever they moved their heads. This created a pleasingly queasy effect that fitted well with the song's lyrics about drunken revellers being watched by CCTV. With Thom and David Byrne standing on either side of me, I hooked up my laptop to the control room speakers and played the finished music video for them, Nigel and the rest of Radiohead. It looked good, though, to be honest, pretty much anything would have looked good with that song.

David Byrne chuckled at the sight of the band all looking so intense in their silver nerd helmets. 'What a great performance!' he said. 'And you can get rid of the helmets later, right?'

'I thought we should keep the helmets in, don't you think?' I said, looking over at Thom, and he and the rest of the band seemed to agree that looking 'cool' was not the object of this particular exercise. The silver nerd helmets stayed in, and the video, which would be the last to feature all five members of the band, became the official promo when 'Jigsaw Falling into Place' was released as a single in January 2008.

What's in the Box?

When David Byrne had left, Garth and I thought about what else we could film before the webcast the following night. Garth had the idea to use the climactic 'head in a box' scene from David Fincher's film *Seven* for something, and a few minutes later I found him in the main studio holding a cardboard box with a hole cut in the bottom, looking intently at Thom, who was sitting on a sofa in front of him and eyeing the box suspiciously. Garth had obviously just explained his idea and was now waiting for a response, like a doctor who has just outlined a risky procedure to a patient. Thom took a deep breath and said, 'Come on, then, let's do it.'

The idea was to use the footage of Morgan Freeman

opening the package in *Seven*, then cut away to a shot of Thom's disembodied head singing the first couple of verses from '15 Step', the opening track on *In Rainbows*. We'd keep cutting back to Morgan Freeman looking horrified and end with Brad Pitt's weirdly delivered line, 'Aw, what's in the box?' The *Thumbs Down* livestream was happening on the radiohead.tv website rather than a corporate platform, so we were hoping we wouldn't get in trouble for using the *Seven* footage, but if there *was* a problem we told ourselves that, as a fan of the band, Brad Pitt would stick up for us.

Once his head was in the box, Thom said, 'Hang on, this is familiar. It's the "No Surprises" video all over again!' For Grant Gee's 1997 'No Surprises' promo, Thom had to stick his head in a glass bowl and sing as the container filled with water, so that he appeared to be submerged for a whole minute (though that part of the film was slowed down slightly to stretch it out) before the water drained and he could breathe

Ta-daaa! Thom-in-the-box for '15 Step'

and sing again for the final section. The result was one of the more visually engaging and memorable music videos ever made, but as the behind-the-scenes footage in *Meeting People Is Easy* shows, 'No Surprises' took many uncomfortable takes to get right, and left Thom literally screaming with frustration, a scenario that Garth and I were keen to avoid.

As we arranged bubble wrap and foam packing peanuts in the base of the box to hide Thom's neck, he complained that his nose was itchy, but he couldn't reach around the top of the box to scratch it. Eager to keep him sweet, I reached in and started gently scratching the tip of his nose with my forefinger, but even as I did so I knew I'd crossed the line. 'Er, I'm not sure I'm comfortable with Adam touching me,' said Thom. 'Does anyone have a pencil?'

All we needed was a minute or so of Thom singing '15 Step', and once we'd got it, we unboxed him and I set about cutting the footage in with the clip from *Seven*. Thom had played it just right, wearing a nonplussed expression that gave way to a slight mad grin at one point that worked well between shots of Morgan Freeman looking about and down at the contents of the box as if to say, 'What the hell am I supposed to do with this?'

Radiohead would be the first to admit that when they signed to EMI in 1991, they were not a cool band and stayed not cool until people realised how good their second album, *The Bends*, was. Then *OK Computer* came out, and from then on, whether or not you thought they were cool, you couldn't deny that this was a group of people who were, in the best way possible, unusually serious and careful about every aspect of what they did, from the writing and recording of their music to their live shows, artwork, music videos and other promotional material. And yet, when they play together, they aren't prissy or precious; they sound free and thrilling, combining the accessible and the avant-garde in a way that few other bands have ever pulled off. Standing in the middle of the five members as they ran through songs for the webcast in the rehearsal room of their Oxford studio, and sounding, if anything, better than the record, I felt very much in the right place at the right time.

No one was more surprised than I that this band invited me and Garth to invade their personal space, put silly helmets on them and stick their lead singer's head in a cardboard box. But nearly 20 years later, that *In Rainbows* period is regarded by new generations of Radiohead fans as a high watermark. Am I suggesting that's partly down to me and Garth? Yes, obviously.

CHAPTER 6

ARGUMENT WITH WIFE LOG

What Is Love?

Before I had children, I thought Love mainly meant finding your partner physically attractive, drinking a lot of booze and then, when the alcohol had lowered my inhibitions, saying, 'I love you.' Apart from that, Love meant watching TV together with snacks (especially Cookies and Cream Häagen-Dazs, honey mustard pretzel pieces, Popchips, Macadamia Nut Brittle Häagen-Dazs, honey-roasted cashews and, most of all, Revels).

After I'd married Sarah and the children came along, I experienced a new kind of Love, one that wasn't based on me getting what I wanted all the time. It was a deeper but more annoying kind of Love that required more of me, and I would look forward to weekends when the children were tucked up in bed, the booze and the Revels came out, and we could go back to the old, snacks and TV version of Love for a few hours.

There are people who will tell you that when it comes to Love, you shouldn't compromise and that tolerating imperfections in a relationship amounts to avoidance. But if the biggest problems in your relationship are on the level of wishing you kissed more, disagreeing about private education and not liking all the same films and music, then I think blowing it all up in the hope that something better might come along is a mistake. That's what I'm telling myself, anyway.

None of us is perfect. Some of us are miles from perfect and might even have been attracted to our partners because we sensed they struggled with a similar level of imperfection. There's no question I can be a dick. Sometimes my dickishness is the result of my ongoing battle with low self-esteem and oversensitivity. Other times I'm just a dick. And then there are the times I think I'm being fun, but the fun doesn't quite land.

Laugh Track

In the summer of 2022, Sarah and I were travelling on a very busy train to Scotland. I was sitting on a single seat on one side of the aisle, and Sarah was on the other side, sitting at a table with three other women we didn't know.

There had been a lot of delays and Sarah had struck up a friendly conversation with the women while I did laptop work at my single seat. The refreshments trolley approached, wheeled by a woman who looked like a nice Scottish granny. I asked for tea but forgot to ask if she had oat milk, which I would generally prefer, so she gave me tea with dairy milk. Across the aisle, Sarah also ordered tea, but she remembered to ask if there was oat milk, and the server lady said yes. (From now on, I'll refer to the server lady as Servalan – a fun but irrelevant reference for any super nerds reading this to the villain in the Eighties sci-fi show *Blake's 7*).

Knowing that Sarah sometimes takes dairy milk, I leant across the aisle and said, 'Do you mind if I give you my tea with the dairy milk, and I'll have the one with the oat milk?' But before Sarah had a chance to reply, Servalan, perhaps not realising that we were together, said, 'She might not want that one.' I wanted to explain to Servalan that we were married, and I had inside information about how my wife likes her tea. I didn't want her to think I was trying to fob off my tea on a stranger.

However, instead of explaining all that – and perhaps wanting to make Sarah's new friends laugh – I said with exaggerated gruffness, 'She's my wife, so she'll have what she's given!'

On hearing this, Servalan and everyone within earshot made the same noise: a shocked and disapproving, 'Ooh!' A few people even shook their heads and looked at Sarah with pity and concern. Sarah, understandably mortified, sank into her seat, looking embarrassed and meek, but that had the effect of making me look even more like the kind of controlling monster I had just parodied. But maybe a husband who makes a joke that lands so badly and embarrasses his wife as I just had *is* a kind of monster? On the other hand, perhaps I'm right and everyone else is wrong.

Keeping a log of the arguments I have with Sarah is a case in point. Some people have suggested to me that it's petty and tyrannical, but in fact it's the opposite. My Argument with Wife Log is a commitment to growth and learning that may even help you manage conflict more effectively in your own relationship. I'm not looking for an award or a pat on the back. I just want to make the world a better, more understanding place.

Argument with Wife Log

SUBJECT OF ARGUMENT	ELEVEN-YEAR-OLD DAUGHTER NOT BEING ALLOWED TO GO FOR A WALK ALONE IN THE FIELDS NEAR OUR HOUSE
MAIN POINTS - BUCKLES	'You're being over-cautious.'
MAIN POINTS - WIFE	'I'm not being over-cautious. There are real dangers out there. Google it.'
MAIN POINTS - BUCKLES	'The dangers are exaggerated. Google it.'
MAIN POINTS - WIFE	'They're not exaggerated. Google it.'
MAIN POINTS - BUCKLES	'Helicopter parenting is having negative mental and physical effects on generations of children. Google it.'
WINNER	WIFE (this one would have gone better for me if I hadn't used the phrase 'helicopter parenting')

SUBJECT OF ARGUMENT	WIFE REFUSING TO WEAR PAPER CROWN FROM CRACKER AT CHRISTMAS LUNCH
MAIN POINTS - WIFE	'I don't like them. It's really not a big deal.'
MAIN POINTS - BUCKLES	'It's an important unifying ritual of festive fun. Put on the hat.'
WINNER	WIFE

SUBJECT OF ARGUMENT	PICKING THE BANSHEES OF INISHERIN AS OUR CHRISTMAS DAY FAMILY MOVIE
MAIN POINTS – WIFE	'It was depressing, pointless crap designed to win awards.'
MAIN POINTS – BUCKLES	'It was a powerful allegory about cis-men yearning for immortality because they can't give birth. And mental illness. And the Troubles in Ireland. And donkey nutrition.'
MAIN POINTS – WIFE	'It was a big depressing wank. We should have watched Top Gun: Maverick again.'
WINNER	WIFE

SUBJECT OF ARGUMENT	ME THROWING AWAY THE RANDOM CRAP THAT'S BEEN IN THE BIG BOWL IN THE HALL FOR YEARS, INCLUDING OLD CHARGERS, MEMBERSHIP CARDS, LANYARDS, PACKS OF PILLS, CABLES, REMOTES, MINI TOILETRIES, SHOELACES, RECEIPTS, INTERDENTAL BRUSHES, HAIR CLIPS, KNACKERED HEADPHONES, FOREIGN COINS, PHONE NUMBERS ON SCRAPS OF PAPER, KEYRINGS, KEYS
MAIN POINTS – WIFE	'There might have been stuff in there I needed.'
MAIN POINTS – BUCKLES	'You haven't needed it for the last ten years.'
MAIN POINTS – WIFE	'Still, you should have checked with me before throwing things away.'
MAIN POINTS – BUCKLES	'Then it wouldn't have got thrown away.'
WINNER	WIFE (but actually BUCKLES)

SUBJECT OF ARGUMENT	WIFE DROPPING OUT OF WEEKEND CINEMA TRIP BECAUSE SHE SAYS SHE HAS WORK TO DO
MAIN POINTS - BUCKLES	'It's the weekend, and this is an opportunity for us to spend some quality time together as a family.'
MAIN POINTS - WIFE	'I need to work. Why are you the one who gets to decide when it's time for all of us to be together? Anyway, all you're going to do is sit in a cold, dark room eating Maltesers and watching Ryan Reynolds. Why does it matter if I'm not there?'
MAIN POINTS - BUCKLES	'You're tearing this family apart.'
WINNER	WIFE

SUBJECT OF ARGUMENT	ARRANGING FOR SON'S PHONE TO MAKE INTERNATIONAL CALLS WHEN HE GOES TRAVELLING ON HIS YEAR OUT
MAIN POINTS - BUCKLES	'Why can't he sort this stuff out for himself? He's 18!'
MAIN POINTS - WIFE	'If we don't sort it out, I'll have to deal with it when there's an emergency. This is what parents are supposed to do.'
MAIN POINTS - BUCKLES	'He can sort this stuff out for himself! He's 18!'
WINNER	WIFE

SUBJECT OF ARGUMENT	THE PIERCINGLY LOUD 'PING!' THAT ACCOMPANIES WIFE'S WHATSAPP NOTIFICATIONS
MAIN POINTS – BUCKLES	'That piercingly loud ping is quite annoying, especially when it happens several times during an evening meal. Is it possible to turn it down or even, I don't know, off?'
MAIN POINTS – WIFE	'I need to see the messages from this WhatsApp group to help me organise our daughter's sporting schedule.'
MAIN POINTS – BUCKLES	'Couldn't you still see them without the "PING!"?'
MAIN POINTS – WIFE	'Is the "PING!" really so bad? Your phone makes a noise when you get texts.'
MAIN POINTS – BUCKLES	'I get about two texts a month, and I switched off the alert last year.'
WELL-TIMED NOISE – WIFE	'PING!'
WINNER	BUCKLES

SUBJECT OF ARGUMENT	WIFE BUYING BIG BAGS OF CRISPS AND LEAVING THEM ON THE COUNTER BY THE FRIDGE WHERE I AM FORCED TO EAT THEM
MAIN POINTS – WIFE	'Just don't eat the crisps. You're a grown-up.'
MAIN POINTS – BUCKLES	'Leaving crisps by the fridge is violence.'
WINNER	ONGOING

SUBJECT OF ARGUMENT	WIFE UPDATING ME ON WHICH FRIENDS AND FAMILY MEMBERS HAVE CANCER JUST BEFORE SCHEDULED MARITAL RELATIONS
MAIN POINTS - BUCKLES	'It's not exactly sexy.'
MAIN POINTS - WIFE	'It's the only time we get to discuss important things.'
WINNER	BUCKLES

SUBJECT OF ARGUMENT	WIFE BEING MOODY
MAIN POINTS - BUCKLES	'I don't understand why you're so moody.'
MAIN POINTS - WIFE	'You're the moody one. It's like a toxic cloud. I don't think you realise how moody you are.'
MAIN POINTS - BUCKLES	'I'm moody because you're moody. I'm normally fun, like on my podcast. Stop gaslighting me.'
WINNER	BUCKLES

SUBJECT OF ARGUMENT	WIFE LEAVING DIRTY PLATES AND COFFEE MUGS BY THE SINK TO CLEAN LATER
MAIN POINTS - BUCKLES	'I always think it's better to clean as you go.'
MAIN POINTS - WIFE	'I always think it's better to fuck while you off.'
WINNER	UNSURE

CHAPTER 7

TOYTANIC

'They called it the ship of dreams, but to me it was the ship of shit'

– CORNBALLS

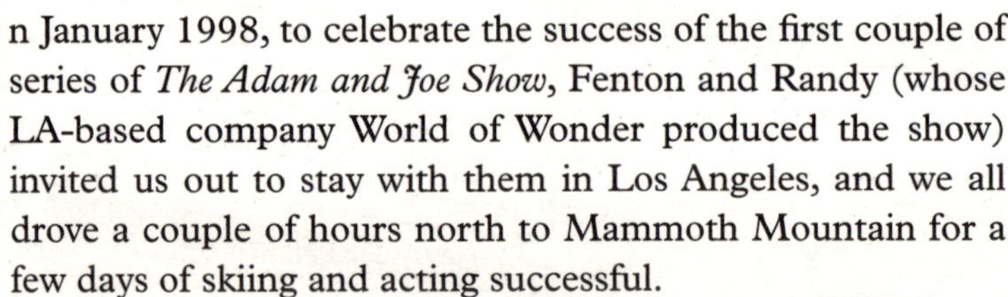

In January 1998, to celebrate the success of the first couple of series of *The Adam and Joe Show*, Fenton and Randy (whose LA-based company World of Wonder produced the show) invited us out to stay with them in Los Angeles, and we all drove a couple of hours north to Mammoth Mountain for a few days of skiing and acting successful.

We stayed in a big, luxurious chalet, and while Fenton and Randy were out skiing one afternoon, Joe and I sat in the bubbling hot tub on the balcony, looking out over the sunny mountains and feeling pleased with ourselves. If there was ever a moment that felt like a Hollywood cliche of 'Success', this was it. And yet, thanks to my gift for combining competitiveness and insecurity, there was an iceberg right ahead.

'*Toytanic!*' said Joe as we turned up the bubbles in the hot tub and my empty bottle of Michelob bobbed about in the middle.

Media pundits had spent the whole of the previous year predicting that James Cameron's film based on the *Titanic* disaster would be one of the most expensive flops in cinema history. Ha-ha! Stupid pundits of the past! In fact, when it

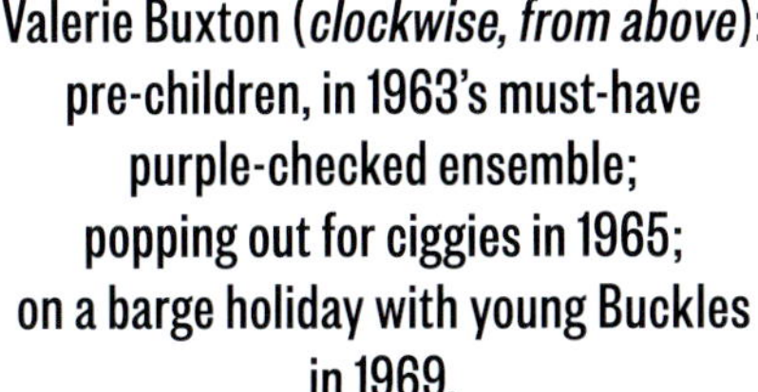

Valerie Buxton (*clockwise, from above*): pre-children, in 1963's must-have purple-checked ensemble; popping out for ciggies in 1965; on a barge holiday with young Buckles in 1969.

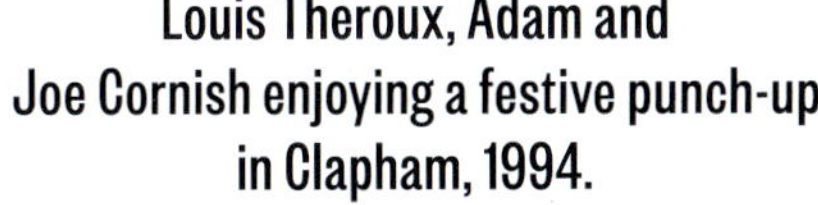

Louis Theroux, Adam and Joe Cornish enjoying a festive punch-up in Clapham, 1994.

The Adam and Joe Show toy movies (guess the film or TV show).

JEDI
Springer
The
Tufty
Club

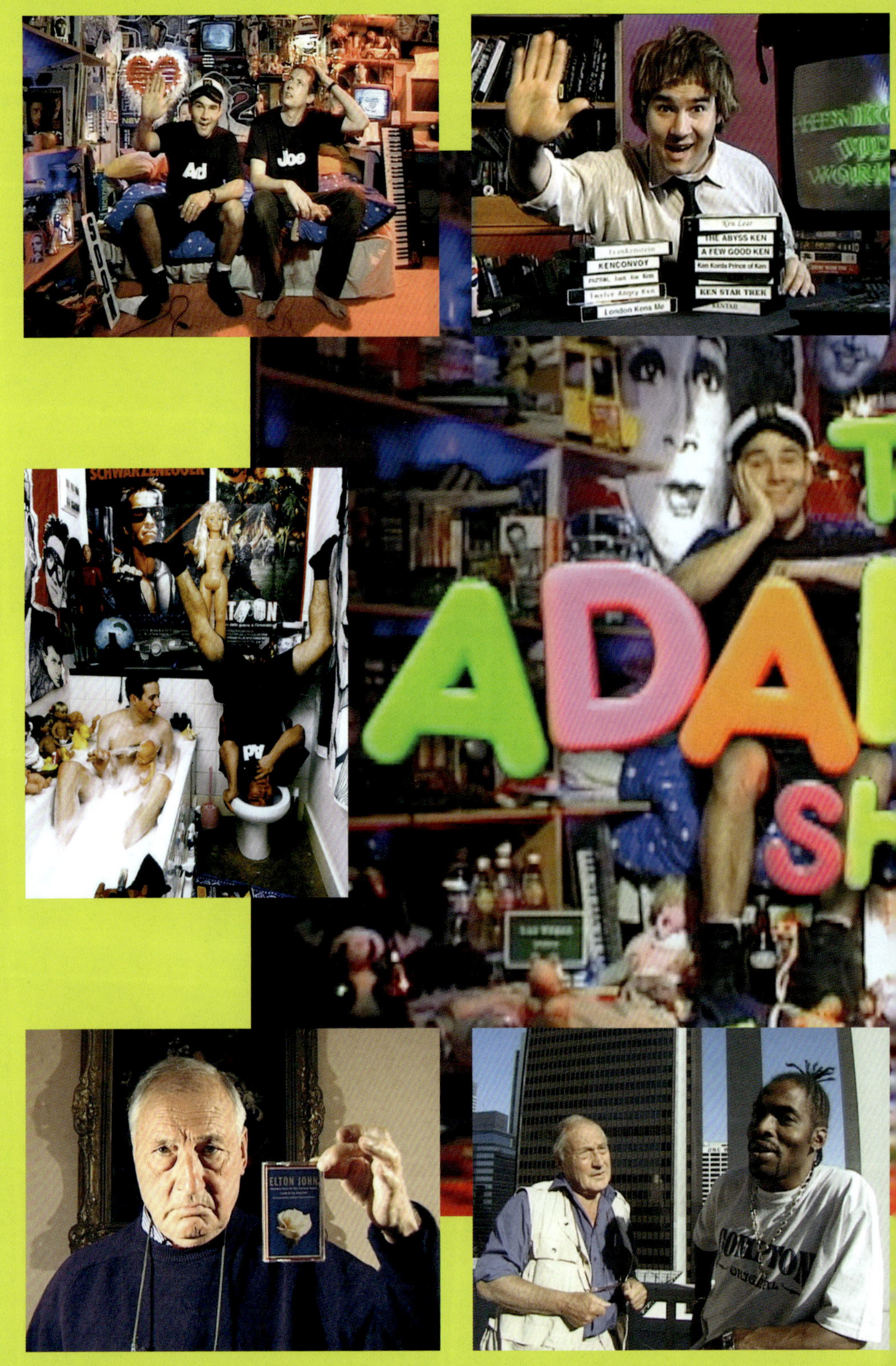

Ad
Joe
Ken Lear
THE ABYSS KEN
A FEW GOOD KEN
Ken Korda Prince of Ken
KEN STAR TREK
KENCONVOY
Twelve Angry Ken
London Kens Me
SCHWARZENEGGER
ADA
ELTON JOHN

ER
A+J
and JOE

Polly Borland

Anticlockwise, from above:
Joe and Zac Sandler in the Borough studio working on *Toytanic*, 1998;
Fenton Bailey, Joe, Adam, Randy Barbato, Mammoth Mountain, 1998;
smouldering for series three, 1999;
Adam with Fran Healy, Dougie Payne and Andy Dunlop of Travis, Denver, USA, 2000;
a couple of infantile c***s at Xfm, London, 2003.

Above: A fraction of the A. Buckles CD compilation empire (with original artwork).
Below, left: 'Sausages' video directed by Garth Jennings, 2007.
Below, right: Adam and Joe 6 Music publicity shot by Perou, 2008 (not our clothes).

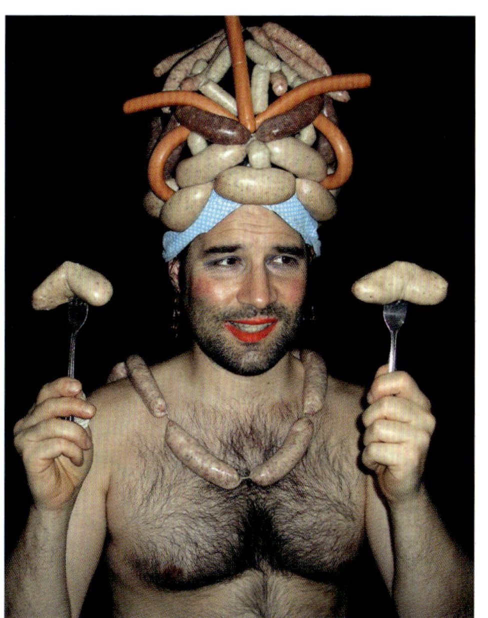

Anticlockwise, from above:
inside the Big British Castle, Saturday morning at 6 Music, 2011, with producers James Stirling and Lucy Winter;
Adam and Joe with Peter Grimsdale, 2015;
Adam and Joe Mount during *Buckle Up* sessions in Kent, 2024;
the *Alien* cherry pie I made before *Bake Off* (with temporary silver cake-ball teeth).

was released at the end of 1997, *Titanic* was a massive hit, becoming the first film ever to make a billion dollars, and in our Californian mountain hot tub that day, Joe said it would make a great toy movie.

I told Joe I was worried that making a parody of a film everyone had seen was too obvious and that we should be making snarky jokes about the kinds of films critics loved but comparatively few people were familiar with – David Cronenberg's 1996 film *Crash*, for example (Joe's toy version was called *Crèche*). The truth is, I was worried that Joe's *Toytanic* would dwarf any of my creative efforts and become a symbolic iceberg that would sink our creative partner-ship (like *Titanic*, see?).

I know this is going to seem crazy coming from one of the most successful and accomplished people in the UK, but ever since we'd started making *The Adam and Joe Show* together, I'd been battling the anxiety that Joe was just much more talented than I was. My worst nightmare was that one day Cornballs might do something like make a film without me that did really well, making it clear that he didn't need me at all. This particular nightmare came true in 2011 when Joe made his debut feature *Attack the Block*, but I got a miniature, cardboard and plastic straw preview of my worst nightmare when he made *Toytanic* in 1998.

For the third series of *The Adam and Joe Show*, World of Wonder rented us a studio flat in Borough, south London. It was a much larger and more private space than we'd had for the first two series, when we were working out of the production company's offices above the Body Shop in Brixton. In the Borough studio we could build sets for the toy movies, shoot links and skits, edit the programmes in the tiny online suite that was set up for us there, and deliver the finished programmes direct to Channel 4. It was the realisation of a fantasy I'd had since art school: to bypass what was then the standard way of making TV and instead create a programme in which nearly every aspect of the production was lovingly (and sometimes passive-aggressively) overseen by the show's hosts.

Making our toy parodies of movies and TV shows was always one of the most pleasurable parts of the process, and both of us loved the days and late nights we spent with glue guns and stuffed toys, listening to music as we constructed sets from cardboard boxes and bits of junk, decorating and lighting them to get as close as possible to the look of whatever film or show we were spoofing. If anything, it was *too much* fun, and the toy movies always took disproportionately longer to make than anything else. For that reason, Joe and I had got into the habit of filming them separately and then coming together to record the voices. For our third series, I was doing toy versions of *Star Trek: The Next Generation*, *Ally McBeal*, *This Morning with Richard & Judy* and *Who Wants to Be a Millionaire?*, while Joe was busy in another part of the studio with *Saving Private Ryan*, *Jerry Springer*, *Shakespeare In Love* and *Titanic*.

We told people this way of doing things gave us more flexibility, but looking back, it also seems to be a symptom of an increasingly unhelpful competitive mania between us.

RAMBLE

BEDEVILLED BY DETAIL

My 2020 lockdown archiving session included all the old footage that we'd shot on Mini DV tapes for *The Adam and Joe Show*. As the tapes were digitising, I saw many of Joe's toy movie rushes for the first time, as he would have loaded and edited them himself when we were making the show.

Again and again, I admired the simple tricks and camera techniques Cornballs used to get shots in a fraction of the time it would take me to make my toy movies. If he needed a shot of a character in the corner of a room, J Corn would hastily tape together two bits of cardboard, light it and shoot it in about five minutes. Given a similar task, I'd spend two or three days painstakingly constructing a model of an entire room, often featuring tiny details and in-jokes that no one would ever notice; then, once my model was complete, I'd realise that because I'd constructed the entire room rather than just one section, it was much harder to position the camera and lights to film what I needed. Further hours would be spent deconstructing the set in order to achieve the effect I was after, which often I never did.

Joe had learned the basics of filmmaking at college in Bournemouth, and his toy movies always looked vivid and vibrant, while mine were sometimes murky and drab. But, I told myself, there was more detail in mine. If you were able to find a pristine copy of my *Star Wars* figurine version of *The Royle Family* (mine was called *The Imperial Family*), you might be able to see that the wallpaper features a design made up of tiny photographs of *Star Wars* action figures that I spent an entire day putting together in Photoshop then printing out and gluing to the cardboard walls. *The Imperial Family* also boasted a *Star Wars* version of the theme tune ('Half the World Away' by Oasis) with new lyrics, sung beautifully by Travis frontman Fran Healy.

Jedi would like to leave this city
Jawas and Banthas don't smell too pretty
And since the evil empire fell
All we do is watch TV

I've had more fun
With my Millennium Falcon
And my blaster on stun
A long time ago
In a galaxy far away,
Far, far away.

Sub-Ramble

I think Joe felt my priorities were conflicted by my friendship with Travis, which had blossomed between the third and fourth series of *The Adam and Joe Show*. Perhaps when I got Fran to sing on my *Imperial Family* theme, Joe felt I was using my celebrity friend to gain an unfair competitive advantage. After I played him the song for the first time we had one of our more tense, wobbly voiced conversations – 'It's not supposed to be the Adam vs Joe Show,' said Joe. I half-expected him to get in touch with Simon Pegg and see if his friend Chris Martin of Coldplay would sing in one of his toy movies.

Yes, I was good at detail, but Joe was always better with the bigger picture even if at times he could be a little slapdash.

While Joe's *Toytanic* rushes were digitising in 2020, I stopped and watched his shots of the cardboard ship moving through the sea at sunset. Joe had hung up a large sheet of filter paper behind the model, and it was backlit, so it glowed sunset orange. He had positioned the camera on a tripod at the front of the *Titanic* model and panned around from right to left, so the stationary ship appeared to be sailing through the shot. It worked so well.

He did about six takes of this sunset shot, but on the second one, I noticed that when the camera panned all the way to the left, you could see the edge of the filter paper and the walls of our studio behind it. *Come on, Cornballs, reposition that filter paper!* I thought as I watched successive takes digitising, but he never did. Sure enough, when I checked the version of *Toytanic* that was finally broadcast, you can still see the edge of the filter paper.

I know it's unlikely to turn up on a YouTube compilation of History's Biggest Movie Mistakes, and when I was watching it in 2020, I may have been in the grip of grief- and lockdown-induced psychosis, but seeing that shot made me realise:

A – A good director doesn't get hung up on irrelevant details

B – Caring about small details is part of who I am, for better or worse

C – Perfect is the enemy of good

D – I've wasted my life

Sometimes, the competition between me and Joe was healthy and encouraged both of us to push the science of toy waggling to its very limits, but other times it threatened to take the fun out of the whole thing and made me wish we'd never turned our friendship into a job.

In August 1998, I was going out with Sarah, the woman who would one day become MY WIFE. The day after we returned from our first foreign holiday together, I went into the Borough studio to find the space completely dominated by a model of the *Titanic* that was about four metres long and two metres high. Joe had constructed it with the help of our friend Zac, using cardboard, bin liners, pipe cleaners and plastic straws. I should have been delighted that they'd created something so epic and hilariously mad for our show, but every inch of cardboard, pipe cleaner and plastic straw made me feel threatened.

When Channel 4 launched its new digital channel, Film4, on 1 November 1998, the first night's schedule included a nine-minute cut of *Toytanic*. Before the launch, I got a call from someone at *Time Out* magazine who was doing a small piece to plug the *Toytanic* screening and wanted to ask a few questions.

Doing press for the first series of *The Adam and Joe Show* had taught us that it was bad for double-act dynamics when one of us got more attention than the other. From then on, we agreed that during interviews we should imply that everything on the show had been made together in creative harmony. Rather than each of us saying '*I* did this' or '*I* did that', we would respond to questions about the production using the special '*We*'. When the *Time Out* journalist asked me about *Toytanic*, it would have been more truthful to say, 'You should probably speak to Joe because I didn't do much on that one except a few voices.' Instead, I answered the journalist's questions as well as I was able, sprinkling my answers liberally with special '*We*'. As it turned out, I ought to have *We*'d a bit harder.

The day the *Time Out* interview was published, Joe called. His voice was quavering. Apparently, a few 'I's had crept into the piece along with the 'We's, and whether I had misspoken or the journalist had misquoted me, Joe was massively and uncharacteristically pissed off. Not only had I broken the Pact of 'We', I had done so with his all-conquering statement of cardboard-and-stuffed-toy genius.

Joe might have consoled himself with the fact that every time I went out in the weeks after *Toytanic* was broadcast, at least one person would come up to me and say, '*Toytanic*, man! That was genius!', before quoting Joe's lines at me ('Everybody on deck! The special effects are starting!') and telling me it was the best thing that 'We' had ever done.

Now that I'm older, I've made peace with *Toytanic*. The other night, I showed it to my children, and they all thought it was amazing. 'Did you and Joe do all that together, Dad?' asked my daughter.

'No,' I replied. 'It was mainly me.'

NCC-1701-D

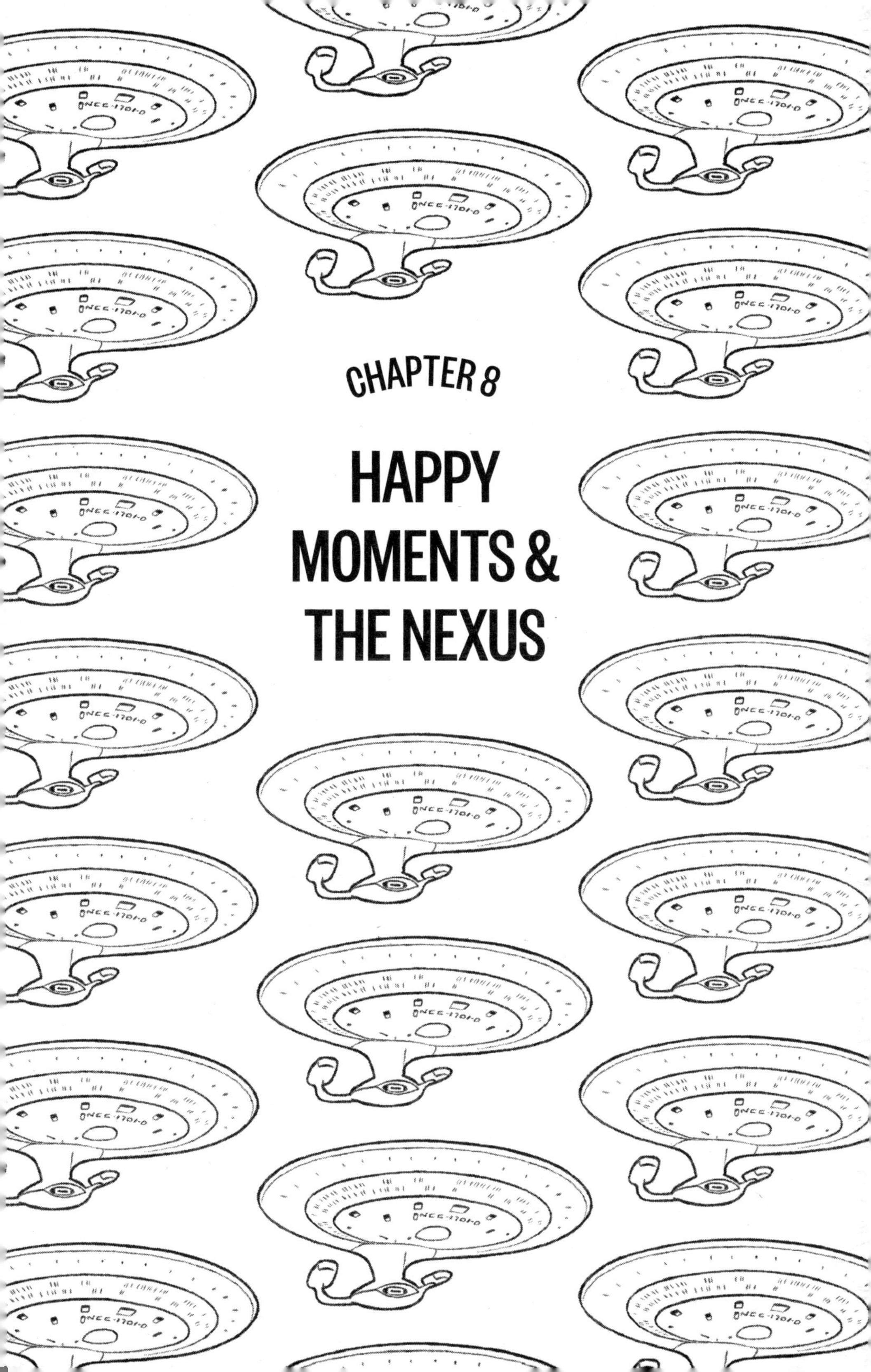

CHAPTER 8

HAPPY MOMENTS & THE NEXUS

I've made a family photo album every year since our first son was born. Sometimes, when I find myself looking through them, I think that as well as taking photos of the children when they were looking happy and adorable, I should have taken a few on bad days too. The impression that the past was a happier, simpler place than the messy present, which photo albums tend to promote, might have been corrected if I'd added a few snaps of tantrums at home or sulks on rainy day trips. And for balance, I could have included some pictures of the children behaving badly, too.

The mundane reality of family life is sometimes captured better in home videos. Here, the atmosphere of toddler cuteness is more likely to be punctured by one of them going barbaric when something doesn't go exactly the way they want it to. Then you remember what having young kids was *really* like. The teenage years bring a new raft of problems but at least they can dress and feed themselves, sort of. No longer having to look out for them 24 hours a day goes some way to making up for the fact that sniffing their heads has ceased to be something that will make you blissfully happy.

There weren't any photographs or videos being taken one afternoon when Frank was one and a half, and Sarah went up to his room to get him after his nap to discover that he'd been awake for a while and had been amusing himself by having a Dirty Protest party. There was shit everywhere. On the wall, on the sheets, on the floor, on his legs, on his hands and on his face (smeared like chocolate pudding). He'd gone nuts with the shit. While Sarah got to work cleaning his bedroom, I washed him off in the bath. He was still a bit sleepy and dazed from the party, and with doleful eyes he said cautiously, 'I done a poo.' Sarah was careful not to make a big deal out of the whole thing and freak him out. I was impressed with her coolness because I *was* a bit freaked out. I hadn't even considered that my son might be the kind of guy who threw faeces around. Now, I was wondering if this was going to be the first of a series of Poo Poo parties. Happily, it proved to be an isolated incident.

What did turn out to be more of a regular occurrence as Frank and his younger brother Nat got a bit older were tech-related tantrums as part of the night-time shutdown routine. If the Wii got switched off before Nat felt he'd had as much time on *Lego Star Wars* as his brother, variously intense meltdowns would ensue, and Sarah or I would have to take him firmly by the arm and march him up to bed. On one occasion, an emotional Nat wrenched his arm away halfway up the stairs, covered his eyes and announced, 'Now you only have one son.' When he was in bed and the light was being turned out, he revised this to the even more dire, 'Now you have no sons. Not Nat and not Frank.'

Their younger sister was challenging in her own way when she was little – I don't miss the extended periods in which night-time coughs ended with projectile vomiting, for example – but when I look back now, children's bedtimes were the best part of my day, and not only because it meant that supper and a glass of wine were just around the corner.

By the time Hope was four, we'd established an elaborate multi-section bedtime ritual with set dialogue and precise choreography, amounting to half an hour of pure happiness. By 7.30 p.m., Sarah would have bathed Hope and got her into her PJs, and I'd stop whatever I was doing in my studio and head up to Hope's bedroom, where my part of the routine would begin. As well as the low child's bed where Hope slept, there was a regular single bed in the opposite corner of her room in case she ever wanted Mum or Dad (though it was usually Mum) to sleep in there. When I arrived, Hope would jump up onto the spare bed, and I'd lie down next to her, thinking how nice it was to lie down. Then, with Hope snuggling beside me, often clutching the very soft kangaroo I'd brought her back from a trip to Australia, I'd read to her, usually two or three books.

I loved reading to the children. Not only was it fun and relaxing, I knew it was good for us too, and what else can you say that about? (Apart from broccoli and wall squats, of course.)

RAMBLE

SCARRY MEMORIES

When I was little, Mum would read to me from *What Do People Do All Day?*, one of a series of books by Richard Scarry set in the fictional, bustling community of Busytown. Scarry's stories and warm, richly detailed illustrations explored the various jobs and daily activities of Busytown's anthropomorphic animal residents in a way that made modern society look fun and appealing rather than meaningless and, well, scary.

In the years before TV swallowed up all my attention, I spent hours poring through the pages of *What Do People Do All Day?*, admiring Huckle the Cat's lederhosen and suspenders, coveting Lowly Worm's Tyrolean hat with feather, and relishing any shenanigans featuring Bananas Gorilla and his multiple wristwatches. But I most loved the pages that showed cut-away sections of Busytown's houses, ships and factories, revealing the workings within. There was something deeply soothing about seeing the interconnected pipes, machines, cables and little animal engineers that kept everything running as it should. Scarry's books left me with the impression that the adult world made sense. Back then, it didn't seem strange that the Busytown butcher was a pig who sold sausages and pork chops to other pig families.

There were times when Hope wanted me to read a book I found tedious ('Not *The God Delusion* again! Why don't we have another go at Jordan Peterson?'), but other times, when it was a book we both enjoyed and when we were lying together, absorbed by the story, I wished I could suspend time and stay in that moment.

With the story over, Hope would take my hands and leap from the big bed to the floor. That was my cue to say, 'OK, jump into your bed now,' which she would then follow with, 'Can you get me some warm water in my bottle?' This part of the routine started when I accidentally turned on the hot tap to fill up her water bottle one night, and she preferred it to the cold option. 'What do you say?' I would recite. 'Please,' came the reply. When I'd delivered the warm water, it was time for the next act. 'Can you sing me a song?'

For a while, our favourite bedtime song was David Bowie's 'The Laughing Gnome', which I sang with full Bowie impression and as many of the puns – 'Didn't they teach you to get your hair cut at school? You look like a Rolling Gnome' – as I could remember. Then we went through a *Bugsy Malone* phase, especially 'Bad Guys' and 'So You Wanna Be a Boxer'. The song that stayed the longest at the top of the bedtime hit parade was 'Cruella de Vil' from *101 Dalmatians*.

At first, I'd just sing the song, but soon I started adding actions. When we got to the line 'the curl of her lip', I would tweak Hope's bottom lip. On 'watching you from underneath a rock', I gave her nose a prod. As we approached the line 'she's like a spider waiting for the … kill', she hid under the covers because she knew that my hand was about to crawl over her back, and on the word 'KILL!' I would pounce with both hands for a tickle. Hope would protest if I missed any of the actions, and I'd have to back up and repeat whichever stage she wasn't happy with.

When the song was over, she would say, 'Let's sleep now,' and we'd lie with our heads together. At first, this bit used to last up to a minute or so (both of us acting as though we might stay like that for the rest of the night) before one of us would break the embrace to move on to the final stage. Later, we'd only lie together for a few seconds before she'd chirp, 'Are you going now, Daddy?'

And so to the routine's even more schmaltzy finale. As I climbed off her little bed, Hope would run through the checklist for the last section so we didn't miss anything: 'Kiss here on the bed and hug here on the bed, then kiss from the door and blow from the door.' With that, she would pucker up theatrically for a kiss. That was followed by the hug, and finally, once I was standing at the bedroom door, we'd blow each other more kisses, which we both had to pretend to catch and put in our pockets.

Even as these moments were happening, I felt them pulling away inexorably, like an ocean liner slowly leaving a dock.

Back then, it felt to me that Hope was a magical creature who had arrived from space, and I dreaded the day she would have to return to her people. I didn't let on that was how I felt at the time because it's probably not good for a child's development to be treated like E.T. and it might have made her brothers feel I loved them less, which was never the case. Even when they put shit on the walls.

RAMBLE

THE NEXUS

Hope's bedtime rituals often made me think of the film *Star Trek Generations* (although I think about that film a lot anyway). There's a bit in which Captain Kirk and Jean-Luc Picard get sucked into an extra-dimensional realm called the Nexus where time and space have no meaning, and anyone who enters is trapped in a hallucinatory limbo that takes the form of a remembered idyll or 'happy place' specific to that person. Captain Kirk's happy place is a cabin in the woods, where he prepares meals for Mrs Kirk in their open-plan kitchen, chops wood and goes horse riding. He's boldly gone to Center Parcs.

For Jean-Luc Picard, the Nexus turns out to be a weird, chintzy Victorian stately home at Christmas, with fake snow sprayed on the windows and peculiar children who call him Papa and dress like Little Lord Fauntleroy. The scene resembles a tacky festive window display from a 1970s department store, but we're led to believe that, for Jean-Luc, this is as good as it gets.

Whoopi Goldberg's character Guinan appears in the happy places of both captains, wearing a small fabric-covered coffee table on her head, and she tells them they have to get back to reality. Kirk's gutted because he's just signed up for quad biking and laser tag, and Picard would dearly love to remain in his festive window display, but he knows, as we all come to know, that by definition, a happy moment is fleeting. You can't live there. Unless you get sucked into the Nexus, of course. Just make sure Whoopi Goldberg doesn't follow you in.

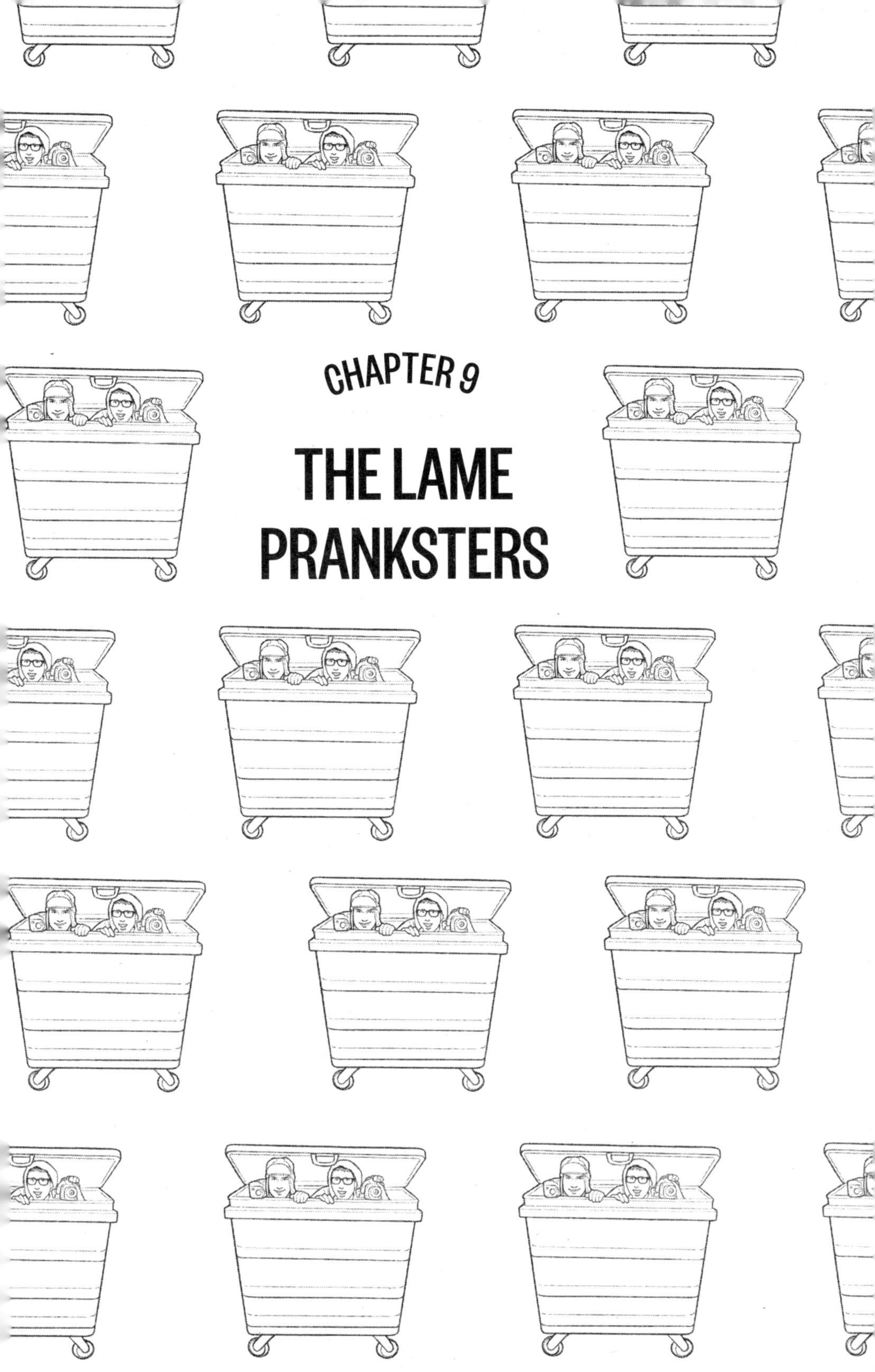

CHAPTER 9

THE LAME PRANKSTERS

I have a problem with pranks and practical jokes. Perhaps it's that I'm nice and don't enjoy exploiting another person's goodwill for the sake of a laugh. Or maybe it's that I'm a conformist coward who gets uncomfortable when he sees the rules of society being disrupted. It's probably a bit of both.

One Saturday evening in 1982, Dad came into the living room while we were having a McDonald's and watching ITV's prank and practical joke show *Game for a Laugh*, and we tensed up. We knew that to Dad, this was a scene of wholesale cultural degeneracy, and we paused shovelling fries into our faces as we awaited his comments. Presenter Jeremy Beadle was delivering a grinning introduction to one of the show's elaborate stunts, and Dad glowered in silence for a minute before muttering, 'Look at that loathsome creep. He needs to join Noel Edmonds and Jimmy Savile in a leaky boat in the North Atlantic at the earliest opportunity.'

One of the few times I saw Dad smile at contemporary comedy was in 1983 when I showed him the *Not the Nine O'Clock News* parody of *Game for a Laugh* that I'd taped on our new VHS machine. Rowan Atkinson played a man who was distraught, having come home to find his wife had been decapitated. Mel Smith played the giggling Jeremy Beadle character, who explained to the distraught man that his wife had been executed as part of a prank. On hearing this, Atkinson's anguish turned to amusement, and he shook his head, chuckling, 'What a bunch of loonies!'

The message I took from Dad and *Not the Nine O'Clock News* was clear: Prankers are Wankers.

Louis Theroux was a Beadle fan, although Louis always got a kick out of any situation that most of us would find awkward or uncomfortable. Presumably, that was one of the qualities that helped him land a job with political prankster Michael Moore on his show *TV Nation* in 1994. After years spent hanging out with Louis at each other's houses, getting off our faces and giggling, it was strange to see Louis on TV. His on-screen persona was stiffer than the version I knew, but the more I watched *TV Nation*, the more I realised that the stiffness was all part of Louis' ability to appear cool under pressure, something I knew I could never be good at. To this day, any hint of confrontation gives me a severe case of Wobbly Voice.

Louis honed his awkward encounter skills towards the end of the Nineties on his show *Weird Weekends*, in which he hung out with the kinds of isolated fringe groups that we in the liberal elite used to consider amusing weirdos, at least until the internet enabled them to get organised. But in between *TV Nation* and *Weird Weekends*, Louis made time to help Joe and me come up with ideas for the pilot series of *The Adam and Joe Show*.

It was Louis who suggested getting my dad to review music videos, which developed into our regular BaaadDad segments, and Louis also came up with the idea for a prank that ended up in our very first episode: 20% FREE.

To shoot the piece, we went into a food store on Brixton High Street, and I filmed as Joe opened any package that advertised '20% FREE', emptying 20 per cent of the contents into his pockets, then putting the opened package back on the shelves. It wasn't long before we were approached by a shop assistant asking what we were doing, to which Joe replied, 'It's OK; we're just taking the free stuff.'

Our producer, Debbie, had got permission from the

owner to film in the shop, but his staff hadn't been warned, so their bewildered responses were genuine. When a few onlookers got involved, the mood shifted to something more angry and menacing, so we called the owner, who emerged from his office to reassure everyone that we were just a couple of loonies doing a hilarious prank. Thereupon, we made our grateful apologies and went back to the office to review the footage.

There was just about enough to cobble a piece together, but a lot of what I'd shot was unusable because my hands had been shaking so badly. As I already knew when it came to pranks, I was no Beadle.

RAMBLE

TRAIN OF SHAME

In the early Seventies, Dr Stanley Milgram conducted an experiment in which he instructed his young, able-bodied students to board a subway train in New York and ask random passengers to give up their seats, even though there was no obvious reason for them to do so. You'd think most people would refuse, especially on the notoriously brusque New York subway, but surprisingly, when asked to give up their seats by Milgram's students, around two-thirds of passengers did so willingly.

The experiment's results demonstrated that the average person tends to be either more obedient or just nicer than you might expect. Either way, the people most dramatically affected by the experiment were not the people being asked to give up their seats, but

Milgram's students. Deliberately disrupting social codes this way was so upsetting that many of them felt physically sick.

When Stanley Milgram himself took part and began asking people to give up their seats for no good reason, he too found that he was mortified. Speaking in 1974, Milgram said of the experiment, 'Taking the man's seat, I was overwhelmed by the need to behave in a way that would justify my request. My head sank between my knees, and I could feel my face blanching. I was not role-playing. I actually felt as if I were going to perish.'

In other words, whether undertaken in the name of entertainment or academic study, pranking is likely to lead to pain somewhere along the line.

After the months of work that went into the first series of *The Adam and Joe Show*, one of the most popular items was the '20% FREE' prank, which took about 15 minutes to shoot and wasn't even our idea. So when we started working on the second series in 1997 we tried to think of other pranks along the same lines. When it came to winding up unsuspecting members of the public, Chris Morris had recently raised the bar to absurd heights in his show *Brass Eye*, and we were struggling to come up with anything approaching the same level of daring ridiculousness. But we told ourselves we had to keep trying because without the pranks, *The Adam and Joe Show* wouldn't be sufficiently 'edgy', and in the late 1990s, if you wanted to get ahead in comedy, you needed to be an Edge-itarian.

You Break It, You Pay for It

Once again, we turned to our friendly Edge Lord, Louis. He suggested we try another prank that, like '20% FREE', relied on a very literal reading of a phrase found on signs in certain shops: 'You Break It, You Pay for It'. The idea was to find a shop displaying the sign and start breaking things. When the shop assistants tried to stop us, we'd point at the sign and say, 'But we're just doing what the sign says. Now we pay for it, right?' It was edgy, alright, but was it the edge of comedy or cuntishness?

Our first attempt at filming the prank took place during our trip to Los Angeles in April 1997. The production team located a big, airy independent store in East Hollywood that sold books, DVDs, CDs and pop-cultural tat, and, as we had with the '20% FREE' prank, we got permission from the owners to film there without the floor staff being warned. Because the store didn't actually have any signs that said 'You Break It, You Pay for It', a production assistant printed out a few and, an hour before Joe and I arrived, stuck them on shelves near some decorative highball glasses that had also been purposely placed for us to smash. Finally, into this Theatre of Lies stepped Joe and me wearing our 'Ad' and 'Joe' T-shirts, with me filming and Joe carrying a rubber mallet because it had been decided that taking a claw hammer into a shop might be considered by some staff and customers to be scary and illegal rather than edgy and fun.

After several minutes of performative browsing, Joe located one of the specially planted glasses, and I filmed him inspecting it for a moment before he dropped it onto the wooden floor where it lay unharmed. Joe gave it a whack it with the mallet, but the sturdy glass spun away, still intact. Only when Joe started jumping up and down on the glass did it eventually break, by which time, a young shop assistant was approaching. 'What are you guys doing?' she asked, and Joe replied, 'We just broke this glass, but it's OK. We're going to pay for it. That's what the signs mean, right? You have to break stuff, then you pay for it?'

'No,' said the shop assistant patiently. 'It just means if you break something by accident, you have to pay for the damage.'

'But we thought the signs meant ...'

'Guys, come on,' she replied. 'You know what the signs mean. You need to leave.'

Back in England, it was decided, to my great sadness, that we should have another go at 'You Break It, You Pay for It'. This time, Debbie got in touch with the owner of a shop in Waterloo that sold china and glassware, and he gave us permission to plant another 'You Break It, You Pay for It' sign, then go in, smash some glass jugs and a bowl or two (using a proper hammer this time), pay for the damage then leave. Again, Joe volunteered for the violence, and I was behind the camcorder.

As before, to ensure a genuine reaction, the staff had not been told what was about to happen. However, whereas the Brixton food store had been staffed by strapping young men, when we entered the tiny china shop we found just one elderly lady at the till. Twice, we chickened out and left, but after a fortifying drink at the pub across the road and a mutual pep talk, Joe and I returned, and finally it was hammer time.

When it became clear we were deliberately smashing things, the elderly shop assistant became frightened and upset. 'It's OK,' said Joe reassuringly, 'We're going to pay for it, like the sign says!' But that failed to cheer her up. A young man poked his head through the multicoloured strip curtain at the back of the shop, and when he saw what was going on, he called the police. A passer-by came in and he too got involved, threatening to punch us if we didn't stop filming and leave. A couple of minutes later, two policemen arrived, and like the fearless gonzo provocateur I'm not, I immediately put down the camera and stopped filming.

It was a relief when the owner turned up and explained the situation to the police and his employees. We apologised to everyone, especially the distraught shop assistant, but by the time we left, only the man who had threatened to punch us saw the funny side.

We didn't plan to use the piece, but a few weeks away from transmission, there were still holes in a couple of shows, and our editor Jon suggested cutting together 'You Break It, You Pay for It'. He did his best with the material, but the finished piece wasn't so much 'edgy' as painfully 'cringey'.

Metapranks

In 2000, for the fourth and final series of *The Adam and Joe Show*, we decided it was time to go 'meta' and parody a new generation of edgy TV pranks we'd seen on programmes like *The Eleven O'Clock Show* and *Balls of Steel*.

I thought too many of the laughs on those shows relied on exploiting the kindness and goodwill of ordinary people to make them look foolish. I decided that the best way to illustrate that would be for Joe and me to exploit the kindness and goodwill of the public in a series of deliberately rubbish stunts that we hoped our viewers would understand were intended to be ironic.

We would perform these stunts in the guise of Martin and Andy, a pair of West Country troublemakers who called themselves the Media Chaos Collective, though Joe and I referred to them as the Lame Pranksters.

For one of these intentionally lame pranks, we went to St James's Park in London with Joe dressed up as an old man shuffling along on a Zimmer frame. The plan was to film discreetly until a real member of the public walked past Joe, which would be his cue to fall over. When the passer-by went to help the 'old man', Joe would jump up and shout (in a West Country accent), 'I'm not an old man! I'm young, and I fooled you! Ha-ha! You're an idiot!'

We imagined that real members of the public would then get angry with us for being dicks, and we would film them expressing their anger, which would serve as a judgement on the kinds of prank shows we were taking the piss out of.

Unfortunately, the first person who went to help Joe was so shocked and upset when Cornballs jumped up and started laughing and shouting, 'I'm not an old man!' that she screamed in fear, and then started crying. Not something you'd see on the average episode of *Trigger Happy TV* or even *The Eleven O'Clock Show.*

Once again, we had to resort to faking an ending, this time using our production assistant John, who did a good job of pretending to tell us off for being pricks, though by that point not much acting was required.

For my money, the best Lame Prankster sketches we did were the ones that reduced the whole genre of confrontational political comedy to a series of childish taunts and gotcha moments. A Labour MP, Steve Pound, agreed to an interview with us on College Green outside the Houses of Parliament. We explained it was going to be a stupid interview, and he said he was used to those. We arrived dressed as Martin and Andy, and Joe filmed as I giggled my way through a few incredibly pathetic wind-up questions that Steve Pound patiently responded to, until he'd had enough and departed.

ANDY – Hello, I'm from the news. What's your name, please?

STEVE POUND – I'm Steve Pound, Member of Parliament in Ealing North.

ANDY – Are you a Labour politician?

STEVE POUND – I'm a Labour Member of Parliament, yeah.

ANDY – If you are in labour, shouldn't you go to the hospital?

STEVE POUND – Well, if I was in labour …

ANDY – … But you can't, because there's no beds!

Steve Pound reels.

ANDY – Um, are you a member?

STEVE POUND – I'm a member of the Party, yeah.

ANDY – Do you know a lot of members?

STEVE POUND – A great many, yeah.

ANDY – Who is the biggest member you know?

STEVE POUND – Well, listen, thanks a lot for your time, but I've really got to get back to the office.

ANDY – Fascist!

Martin and Andy run away.

ANDY – We learned him! System: nil! Revolution: one!

MARTIN – Chaos!

ANDY – Subversion!

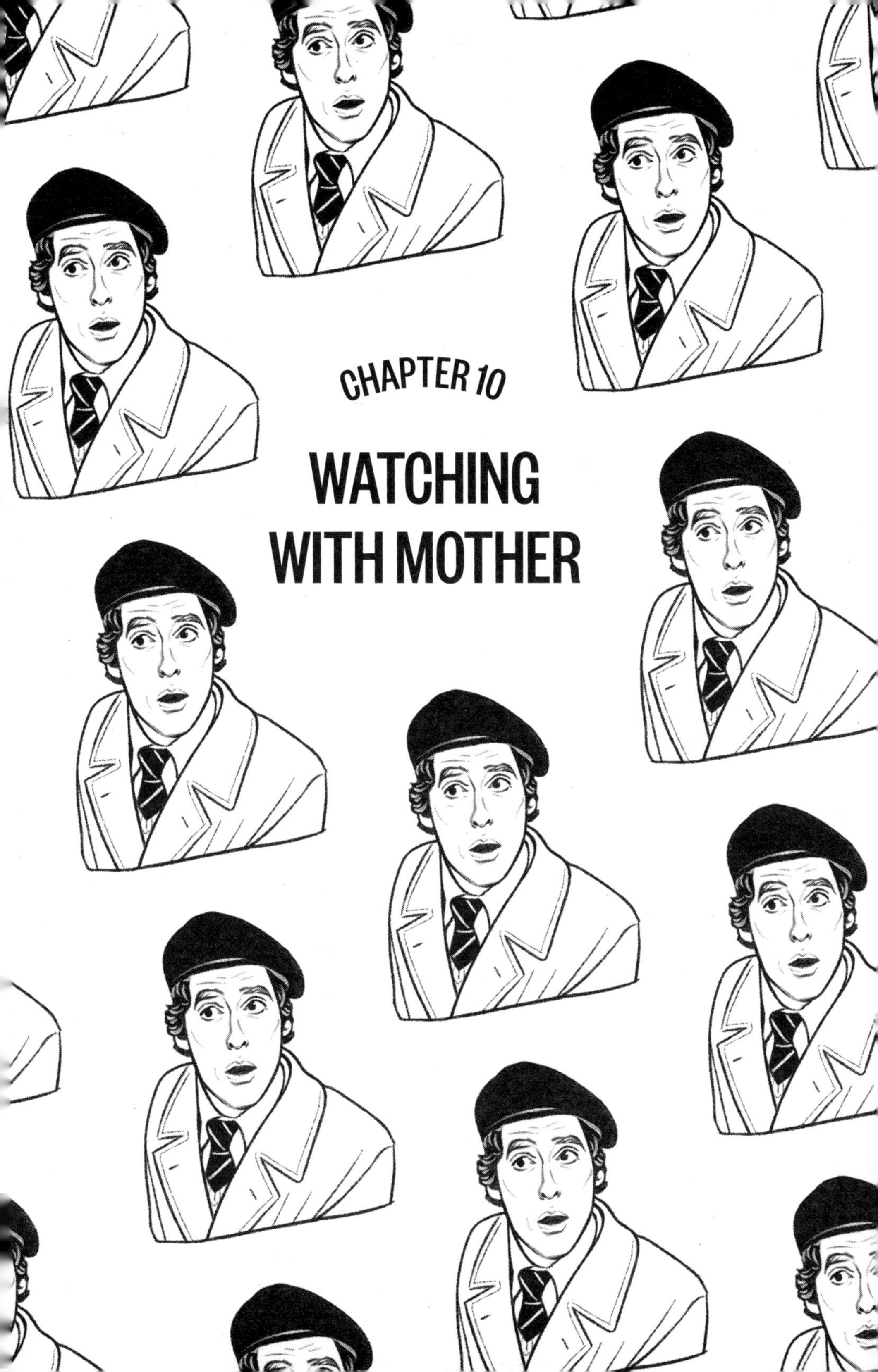

CHAPTER 10

WATCHING WITH MOTHER

Unlike my dad, Mum loved comedy, and I can clearly recall the sound of her laughter as we watched TV shows together in the late 1970s and early 80s when Dad was away on his travels. Mum introduced me to the joys of *The Two Ronnies*, a sketch show whose USP was that it was hosted by two blokes called Ronnie, who wore similar glasses. It was also very funny, sometimes involving mind-bendingly clever feats of wordplay, as in a *Mastermind* sketch in which Ronnie Corbett's specialist subject was 'Answering the Question Before Last'. So, because the previous question had been about what you kneel on in church, when asked, 'What do tarantulas prey on?' Corbett replied, 'Hassocks.' And to the next question, 'What would you use a rip chord to pull open?', he answered, 'Large flies.' Mum hooted, and I laughed along, jazzed at being allowed to stay up beyond my bedtime.

Elsewhere, the Ronnies' gift for combining the brilliant and the lowbrow was on full display in their parody of Jack the Ripper-type Victorian-era melodrama, *The Phantom Raspberry Blower of Old London Town*. These recurring serial sketches (written by Spike Milligan) focused on the hunt for a cloaked figure who sneaked up on unsuspecting members of the public and then, to my ecstatic joy, blew a long, loud raspberry until his victims collapsed in shock. It was the sort of thing Dad would have called 'moronic', but it made me and Mum howl.

In those days, we also tuned in regularly to the *Mr Bean*

forerunner *Some Mothers Do 'Ave 'Em,* in which a chronically naïve child-man called Frank Spencer (played with sinewy comedic genius by Michael Crawford) staggered from one slapstick catastrophe to the next. I loved the elaborate stunts, famously performed by Crawford himself – Frank rollerskating through traffic and passing underneath a truck was better than anything I'd seen at the cinema – but *Some Mothers Do 'Ave 'Em* also induced acute anxiety.

This wasn't simply because Spencer was so frequently in physical danger and caused so much property damage that would have been ruinously costly to repair. The feeling of worry bordering on depression that I sometimes got watching *Some Mothers Do 'Ave 'Em* had more to do with being expected to laugh at Frank's routine abject failure and the contempt people had for him. And then when Frank's long-suffering wife Betty got pregnant, well, that was a whole other level of melancholy mystification. What kind of father was Frank going to make? What *Eraserhead*-style journey of hellish parental isolation was Betty embarking upon? How had Frank and Betty managed to have sex without the bed crashing through the floor and landing in a meeting of the Christian Association or some other Spencer-worthy cringe-tastrophe?

Less stressful to watch with Mother was a sitcom about a Royal Artillery concert party based in India during the Second World War called *It Ain't Half Hot Mum.*

Like much TV in the 1970s (and, indeed, beyond), *It Ain't Half Hot Mum* leaned heavily on what would now be considered offensive and hurtful stereotypes and belittling attitudes of every kind, though none of that was the intention of the show's creators, Jimmy Perry and David Croft, who also wrote several other well-loved British sitcoms, including *Dad's Army* and *Hi-de-Hi!* Back then, *It Ain't Half Hot Mum* was just a bit of fun that also happened to be racist, homophobic and colonialist, but, sitting at my mum's feet in my PJs while she chuckled away, I adored it.

One of the things I remember finding funny about *It Ain't Half Hot Mum* was the character of the amiable Indian bearer Rangi Ram (played by white actor Michael Bates in brown face), who kept his turban secured with the same kind of elasticated belt with silver 'S' buckle worn by many of my school friends. I also liked the title sequence in which the men of the concert party, in heavy make-up and red shirts that made them look like an expanded lineup of Kraftwerk, stood on stage and delivered the theme tune: 'Meet the gang, cos the boys are here, the boys to entertain you. With music and laughter to help you on your way, to raising the rafters with a Hey! Hey! Hey!' I think I was probably channelling the spirit of the theme tune for *It Ain't Half Hot Mum* when I wrote the lyrics for my podcast theme: 'My name is Adam Buxton, I'm a man. I want you to enjoy this, that's the plan.'

The character that made Mum laugh the most was Battery Sergeant Major Williams, played by Windsor Davies. With villainous moustachio standing to attention above a gap-toothed snarl, the Welsh sergeant major existed in a state of semi-permanent red-faced fury and was the source of most of the show's now unrepeatable tirades. But it was one of his milder catchphrases that tickled Mum the most. If any of his charges had the temerity to complain to the sergeant major, his reply was always, 'Oh, dear. How sad. Never mind.' Mum would guffaw, 'Oh, he's so awful!'

It's hard to say how young Buckles was affected by regular exposure to a show that no amount of trigger warnings or cultural context disclaimers would convince the BBC to repeat now, but I don't *think* it turned me into a racist homophobe. Then again, in 2025, that's precisely the kind of thing a racist homophobe *would* say, isn't it? In 1979 all I knew was that I liked watching TV with Mum, and if it was funny, so much the better.

The comedy film that made the biggest impression on us both, which we rented on video when I was home from school one weekend in January 1985, was *Monty Python's Life of Brian*. Our favourite parts were Michael Palin's Ex-Leper '*Welease Wodderwick!*', and, most of all, more than anything, 'Always Look on the Bright Side of Life', which managed that rare trick of being moving as well as funny and slightly horrific. Dad happened to be home and came in while we were watching Eric Idle whistling away on his cross. He stood stony-faced for a minute or so before trudging out again, observing curtly that crucifixion was not a laughing matter. Of the two of them, Mum was the more religious and stayed faithful to the end, but when it came to some light blasphemy, she was able to look on the bright side.

I don't know how much Mum enjoyed *The Adam and Joe Show.* Even for someone who appreciated juvenile humour, it might have been a bit much, and in the years we were making the show, in the latter half of the Nineties, she wasn't in the mood to laugh much anyway. Her children had all moved out, she and Dad were barely speaking, and life at home – while far from penury – was not the upper-middle-class idyll she had imagined for her late fifties. Dad was sleeping on a camp bed in his study, surrounded by books and papers on makeshift shelves constructed from fruit crates. Mum got the double bed at least, but her dresses hung in the tall cardboard garment boxes they'd arrived in from Earl's Court a decade earlier because there was no room and no money for a wardrobe. Above her bed was a big hole in the ceiling that had opened up when the water tank leaked. It never got repaired.

When I started getting regular paycheques for *The Adam and Joe Show*, I said I'd chip in for whatever needed doing at the house, but Mum wouldn't have it. Instead, she got a job behind the counter at Liberty, where she wore the silk Liberty scarves that she'd bought in more prosperous times. On the few occasions that we watched *The Adam and Joe Show* together, Mum struggled to get beyond Dad's involvement.

'It's all very well him embarrassing himself on TV, but when's that hole going to get fixed?' she said.

Life got better for Mum in the early 2000s, when the Clapham house was sold and she went to live in Sonning. She was delighted when I got married; both Mum and Dad loved Sarah, and when Frank was born, Mum transitioned into doting granny mode more smoothly than I transitioned into husband and dad mode. At least half the times she came to visit when the children were little, I'd be tired and stressed, and if the white wine was flowing and the conversation got political, I'd snap at Mum when her *Daily Mail* side came out, then feel bad when she'd left.

A happier memory from those days was Mum crying with laughter as she watched a music video I appeared in for a 2003 track by Swedish indie pop band the Wannadies called 'Little by Little'. It was one of *two* videos for the track directed by Garth Jennings, who cast me as the fictional 'Master of Dance and Movement' Maurice Colon. Garth strapped fur-covered stilts to my feet, gave me tight leggings and a little black waistcoat to wear and then let me loose for improvised choreography in a photographic studio. With nothing on beneath the waistcoat, my flabby belly wobbled about over the leggings as I staggered around and 'danced' as madly as I could. Under normal circumstances, vanity would prevent me from displaying my body this way, but this was one of the very few times I've managed to get beyond my physical self-consciousness on camera. It was worth it for Mum's reaction. 'Look at your hairy tummy!' she spluttered, clapping her hands with glee.

The most offensive thing I ever watched with Mother was not in the 1970s, but a romantic comedy from 2019 called *Long Shot*, starring Seth Rogen and Charlize Theron.

The reviews for *Long Shot* led me to believe it was going to be an intelligent, fun romantic comedy with some thriller elements thrown in, i.e. perfect to watch with Mum, Sarah, the kids and Rosie. In fact, it was a tonal *smörgåsbord*, with every dish liberally sprinkled with 'Fuck', 'Shit', 'Motherfucker' and jokes about drugs and wanking. I've got nothing against any of that in principle (in fact, it's quite a good description of *The Adam and Joe Show*), but it wasn't ideal for Family Movie Night at Castle Buckles.

The experience of watching *Long Shot* was further complicated by the fact that Mum had consumed most of a bottle of Prosecco that she'd brought with her and was pretty well hammered. Shortly after a sex scene in which Charlize Theron instructs Seth Rogen to 'fuck me from behind and smack my butt really hard while you choke me a little bit', Mum burped then got up from her chair effortfully and tottered off to the kitchen to refill her glass. 'Let me do that, Mummy,' I offered, but she insisted; she was fine, thank you. A few minutes later, she wobbled back into the room, stumbled at the edge of the rug and emptied the whole glass of Prosecco onto Rosie. I suggested more than once that we abandon *Long Shot*, but Mum was quite insistent that we should persevere, even though, as the film progressed, she started nodding off every few minutes, coming round with a jolt when there was a loud 'Motherfucker!'

Mercifully, the children had checked out and gone to their rooms, and Mum appeared to be unconscious when we got to the scene in which Seth Rogen masturbated over a video of Charlize Theron and a big glob of jizz shot into his beard. That seemed to me a good place to call it a night, and I gently shook Mum awake and walked her up the stairs. As she clung tightly to my arm, I was struck by how unusual it was to feel (and there's no un-pathetic way to say this) that she needed me. In her bedroom, she apologised. 'I don't know what's wrong with me,' she complained. I told her not to worry and helped her change into her nightie. Then she paused to study her face in the mirror and snapped angrily, 'I hate getting old.' Well, you're not *getting* old, I thought. You *are* old, Mum.

Sometimes, when I look in the mirror, I'm surprised to see

the effects of ageing are still there. I keep expecting them to clear up, as you would with most other illnesses or injuries. I had assumed this delusional phase would pass and that if I made it to 70 or 80, I'd have adjusted to old age, but seeing my mother scowl at her reflection, I realised that might take a little longer than I'd hoped.

Downstairs, I said to Sarah that I was worried about how much Ma was drinking. She suggested the drinking was her way of blocking out the reality of old age and her mind slowing down. Or maybe it was just her way of dealing with *Long Shot*. I sympathised. By the time the credits rolled, not only was I less keen on Seth Rogen (especially his jizzbeard), I realised that Ma, resilient and upbeat for as long as I could remember, was in trouble. I knew her independent life in her cottage in Sonning on Thames couldn't carry on much longer, and in all likelihood 2020 would be the year she came to live with us in Norfolk, where she would probably stay in the flat where Dad spent his last few months in 2015.

It would be a new phase for us all, adjusting to her needs and beginning a final chapter in which we got to know each other better and hopefully didn't discover we found each other incredibly irritating. Clearly, I'd learned nothing from moving Dad in with us. In the meantime, we needed to stock up on Prosecco and find some less spaff-tastic films to watch.

Ad
Joe

CHAPTER 11

BIG TIME

In a taxi with Sarah after an evening with friends in July 1998, we were staring at each other amorously and I said, only slightly facetiously to give myself a get-out, 'So, are we going to get married, then?'

'Yes,' said Sarah. 'It's so weird that you're the one. You're the man I'm going to marry. I just know it now for certain.' Though neither of us considered it a formal proposal, and we didn't get married until 2001, it was still one of my best journeys by taxi.

On the whole, things were going well in my professional life, too. Channel 4's decision to repeat the first and second series of *The Adam and Joe Show* in the spring of 1998 had turned us into minor celebrities. We did the rounds of Sunday supplement interview profiles and appeared on the nation's biggest television programmes, *The Big Breakfast*, *T4* and *Bedrock*. We even won a prestigious Royal Television Society Award for Best Newcomers, presented to us at a black-tie ceremony with a kiss from beautiful brainiac Carol Vorderman, one of the objects of Ken Korda's affection. It could only have been better if we'd got a snog from Bodger and Badger and a handjob from PJ & Duncan.

A VHS of *The Best Bits from Series 1&2* from *The Adam and Joe Show* was hastily released, and we signed a contract to write an Adam and Joe book, which wasn't so hastily released. We'd been fans of comedy book tie-ins for *The Young Ones*, *Not the Nine O'Clock News* and *Monty Python*, and we were keen to make our book as detailed and carefully produced as those had been, which meant ours wasn't published until late the following year.

The other professional high points for me in 1998 were the music videos Joe and I made for two of my musical heroes. Dad starred as a prophet of doom in the video for 'Dog Gone' by Pixies frontman Frank Black, and in our video for 'Sweet Johnny' by Welsh psychedelic pop geniuses Gorky's Zygotic Mynci, the band appeared as collectable dolls intercut with toy versions of classic music videos including 'Firestarter', 'Bittersweet Symphony' and 'No Surprises'.

The Gorky's video was the first thing we filmed in our new workspace around the corner from Borough Market in south London. Here, World of Wonder had rented us a small studio flat with a bathroom, kitchenette, edit suite and enough space for us to reconstruct the bedroom set and work on toy movies.

The only thing that detracted from the joy of our new Borough media hub was the presence in the building next to ours of PWL, pop producer Pete Waterman's Hit Factory, home of Kylie and Jason, Rick Astley, Sinitta and, around the time we were there, Steps. The problem wasn't the music, but the parking.

The day of our Gorky's Zygotic Mynci shoot, I had driven my Ford Fiesta to transport various bits of gear, and while I was unloading in the small courtyard, I bumped into one of Pete Waterman's pop henchmen, a dead ringer for late-Nineties Ray Winstone. His first words to me were not 'Welcome to the neighbourhood' but 'Who the fuck said you could park there?' When I told him we were moving into the flat and said truthfully that I had understood it was OK to park outside, Winstone barked at me that I needed to move my car immediately and added that I was 'a lying cunt'. That set the tone for most of our mercifully infrequent interactions with the Hit Factory for the next couple of years.

Though we never encountered Pete Waterman himself

while we were working from the flat in Borough, and I know people who swear he is a wonderful and prodigiously talented human being with a deep love for all kinds of music, our occasional encounters with his more frightening employees reinforced my snobbery about the shrink-wrapped, processed plop crapped out by his Shit Factory.

When Joe and I were getting into music in the early 1980s, the Top 40 was a wildly unpredictable and varied landscape where the sparkling smoothness of Duran Duran, Lionel Richie, Spandau Ballet, ABC and Imagination coexisted with the avant-garde oddness of Talking Heads, XTC, Grace Jones, the Associates, Laurie Anderson and Kate Bush. Maybe I was just nostalgic for my youth, but by the late Nineties it felt to me that the weirdos had been squeezed out in favour of sanitised pop from manufactured acts like B*Witched, Boyzone, Another Level, Five and PWL alumnus Steps. I channelled my prejudice into a new project for Ken Korda in which he cynically put together a band aimed at the wallets of young teens, a process that was still a couple of years away from becoming the mainstay of British TV entertainment via shows like *Popstars*, *Pop Idol* and *The X Factor*. This piece of pop prescience was to be just one of the magical handcrafted gems in the comedy crown that was *The Adam and Joe Show* series three.

RAMBLE

SERIES THREE

I went big on the hyperbole in that last sentence because, in many ways, everything we wanted to do with *The Adam and Joe Show* came together in our third series. I spent weeks writing about every single item we shot for that series, and then my editor, Jack, cut it all out because he said it was 'too in the weeds and quite boring'. As a compromise, I asked if I could include some highlights in this Ramble, and he said, 'OK, as long as you keep it short.' Then he punched me in the nuts and closed the door of my cage.

For series three, we got BaaadDad out into the world more. We filmed him riding around Los Angeles in a Humvee with hip-hop superstar Coolio, who also gave Dad some help with his rapping. In London, Pa got painting lessons from art-world troublemakers the Chapman Brothers. We also travelled to the hedonistic mecca of Ibiza, where BaaadDad partied with a drunken 18–30s holiday mob and watched the owners of Manumission nightclub shagging on stage and then claiming it was art. Off camera, Dad went ballistic in a carpark after I accused him of being unprofessional when he refused to touch the bum of a sexy pole-dancing man in Trade (see *Ramble Book* Chapter 21 for a more sensitive account of this).

Elsewhere in series three, Joe and I turned an empty clothes store on Carnaby Street into Dr Spankle's Hollywood Wax-O-Rama, a West End tourist attraction to rival Madame Tussauds. Once inside, befuddled visitors were guided through a series of classic cinema moments recreated with barely moving mannequins in shoddy costumes. There was a mannequin that we pushed around next to an IV drip while opera played (*Philadelphia*), a mannequin sitting on a chair wearing a blonde wig and a white dress which opened its legs to reveal another blonde wig (*Basic Instinct*) and a mannequin admiring another mannequin standing in a shop window (*Mannequin*).

Series three also featured some wonderfully well-observed 'Guide To' segments in which we provided helpful tips for dealing with challenges like sharing a bed with someone, forgetting people's names, being a terrible driver and being served by condescending men in cool record shops.

Toy movie highlights included Joe's version of *Saving Private Ryan*, which I think most people would agree was more powerful than the original. I channelled years of loyal late-morning viewing into *This Morning with Richard and Chewie*, and my *Stuffed Trek: The Toy Generation* looked out of this world (even though someone appeared to have beamed out the jokes). Oh yeah, and there was *Toytanic*, which was fine, I suppose.

For Vinyl Justice, we got stoned with Mark Morriss from the Bluetones and played with his John Holmes realistic rubber cock. We made up a new theme for *Beadle's About* with Pixies frontman Frank Black. We used synthesiser genius Thomas Dolby as a ventriloquist's dummy. We danced to 'MMMBop' by Hanson with Alexis Arquette, her dog and masked cross-dressing pals at her Hollywood house. We showed Ray Manzarek, keyboard player of the Doors, how to improve his riff for 'Light My Fire'. And, of course, the Fall's Mark E. Smith bullied me, assaulted Joe, told him he looked like a 'fucking egg' and extorted £200 from us.

Other precious musical moments came in the form of videos for more of our songs, including another Zac Sandler number from our school days, a slice of country and western called 'My Name Is Roscoe':

My name is Roscoe
That's Roscoe H Spellgood
I like to go a long way in a short time
That's why I increase my velocity when possible,
Cos speed equals distance over time

We hired an incredibly expensive New York taxi for our cinematic homage to a figure we'd admired throughout our teens who, according to Zac's lyrics, was 'a loverly persjuan, and a very good actor'. Although the 'Robert De Niro Calypso' was not, in fact, a calypso, it was a fine piece of songwriting that will undoubtedly accompany many news reports on the sad day that the credits finally roll for De Niro.

Another musical tribute to an acting legend was supplied by Joe's authentic cockney knees-up 'Song for Bob Hoskins'. For the video, we filmed a tightly choreographed dance number (for which the directions were: jump from one foot to the other), with my dad and brother Dave joining members of our production team dressed up as pearly kings and queens in a Dickensian street set. As far as I'm aware, the song was not used in news reports when Hoskins died in 2014.

Tickle me fancy,
Have a banana,
What a palaver,
Old bull and bush!
Apples and pears,
Scruffle me nuts,
I'm off to Stepney,
To waggle me brush!
Rattle me spoonies,
Nibble me knob,
Shiver me timbers,
Corn on the cob!
Shuffle me bobkins,
Tackle me tits,
Toddy me pipkins,
Fiddle me nips!

And, of course, there was Ken Korda's attempt to jump on Pete Waterman's pop bandwagon. Reasoning that 'kiddies love phones', Ken decided to call his band 1471 after British Telecom's call-return service (soon to be made obsolete by the spread of mobile phones). I hadn't enjoyed auditioning the members of 1471 under false pretences, but once they'd forgiven us, they rolled brilliantly with everything thrown at them. Sean, Shirley, Phil and Lou were given the stage names Jell-E, Bronwyn, Pippin and Funty, and spent an afternoon being verbally bullied by Ken in the studio, where they recorded their first single, 'Please, Please Hold the Line'. As well as lyrics about drunk dialling to appeal to alcopop-swilling teens, the song boasted a catchy playground chant that Ken hoped would also hoover up an even younger demographic:

Last night, you said to me
I was the only one
Said you'd call me up
And we could have some fun
But when I tried to call
I found that you weren't home
Don't tell me you weren't there
Cos I got a busy tone
I must have been pissed
I can't recall
What I did last night at all
You were called today
At 09.00 hours
Sorry, can't call back
Caller withheld their number
Please, please, hold the line
The caller knows you are waiting, oh yeah
Who's the naughty fella?
Who's the naughty fella?
Mr Caterpillar!
Mr Caterpillar!

Producing the kind of top-quality material that made up series three brought a great deal of joy and satisfaction. But working intensively on a single project for months on end with someone you love but also feel competitive with while trying to maintain personal relationships outside work can also leave you feeling that you want to do something else with your life entirely.

By February 1999, when we were shooting links before transmission in April, we had decided to kill off *The Adam and Joe Show.*

For the last link in episode six, Joe and I were seen delivering a farewell from the bed, when suddenly BaaadDad jumped out dressed as a Seventies radical and shot us to death. This bloody conclusion was intended as a reference to Sidney Lumet's 1976 film *Network*, a satire on the dehumanising influence of television that ends with a messianic newscaster being executed similarly. But if you hadn't seen *Network* (and even if you had), it probably seemed like an odd way to wrap up an otherwise fun and silly series.

Welcome to Megastardom

In July 1999, a few weeks after our third series had finished airing, Channel 4's head of programmes, Tim Gardam, wrote a letter to Joe and me in which he said:

> *I should have written before the series finished. However, I have been looking back at our programmes so far this year, and it struck me yet again how good your latest series was. And how well it did with the audience – the best yet.*

Indeed, for a low-budget, late-night show, our ratings were good, sometimes as high as 1.5 million, and we were still getting good reviews and enthusiastic profiles in broadsheets and magazines. That was the summer I reached peak minor celebrity, and one day when I was driving around London, running errands, it seemed as though everywhere I went, people were pleased to see me.

At the Virgin Megastore on Oxford Street, I went to pay for my copy of *Terror Twilight* by Pavement, and as the man behind the till saw me approaching he started to nod approvingly while holding out his hand for me to shake. I wondered if he might be congratulating me on my album choice, but then he bowed and said with faux solemnity, 'Great show, sir.' Then, at the bank, the woman next to me at the counter slid over a paying-in slip on which she'd written, 'We Love Your Show.'

My final bit of recognition that day happened when I was back in my car, crawling home in the London traffic. My Ford Fiesta, bought from a friend after I'd passed my test (on the third attempt) a couple of years previously, had starred in the video we made for 'My Name Is Roscoe'. It had been painted orange with '01' on the front doors like the General Lee, the car driven by Bo and Luke Duke from *The Dukes of Hazzard*, a TV show we enjoyed in the early Eighties in which the bumbling local sheriff of Hazzard County was called Roscoe.

I was very pleased with my Ford Fiesta's *Dukes of Hazzard* makeover, so I left the paint job and decals untouched after we'd finished filming. For a few months after the 'Roscoe' video was broadcast, I would get frequent waves from pedestrians as I drove by. On this occasion, I'd been recognised by a woman in the car next to me in the slowly moving traffic queue, and she was so busy grinning and giving me the thumbs up that when the traffic stopped, she failed to notice and ploughed into the back of the car ahead. OK, maybe 'ploughed' is putting it too strongly, but she gave the guy in front a good dent, and he was sad.

RAMBLE

RETIRING THE GENERAL

When my friend Nora came to visit and saw the orange Fiesta parked outside my flat, she exclaimed, 'What the fuck?' For a second, I thought she was impressed, but the expression on her face said otherwise. She was staring at the roof, which, like the car from the TV show, was emblazoned with what most of my friends thought of back then as *The Dukes of Hazzard* flag, but which nowadays is more widely recognised as the Confederate flag. You know, the one frequently displayed proudly by American white supremacists. Nora wasn't a *Dukes of Hazzard* fan, and initially I thought she was making too much of it. But after I'd done a little more reading, I had the flag removed while wondering if I'd just spent weeks being waved at by white supremacists.

We Fear Change

Despite Channel 4's enthusiasm for *The Adam and Joe Show*, from their point of view it had two big problems: firstly, the time it took to produce, and secondly, how scrappy it looked compared to everything around it. In my mind, that had always been the point: to create a TV show with the home-made charm of a mixtape lovingly and painstakingly compiled by a friend that would stand in stark contrast to the slickness and predictability of most other entertainment shows. But even with our production team at World of Wonder doing all they could to speed up the process, our hands-on, obsessional approach to every detail in the show was driving everyone nuts, us included. Something had to give.

Our champion at Channel 4, Peter Grimsdale, had moved on, which meant any future Adam and Joe projects at the channel would be dealt with by the Entertainment department. One of the commissioners from Entertainment invited us to a swanky private members club in Portman Square to talk about what we were going to do next, and we were joined by a comedy producer who'd expressed an interest in working with us. The club was made up of several high-ceilinged rooms scattered with Regency furniture, like a chintzy stately home that had been invaded by media tosspots with record bags, Adidas trainers and T-shirts for obscure bands. We fitted right in.

I ordered a sea breeze from a server who looked like (and probably was) a model and lit up a Marlboro Light. After the preceding weeks of being patted on the back following the transmission of the third series, I prepared my ego for a little more stroking before we got down to business. Instead, the commissioner and the producer began by listing all the things they felt hadn't worked on *The Adam and Joe Show*. The pranks were too low-stakes and lame, they said. The observational material in our 'Guide To' segments was out of place and not strong enough. Vinyl Justice was a good idea, but we'd 'botched it'. 'Maybe you wanted it to look guerilla, but it just looked amateurish,' said the producer. 'I wanted to know more about the records, but we didn't see more than a few seconds before the arsing about started again, and that got tiresome pretty quickly.' The fact that I'd had some of the same concerns about these segments made the criticisms sting a little deeper.

Struggling to conceal my indignation, I told myself I needed to toughen up if I wanted to keep working on TV.

I also reminded myself that Joe and I had in the past parodied some of the shows the commissioner and the producer had worked on, so that may have contributed to the roasting they were giving us now. If so, fair enough, I thought. I put on my best *mature and interested* face, listened to everything they had to say and thought, *Well, you can both fuck off if you think we're going to do anything with you two twats.* These were not my most Zen and enlightened years.

A Bold Reinvention

As the new millennium dawned and the world breathed a sigh of relief that suddenly having so many zeroes in the date hadn't killed all the computers, Joe and I resolved to play the game. We needed to come up with a show that would be quicker and less exhausting to make with production values that were less off-putting to the average viewer.

We decided our brave new direction would be a media parody show called *Adam and Joe's TV Show*. Yes, that was the title we'd had for five minutes back in 1996 before Channel 4 insisted on *The Adam and Joe Show*, but now it worked better because we were going to focus exclusively on TV. And films. Obviously, we'd keep on doing the toy movies because they were popular, and no one thought *they* looked amateurish … at least not in a bad way. We'd also keep Ken Korda because he was a character that could be slotted into all kinds of formats easily. And it was fun being Ken. And we'd find some way to keep BaaadDad, too.

We also intended to carry on wearing T-shirts with our names on and waggling stuffed toys on *Adam and Joe's TV Show*, but when it came to sitting on a bed in a poster-covered bedroom we decided that was too sad for men who had recently turned 30. So we designed a new set to show we had completely moved on from *The Adam and Joe Show* and, with our new producers Ruth and Grainne, we got to work making a pilot that would show Channel 4 we'd taken all their comments on board and were not afraid to embrace radical change.

Segments for our new pilot included Joe's stuffed-toy version of *Fight Club* and a BaaadDad piece in which he attended a 'Toff ball' with more drunken teens. These were filmed much the same way they would have been on *The Adam and Joe Show*, i.e. with us doing the camera work and Joe doing most of the directing. Other segments, like our spoof of *The 1900 House* and a Ken Korda profile of DJ Pat Sharp, were filmed with a professional crew, and for our links we spent the day in a small TV studio in Soho where the art department had built our new set, which looked like the inside of an old television.

The walls of the set were made up of giant models of circuit boards rigged with twinkling lights, brightly coloured wires and huge speakers. In the centre of the floor were a couple of big capacitors for me and Joe to sit on. I thought it looked excellent. We also had a professional studio crew with broadcast-spec camera equipment, headsets, clipboards, walkie-talkies and all that jazz. There was even a make-up person, which we'd never had before except when we went on other TV shows.

On *The Adam and Joe Show*, we'd shoot links on the bedroom set in the evening because we didn't like getting up early. Joe and I would work late into the night, just the two of us getting tetchy when a mic wasn't working or a light blew. Shooting the links for our new pilot in a real TV studio during daylight hours with a crew fussing around us was a welcome novelty. We enjoyed feeling important and having other people there to make sure everything was plugged in, tell us what we needed to do next, and laugh encouragingly as we delivered our links. And we loved how good we looked under those studio lights with all that make-up.

One night, a few weeks after we'd finished the pilot for *Adam and Joe's TV Show* in March 2000, I got back to my basement flat in Clerkenwell and embarked on a booze-fuelled internet ego-surfing mission. I returned to the Channel 4 comedy message boards where Joe and I had once chatted excitedly with users who had been full of praise for us when *The Adam and Joe Show* first aired in December 1996.

Now, the chat was about new Channel 4 comedies, like *Jam*, Chris Morris's trippy sketch show, *Trigger Happy TV*, in which Dom Joly fearlessly played out his character sketches for an unsuspecting public, and Sacha Baron Cohen's *Da Ali G Show*, which took the art of the wind-up interview to giddy new heights. Though *The Adam and Joe Show* had elements that were similar to parts of these new comedies, I worried that we seemed quaint, not to say irrelevant, by comparison. These fears were confirmed when I came across a thread on the message board from someone who had managed to get hold of our new pilot and written a long, eviscerating review. They called it 'a tired fucking waste of time' and announced that we had 'run out of ideas'.

We'd had bad reviews for *The Adam and Joe Show* before, but only from TV critics who didn't get it and could be dismissed as dickheads. Now, we were being slammed by our *own* people, the comedy nerds, and the criticism hit home once again. The pilot contained some good segments, but they weren't so different from things we'd done before, just a little more slickly produced. When it came to the new TV set and the links, which had felt good on the day, everyone came to agree they hadn't worked at all.

When Channel 4 suggested that we try to be more accessible, they were probably imagining a conventional TV studio with a crew, a desk and an audience. Instead we'd used the bigger budget to make our show even weirder. It didn't help that the set looked like the inside of the kind of boxy 4:3 aspect ratio TV that would soon be made obsolete by flat

16:9 screens. As the internet nerds pointed out, by reducing our links to thin pastiches of insincere TV presentation, we'd managed to arrive at the worst of both worlds and effectively eradicated much of the homemade charm that had made the show appealing in the first place. It was like the bit in *Wayne's World* where Rob Lowe turns up and convinces Wayne and Garth to sell out, except without Rob Lowe.

Series Four - The Same but Different

Keen not to discard everything we'd created for the pilot, and in the absence of any radically new ideas that we could both agree on, we decided to return to the bedroom set in Borough and make one more series of *The Adam and Joe Show*.

Working on the principle that we would now focus exclusively on media parodies, we dropped Vinyl Justice and our observational 'Guide To' segments. Instead of trying to do more pranks, we parodied the edgy stunts of other TV shows with our Lame Prankster characters, Martin and Andy. Similarly, BaaadDad's segments were framed as spoofs of investigative shows like *MacIntyre Undercover*.

In an effort to speed up the production process, we made fewer toy movies and hired a model maker to help us build sets. We resolved to shoot our links with a camera crew during daylight hours, having written scripts beforehand, rather than trying to come up with ideas on the set in the middle of the night while we were stoned. We even tried working with other writers for the first time, but it quickly became clear there was a gulf between the way they saw us and the way we saw ourselves. The only writer we met whose name made it to the credits for the fourth series was future bestselling author and quiz show creator Richard Osman. Richard's sensibility seemed most in line with ours, although now I don't

Adam and Joe on the 'TV set', 2000

remember at all which bits he was responsible for (and no, it wasn't Quizzlestick – that was all Cornballs).

Once again, I'm sorry to tell you my editor put his stupid red pen through several pages filled with detailed descriptions and fascinating analysis of the whole of our fourth series, but I managed to sneak three chunks back in. Don't mention it.

Toy Movies

There were a lot of films that might have made good toy movies released in 1999, when we started work on the pilot for the fourth series. *The Sixth Sense*, *The Blair Witch Project*, *Magnolia* and *Notting Hill* all had elements that would have been fun to recreate with stuffed toys, but there was something about being told how meaningless our lives are by Brad Pitt, Edward Norton, Helena Bonham Carter, Jared Leto and Meat Loaf that made *Fight Club* the obvious place to start.

Like so much popular culture in the Nineties, *Fight Club* was soaked in irony while wanting desperately to be cool *and* taken seriously. So it made me happy when Joe said his toy version of *Fight Club* was going to be called *Tufty Club*, a reference to the children's road-safety awareness organisation whose mascot was a squirrel called Tufty Fluffytail. In Joe's toy movie Brad Pitt's character, Tyler Durden, was played by a fluffy toy squirrel whom Cornballs named Piler Turden (in the tradition of his scatological retitling of bad films on our cinema trips in the Eighties, e.g. *Crocodile Dundee II*, which became *Crock O'Shit Dungheep Poo*). 'The first rule of Tufty Club is: you do not cross the road between parked cars. The second rule of Tufty Club is: YOU DO NOT CROSS THE ROAD BETWEEN PARKED CARS ...'

The last toy movie I made for *The Adam and Joe Show* was ostensibly a parody of the BBC Two film-analysis programme *Scene by Scene*, hosted by Irish film critic Mark Cousins. Previous guests on the real *Scene by Scene* had included Martin Scorsese, Bernardo Bertolucci and David Lynch. In my toy version, Cousins talked to director Guy Ritchie about his gangsters-and-boxing caper *Snatch* (my toy version was called *Twat*). Primarily, it was an excuse to wheel out my impression of Mark Cousins and apply the musical lilt of his delivery to lines like: 'Casting the fillum with *Eastend Toys* actor Muck Reed, alongside Hollywood star Brad Pish was a marvellously postmodern masterstroke, as we'll see in this next scene ...'

It was also nice to get in a featherweight jab at Guy Ritchie, who'd been at boarding school with me in Sussex when he was a nicely turned-out, softly spoken ten-year-old. I liked Guy, and he took the edge off my homesickness during several weekends at school when he taught me how to play cards.

Nearly 20 years later, I was at the British Comedy Awards when *Lock, Stock and Two Smoking Barrels* won the award for best comedy in 1998, and I was excited to see Guy, flanked by a couple of big *geezers*, at the aftershow party. I said hello, but he didn't remember me. When I reminded him about playing cards and being at boarding school in the country together, he said, 'I went to a lot of schools,' and then he disappeared into the celebrity throng.

So, to teach him a lesson, I called him *Guy Richtoy* in my toy movie, implied that he'd changed his accent to appear more streetwise than he really was, and accused him of being a hooky Tarantino. He was never heard from again. The moral? If you've been inside with Buckles, you'd better give him a nice hug when you next see him, or Buckles is gonna get butt-hurt.

The 1980s House

One of my favourite segments in the fourth series was our parody of Channel 4's hit reality show *The 1900 House*. Billed as 'an experiment in living history', *The 1900 House* showed a family from 1999 living for three months as their counterparts would have done a hundred years previously in a house that had been specially de-modernised to demonstrate how technology had transformed our lives in the twentieth century. Spoiler: Life for a middle-class family in 1999 was more convenient than a century ago.

In *The 1980s House*, a family from the year 2000, the Fatboy Slims, volunteer to wash, dress, cook, eat and live every intimate detail of their lives the way they would have done all the way back in the 1980s. Joe played the family's patriarch, web designer Paul Fatboy Slim. I played his wife, Joyce, who designed websites. A couple of actors played the kids, 16-year-old website-design student Catherine and 11-year-old internet-obsessed Joe.

We made three *1980s House* segments, and Cornballs and I enjoyed ourselves by trotting out deliberately cliched references to the decade of our youth that included Roland Rat, Ready Brek, Swingball, *Blitz* magazine, and long-forgotten alcoholic drinks of the period like Bezique, Mirage and Taboo.

One of the first shots we got was of Joe setting off for work in a baggy suit and a wig in the style of Limahl from Kajagoogoo. According to Joe's voiceover, Paul Fatboy Slim was driving to work the way all professional men of the Eighties did, in a Sinclair C5 having snorted a line of cocaine, washed down with champagne.

As soon as we started talking about *The 1980s House*, we knew there had to be a C5 in it. The battery-powered recumbent tricycle had been a disastrous flop when inventor Clive Sinclair's company unveiled it in 1985, but as a teen I'd seen Gary Numan driving one around the stage on Jimmy Savile's TV show *Jim'll Fix It* and thought, Now *that* is cool. There was something thrilling about getting to ride in an actual C5 after all that time, though when we heard that it had cost us several thousand pounds to hire it for one morning, it took the edge off somewhat.

We needed to cast a quintessentially Eighties figure as the authenticity expert for *The 1980s House*, and Joe and I were overjoyed when the production team told us they had secured the services of Leee John from electronic funkers Imagination, who had created some of the best pop music of the early Eighties. Have you heard Imagination's 'Just an Illusion' recently? It's better than all music before or since. Anyway, Leee was completely delightful and was happy to be fed authentic Eighties words and catchphrases like 'Mega!', 'Wicked!', 'Flippin'eck, Tucker!' and 'Hello, Peeps!', which he delivered with great conviction (if I ever get invited on Graham Norton's chat show, that's the anecdote I'm leading with).

'A Place with People, Innit'

One of Joe's daytime TV watching staples was a morning show called *Shopping City*, in which presenters Lowri Turner, Esther McVey and Tommy Walsh fronted consumer reports and chatted with shoppers in a different UK mall each week. Cornballs suggested doing a version where we ran around malls, garden centres, cinemas, supermarkets and other public spaces, interacting inanely with random passers-by, forcing them to take part in ridiculous on-the-spot challenges and babbling rapidly at them about nothing. We named it *People Place* and planned to start each segment by saying, 'Welcome to the show that goes wherever there's a place with people in it.' Later, I insisted we change this to the far more hilarious, 'Welcome to the show that goes wherever there's a place with people, innit.'

To give the pieces a genuine feel and help convince members of the public that we were legit, we had a proper camera crew with us who'd worked on similar shows, and I designed a *People Place* logo that we had printed onto a large board for location shots and made into patches that were sewn onto our revolting mustard-yellow-turtleneck-and-jogging-bottom uniforms. We wanted to appear as sexless as possible and chose our presenting names accordingly. I was Nikki Boxx and Joe was Lindsay Munk.

We shot the first *People Place* segment at the Putney Exchange shopping centre in southwest London, and at first we had fun shooting scripted pieces to camera and doing our best to be believably *Daytime TV*. But when it came to babbling at members of the public, I struggled, and soon I was engulfed by that same paralysing wave of self-consciousness that crashed over me on my first morning delivering CD603 travel reports back in Cheltenham. Apart from anything else, I was physically and mentally unable to waffle at the same pace as Cornballs, who could babble like a speed freak on cue, though as far as I'm aware he was never on anything stronger than cannabis and full-fat Coca-Cola. Joe has objected in the past to my characterisation of him as being occasionally haughty and superior, but there's no question that, in those days, he was able to tap into those qualities when required to. It could be trying off-camera, but it was great for *People Place*.

Whereas I'd get rattled whenever we approached someone with a microphone and they told us to fuck off, which usually happened at least once every time we did vox pops, Joe didn't care in the least. His height was useful in that respect. He seemed most at ease when looming over someone with an insincere grin, firing ludicrous questions and commands at them and steamrolling every answer with more patronising prattle.

'*What have you got in your bag? A loaf of bread! Do you like bread? How many slices do you think are in there? Just have a guess! Do an impression! Do it again! DO IT AGAIN! That's great! Back to you, Nikki.*'

After a while, we realised our *People Place* filming days went best if Joe did most of the blathering with members of the public and I came up with random vacuous info plops that we could use as cutaways.

'*Nothing perks you up at the end of a long drive like a nice cup of tea, but what if you reach out and find there's no cup? Not a problem with this rotating mug tree. Just give it a whizz, and mugs there is.*'

I recall being grumpy on several occasions while we were filming *People Place*, although that had more to do with the relentless filming schedule than with the pieces themselves, which, thanks mainly to Joe, ended up being some of the best parts of the series.

Death to the Squares

The fourth series of *The Adam and Joe Show* was shown as part of the launch of Channel 4's new digital station, E4, in January 2001. Nice as it was to be part of Channel 4's new venture, it was hard not to feel that we were being sidelined by what everyone still thought of as 'the main channel'.

Far more distressing for me, however, was the news that E4 expected us to deliver the finished programmes in the new widescreen format after we'd already shot several pieces in the 4:3 aspect ratio standard to analogue TV back then.

To me, the switch to widescreen was a symbol of television's wrong-headed determination to compete with cinema. I loved the beautiful, boxy 4:3 image, which was so much closer to the human eye's natural field of view. Widescreen was all very well for panoramic vistas of nature or spaceships blasting away at each other, but for drama on a human scale,

Adam and Joe with the People Place Worm Circus

I preferred talking heads on the bulging, thick glass screen of a cathode ray tube.

Suddenly, we were in a world of wide, flat-panel TV sets with plasma and LCD displays that allowed 16:9 movies to fill the whole screen, but in those pre-HD times, the picture was crap. It was sharper than analogue TV but ugly and unforgiving, and if you were looking at it from the wrong angle, it would disappear altogether. Widescreen images had been developed for audiences in the cinema, not for living rooms, so why were we throwing out the lovely square world of telly for a shit version of the movies? It may seem ungrateful, but I blame George Lucas.

When I eventually stopped crying about aspect ratios and the terribleness of early flatscreen TVs, I was able to enjoy the overwhelmingly warm critical response we got to the fourth series of *The Adam and Joe Show*. But I was aware that Joe and I couldn't keep working together in the same way. The problem was that we'd begun to associate our relationship not with the fun and silliness that had bonded us back at school, but with the competitive stress of work, keeping one eye on who was performing best in the show and another on where our 'careers' were going next.

We had been incredibly lucky to find a backdoor into TV thanks to Fenton and Randy at World of Wonder, and Peter Grimsdale at Channel 4. Nowadays, it seems barely conceivable that we were able to spend five years making such a peculiar show in such an eccentric way. And yet, for all its technical shortcomings, lapses in taste and apparent determination to become outdated within days of transmission, *The Adam and Joe Show* was, to our delight and amazement, embraced by a loyal hardcore who appreciated our efforts to '*fight back at the constant bombardment of advertisers, promoters and manufactured lifestyles*'. The other 99 per cent of our viewers were ten-year-olds up past their bedtime who liked the toys, the swearing and the bright colours.

CHAPTER 12

QUALITY TIME

When I was even more deluded than I am now, I imagined that when my children were in their teens, weekends would be spent with all of us together, bantering on dog walks, laughing on picnics, having passionate discussions about current affairs over supper, then dancing around the kitchen to eclectic music mixes late into the night. Of course, I understood that from time to time, there'd be dramas, as you'd expect with teenagers, but weekends would be when we all came together to support one another through our respective challenges, like an endearingly dysfunctional family from a Richard Curtis film.

I'm not saying we *never* have heartwarming family moments at Castle Buckles; there have been some epic frisbee afternoons that even Rosie got involved with, many very spiritual rounds of the Name Game, and during the first lockdown, I forced everyone to learn the Cup Dance, but the reality of spending time together as a family in the early twenty-first century is typically a more atomised affair. It's hard to get teenage children excited about the prospect of dog walks and picnics when they'd rather be alone in their rooms, marinating in box sets or scrolling listlessly on devices. Hang on, has my dad finally possessed my laptop? Or have I just turned into him?

One weekend in late August 2021, with the autumn term about to begin after a summer holiday torpedoed by

'Pingdemic' isolations, I was in my office continuing to sort through my parents' photos when it struck me how crazy it was to be sitting alone, getting emotional about the past and missing Mum, while my children were all still home and we could be spending time together in the present. So I closed my laptop and went knocking on bedroom doors to canvas support for the year's first trip to the cinema.

The only holdout was Sarah, who said she had too much work to do. After a brief ratty exchange in which she suggested I was only interested in spending time with the family when it was convenient for me to do so (see Argument Log), the rest of us decided on a trip to see *Free Guy*, starring Ryan Reynolds, Jodie Comer and Taika Waititi, because it looked fun and had good reviews. 'I thought you said we weren't going to see any more films that look fun and have good reviews because they always turn out to be shit,' said Frank when he'd finally come down from his room ten minutes after I'd shouted up the stairs that if we didn't hurry, we'd miss the start of the film.

By the time we arrived at the Odeon in Norwich, we'd missed the start of the film. It was only four minutes in, but Hope felt it would be too disrespectful to the artists behind *Free Guy* to miss even a second of the five-star action. Frank jabbed at his phone and announced there was another showing in an hour over at the Vue cinema in nearby Castle Mall.

Castle Mall was never the most uplifting spot in Norwich, but pandemic times had intensified the bleakness. Every other shop was shuttered, and the ones that were still open seemed at that moment to indicate a yawning spiritual chasm at the core of twenty-first century life in the affluent West. On the evidence of Castle Mall, what we absolutely can't do without as a society are phone cases, doughnuts, sweets, snacks, mobility scooters and, best of all during a pandemic, an arcade with buttons, joysticks and touch screens all crawling with every variant of Covid.

I wondered what Castle Mall would be like in another 20 years. Perhaps they'd open up a walk-in euthanasia clinic, like the one in the sci-fi film *Soylent Green*. They could put it right next to the cinema, so when your film finishes you'd have a choice of exits. Then, if you choose the Dying Room, instead of projecting images of nature on the walls, as they do in *Soylent Green*, they'll show you a blooper reel from whatever film you've just seen, so you can slip into oblivion as that year's version of Ryan Reynolds and Taika Waititi run through some semi-improvised wisecrackery.

As we made our way up through the semi-deserted levels of Castle Mall to the Vue cinema on the top floor, we passed a large model of Norwich Castle as it might have looked 900 years ago. Sections of the walls were cut away to reveal little painted medieval figures enjoying a banquet and doing castle chores. We still had some time before the next showing of *Free Guy*, so we paused to study the miniature scene. I wondered if any real peasants from 900 years ago felt there was a yawning chasm at the centre of *their* lives. Unlikely. Rather than wrestling with existential angst, they were probably busy with castle work and trying to stay alive until they were 40.

We arrived at the cinema with half an hour still to wait, so we sat down by the big window overlooking the real Norwich Castle, and I took orders for drinks and snacks. Frank said he didn't want anything as he was going through a straight-edge phase. Hope asked for some popcorn and a bottle of water. I told her I had water in my Chilly bottle, but she scrunched up her face and muttered about me having had Covid a few weeks ago. I was no longer contagious, and I carried the Chilly bottle precisely to avoid having to buy expensive plastic bottles of water and hastening the demise of the planet, but she wanted her own bottle of water and I didn't want to spoil our first day out for months by turning it into a big deal. Anyway, I told myself, I should have been happy she was asking for water instead of Coke. When I was her age, I definitely would have wanted Coke. I asked Nat what he wanted. 'Sweet popcorn, please. And a Coke.' That's my boy.

At the counter, I asked for a bottle of water, then a medium Coke ('The large size is grotesque,' I could hear my dad saying) and a large sweet popcorn (which was not grotesque because I was about to snaffle an empty cardboard tub and divide the popcorn between Hope and Nat, thereby winning).

'It's going to be cheaper if you have a *large* Coke with the large popcorn because then it's part of a deal,' said the young woman behind the counter.

'No, thanks. I don't want a large Coke. Couldn't you just give me a medium Coke and ring it up as large?' I asked.

'I'm afraid that's against policy,' came the reply.

'So I'm paying more for wanting less?' I said, transitioning into dick mode.

'It's because we're doing a promotion for large Coke and large popcorn,' said the counter lady.

'Right, OK. Could you give me a large Coke but not fill it right up?'

The counter lady pulled a large cup from the top of the stack behind her, pushed it against the serving lever, and then, with a scowl that suggested this was the stupidest thing she'd ever been asked to do, removed the cup from the Coke dispenser before it was full. I had won.

The elation didn't last long because as we took our seats in the auditorium, the adverts were starting, and one of them, for McDonald's, struck me as one of the most depressing things I'd ever seen in my life.

The ad, which I googled when I got home and which turned out to be called 'Me Time', featured a series of vignettes in which ordinary people were seen stealing a break from the pressures of their lives, whether at home or work, for a tiny moment of bliss as they bit into a Big Mac, sipped a McDonald's coffee, munched on a wrap or chomped a McNugget. The subtext seemed to be: life is grim, lonely and exhausting, but it's not all bad because sometimes you get to tip the last shards from a container of McDonald's French fries down your throat as you sit alone in your car.

As is so often the case with adverts, the sugar coating intended to make the shitty pill go down was a beautiful piece of music that had nothing to do with Ronald McStinkles and his revolting food. (I used to love McDonald's when I was little, but have you had a Chicken McNugget recently? A bogey is tastier, seriously. Although perhaps that's just one of my delicious privileged bogies.)

The Flamingos' 1959 version of 'I Only Have Eyes for You' was a song I discovered in the early 1990s when I bought the soundtrack for George Lucas's film *American Graffiti.* I loved the sweetness of the tune, the strangeness of the slow doo-wop groove and the woozy, dreamlike atmosphere conjured by the minimalist production. At the start of the Nineties, it had only been used a handful of times in films and certainly hadn't turned up in any TV ads, but by 2021 'I Only Have Eyes for You' had been plundered so often that the McDonald's 'Me Time' ad wasn't so much the last nail in its coffin as another piece of obscene graffiti on its headstone.

But Buckles, you massive elitist snob, if you think the song is so beautiful, you should have been happy that Ronnie McDonny was helping more people discover it. Well, no, I wasn't happy because part of what gives a piece of music its power and meaning are the associations we have with it. Even if a song is maddeningly bad, you can love it because it reminds you of having a wonderful time when you first heard it. Conversely, even the loveliest piece of music can trigger real pain if it was once the soundtrack to a traumatic experience, like, for example, watching a McDonald's advert before sitting through *Free Guy* on your first day out after months of being locked down during a pandemic, and trying to plug a yawning spiritual chasm with popcorn.

Given my frame of mind, *Free Guy* didn't have much of a

chance of being enjoyable. It was fine, but the joke of a relentlessly upbeat character experiencing an existential crisis when confronted by the harsh reality of the outside world had been done with more charm in films like *Elf* and *The Lego Movie*, as I made sure to inform the kids when we left the cinema.

Back at Castle Buckles, everyone disappeared to their quarters, and normal atomised family service resumed. With a heavy heart, I plonked myself down at my computer and gazed around my office at all the accumulated unimportant stuff.

Contents of the Case Pt.2

Staring down at me from the top of a shelf in the corner was my dad's black briefcase, the same briefcase I wrote about in *Ramble Book*, which he used to keep locked in his office when I was little with a label taped to the top that read, 'IN THE EVENT OF MY DEATH THE CONTENTS OF THIS CASE SHOULD BE DESTROYED, UNOPENED.' You'll have to read *Ramble Book* if you want to find out about the exciting McGuffin I finally discovered in there a few weeks before Dad died, but what I didn't reveal was that there was other stuff in the mysterious case, too. I can't pretend the bonus content is as dramatic as the main item, but after the *Free Guy* Quality Time expedition, I got it out again for the first time in several years.

Some items in the briefcase seemed more significant than others, though I guess they were all things Dad wanted either to keep safe or keep secret. There was the photo of my mum and me on the *QE2* in 1970, more recent snaps of a woman I didn't know (fully clothed) and some photos of cows (nude). I assumed the woman was the mysterious 'friend' I heard Mum mention bitterly once or twice before she and Dad split up. Not sure about the cows. Along with the photos were several pages written by my brother when he was 12, cheery diary entries from a family holiday in 1986, and beneath those was a letter that I'd written to Dad in November 1992.

Back then I was in my second year at art school in Cheltenham. Every weekend, I'd get the train back to London so I could work a few shifts at the Rock Island Diner, and if I wasn't staying with my girlfriend Karen, I'd stay in my old bedroom in Clapham and get a bit of washing done at the same time. I was having fun. More fun than Mum and Dad, who argued constantly about money until my brother, the last of us children living at home full time at that point, got tired of the immersive *Who's Afraid of Virginia Woolf?* experience and moved out.

I felt sorry for Dad, more so than for Mum, who it seemed to me was too hard on him. Years later, she explained the reasons she'd been so bitter and said she'd resented me taking his side, but in 1992, I was more tuned in to how joyless Dad's life had become, and my letter was intended to remind him that all was not lost, and that perhaps he needed to look on the bright side of life.

49 All Saints Road, Cheltenham
12th October 1992

Dear Daddy

I never really get a chance to say much to you when I'm back from college of a weekend because I'm usually collecting underwear and preparing to leave for work at the restaurant. I'm really writing because I heard all about David's decision to move out the other day, and I assumed you were being stoical and not mentioning it to me yourself. It looks as if you got blamed for the whole thing and it made me think you must be feeling either indignant or depressed at being labelled Bad Dad.

If this is the case, I wanted you to know that none of us thinks you are solely responsible for David's decision to leave, anyway the whole business of portioning the blame with that kind of thing is silly and useless. The problem, as far as I can tell, is that you and Mummy are clearly not getting on and seeing that is bound to be distressing for David as he's always around; but I know you are fully aware of that.

The letter ended with me giving Dad a pep talk (and trying very hard to strike a tone that Dad would appreciate). After the *Free Guy* Quality Time expedition, and considering my general outlook in the months after Mum died, it struck me as good advice for myself.

You deserve a break, to remember what you're doing it all for. We should go for a meal and see a film, and if the restaurant is bad, we can overcompensate with drink. Then if you hate the film, don't see it as symptomatic of modern society's terminal decline, rather enjoy the ensuing critical post-mortem. What I am trying lumberingly to say is, that sometimes I feel you take things more seriously than necessary. No one minds that you hate pop music or most of what you see us watching on TV, the problem is, you seem saddened by it. We are not suggesting you embrace the things that, whether you like them or not, form most of our lives, but I don't think you should let them get to you so much.

You must think I'm about to come out with something like 'You should get out and enjoy yourself Nigel', or something else equally trite and patronising. I hope you don't feel I have been impertinent or excessively naïve in writing this letter.

Just remember we're with you, and do try to get out and enjoy yourself, Nigel.

Love Ad

Family Supper

A few weeks after the *Free Guy* mission, the whole family was sitting down to a meal prepared by Frank, who had become quite a good cook during the lockdowns, finding and embellishing recipes from Instagram. That night, he had made us his signature dish: special egg-fried rice with mystery hotness. He'd also written a song that day. Not a comedy song or a jingle, but an actual angry punk-folk *song.* I had some slight reservations about the subject matter – the agony of being on a plane near a crying baby and realising you've left your noise-cancelling headphones in the Uber – which I thought could possibly be accused of being a bit *One Percentric,* but it was a whole song, and Frank performed it for us all on his guitar, something I had neither the skill nor the guts to do when I was his age.

Hope was buoyant after being selected for a prestigious local netball team, and she and Sarah exchanged info about the politics and personalities involved as I struggled to keep my pride from being overwhelmed by my strong indifference to sport.

Nat, meanwhile, seemed, at last, to be emerging from the Kevin the Teenager hole that he had spent much of the previous few years moodily barricaded within. He had started to perk up the morning he discovered that, due to the pandemic, his GSCEs had been cancelled, an event that had adverse consequences for thousands of teenagers but was for Nat 'the best day of my life'.

Whereas once a family meal would have been an opportunity to catch up on some sleep, his head either thrown back in stupefied boredom or rested on the table, these days Nat was more likely to chat and laugh with the rest of us. He was becoming more curious about the world and seemed especially delighted by words and phrases that were new to him.

When I'd described a cornfield as 'undulating in the wind' a few nights before, he'd snorted, '*Undulating?* Like *that's* a word! He was also indignant to discover that the idiom 'as the crow flies' cannot arbitrarily be attached to the end of any sentence as decoration, something we pointed out after he'd said, 'I think we should go to the pub for lunch, as the crow flies.'

That night, he told us he'd visited Grandma in the afternoon and had been surprised when she mentioned that Grandpa had once been a high-powered lawyer, like Sarah. 'You never told me Grandpa was a lawyer!' declared Nat at the supper table. Sarah pointed out that in her study next to the piano that Nat had started playing nearly every day, there was a large portrait of Grandpa in his barrister's robes and wig. And hanging in the downstairs toilet was Grandpa's obituary, which appeared in the local paper.

'Haven't you ever read Grandpa's obituary?' asked Sarah. 'His *what*?' said Nat, and she repeated, '*Obituary*.'

Nat stared back, flummoxed, then said, 'Grandpa had a *bitchery*?'

Best Ever TV Show
Best Ever TV Show
Best Ever TV Show
Best Ever TV Show
Best Ever TV Show
Best Ever TV Show
Best Ever TV Show
Best Ever TV Show
Best Ever TV Show
Best Ever TV Show
Best Ever TV Show
Best Ever TV Show

CHAPTER 13

THE LOST PROJECTS

A few months after the fourth and final series of *The Adam and Joe Show* finished airing in March 2001, I pretended to put away childish things and married Sarah. For our honeymoon, we toured around the West Coast of America, ending up in a suite at the Venetian hotel in Las Vegas on Monday, 10 September. After an evening of shoving quarters into one-armed bandits and glugging sugary, complimentary Sea Breezes, we wobbled back to our suite, collapsed on the vast double bed, ordered room service, turned on the giant TV and started watching *Tomb Raider*, starring Angelina Jolie and Chris Barrie from *The Brittas Empire*, until we lost consciousness. In terms of sheer honeymoon class, we were smashing the absolute shit out of it.

The TV was still on when we woke the following morning, but Lara Croft and Gordon Brittas had been replaced by some weird show in which they were imagining, complete with realistic graphics, what it would be like if an aeroplane hit a skyscraper in a major US city. 'American TV is very odd,' I said, genuinely confused. 'Why are they holding that graphic of a smoking tower so long?' Then another plane flew into the neighbouring skyscraper.

A little while later, Dad called from the UK. He made some subdued small talk for a while then announced, 'The world will never be the same again.' Alright, Dad, I thought. Steady on.

When we eventually got back to London after a week of

airport queues, delays and cancellations, the world didn't just feel changed; it felt as though it could end at any moment. Everyone (apart from me, obviously) was acting crazy and paranoid, and speculation over where the terrorists would strike next was rife. Normally sensible, non-racist people exchanged stories like this one: 'A friend of a friend was walking down Oxford Street the day before 9/11, and they saw an Arab man drop his wallet, which was bulging with money. When my friend's friend chased after him and gave him back his wallet, the Arab man was grateful but flustered and said, "Get out of London in the next three weeks!"'

This story was obviously a nonsensical confection of fear and xenophobia, but when someone told it to me, after rolling my eyes there was a moment when I wondered if maybe I should get out of London, because why take any chances?

People were stockpiling food. Sales of gas masks rocketed. Production halted on films depicting violence and horror because it was felt there was now a surfeit in the real world. Meanwhile, Ant & Dec stopped presenting *SM:TV* and *CD:UK* on Saturday mornings in order to concentrate on developing their primetime television careers. Saturday morning TV was never the same again. But life went on, and now that Sarah and I were married, we felt the next logical step was to try for a baby. By the time coalition forces were hoping they'd blown up Bin Laden in the Afghan caves of Tora Bora in December 2001, Sarah was expecting our first human child.

Meanwhile, Joe and I were enjoying a break from each other before we thought about our next project together. After becoming friendly with Travis, I had joined them as court jester and videographer on their tour bus in Europe and America, then hung out with them while they were recording in Los Angeles.

As for Joe, he was spending a lot of time with director Edgar Wright, with whom he was collaborating on a couple of screenplays, including one based on the Marvel superhero

Ant-Man. Years later, I saw Simon Pegg at a *Hot Fuzz* party, and we compared notes on those early years of Joe and Edgar's collaborations. We admitted we'd both been jealous and insecure.

In early 2002, a senior executive at Channel 4, let's call him Telly Mann, took me and Joe for a swanky lunch at the Ivy restaurant in London's West End and told us it was time we thought about what we were going to do next on TV. We said we'd quite like to do something that was a bit like *The Adam and Joe Show* again, but Telly Mann said it was time to stop noodling about in the margins with our home-video silliness and step up to the mainstream with a 'proper' show, something in a real studio with an audience, writers and better production values. We said we liked our homemade noodling, and as long as there were stupid films and TV shows to take the piss out of, we could probably keep noodling indefinitely. Telly Mann made it clear that wasn't going to happen at Channel 4.

My instinct was to suggest that Telly Mann should stick 'proper' TV up his bum, but then I remembered my instincts frequently turn out to be wrong, so Joe and I made one final attempt to come up with some ideas for TV shows that might be more accessible to mainstream audiences.

Here's a selection of some of the ideas we pitched unsuccessfully to Telly Mann and other TV executives in the early 2000s. As you'll see, you were robbed of some very special television.

UNTITLED IDEA FOR AN ENTERTAINMENT SHOW ON A PLANE

PITCH: Chat show with musical guests, comedy inserts and pranks (*TFI Friday*, basically) but on a plane. Could be sponsored by Virgin.

Joe would be the captain of the plane, and I'd be one of the flight attendants along with someone like Gail Porter or Sara Cox. We'd wheel a trolley laden with booze and funny props up to first class to talk to Brad Pitt and Jennifer Aniston about what they were going to watch on the in-flight entertainment system. We could interview Jamie Oliver in the galley where he'd be preparing the meals, talk to fascinating 'real' people in standard class, draw a cock on Richard Branson's face while he was sleeping, then try to smoke a joint with Shaun Ryder in the toilets without setting off the smoke alarms.

RESPONSE FROM TV EXECUTIVES: None.

NEWsic*

PITCH: A spoof music show featuring real music artists.

This would be a spin-off of a segment we had on *The Adam and Joe Show* in which I played a pretentious MTV-style presenter called Jazzz Tits (definitely not based on Zane Lowe). As with those segments, Jazzz Tits would deliver all the latest news on made-up bands like Dirty Shirty, Hate Basement, The Vessel In The Pestle, and Fointy Pinger in between stupid interviews with real musicians (guests on *The Adam and Joe Show* had included Justine from Elastica, Stuart from Mogwai, and John and Steve from the Beta Band). We'd also include specially shot performances to create a comedy hybrid of music shows I'd loved growing up, like *Rapido*, *SnubTV* and *The Tube*.

RESPONSE FROM TV EXECUTIVES: None.

What made the lack of enthusiasm for this idea especially galling for me was that Vinyl Justice, the *Adam and Joe Show* segment in which Joe and I raided the record collections of celebrities, was turned into a show on America's VH1 in 1998. The US *Vinyl Justice*, which starred comedians

Wayne Brady and Barry Sobel, only lasted one season, but that was one more season than NEWsic* ever got.

STUPID QUESTION TIME

PITCH: A pop culture review/discussion programme with me and Joe hosting.

RESPONSE FROM TV EXECUTIVES: None.

These kinds of shows pop up on TV all the time, and ours didn't add anything new other than the funny title that Joe came up with (later used by an unrelated Radio 1 show in 2019).

In 2001, Cornballs hosted a TV show that was not dissimilar to *Stupid Question Time*, along with presenter Lauren Laverne and actor Nick Frost. It was called *This Week Only*, and it might have lasted longer were it not for the fact that two weeks into the show's run, 9/11 happened. I'm not suggesting the attacks were carried out as a response to *This Week Only*. I'm sure the terrorists would have agreed it was a fun show and Joe was a good host. Regardless, TV executives feared that 9/11 would dampen the public's appetite for chuckling at current affairs, and *This Week Only* was not recommissioned.

KEEPING UP WITH THE JONESES

PITCH: Sitcom about some of David Bowie's characters sharing a house.

Ziggy leaves his make-up strewn around the bathroom. Thomas Newton (Bowie's character in *The Man Who Fell to Earth*) never leaves his room, which is blue, blue, electric blue. The Thin White Duke is paranoid about everything, keeps going on about Nietzsche, stores jars of his urine in the fridge and snorts lines of Vim while doing the housework. Meanwhile, the Diamond Dogs keep crapping in Screaming Lord Byron's turban.

RESPONSE FROM TV EXECUTIVES: We pitched this in early 2000 to a group of young, hipsterish execs in a big meeting room at VH1 in Los Angeles. We thought the meeting had gone well, but there was no follow-up call.

TRIVIA: In 2006, David Bowie made a TV ad for Vittel mineral water, which was eerily similar to our pitch. Am I saying someone in our meeting stole the idea and sold it to Vittel? Yes, that's what I'm saying.

ADAM AND JOE'S FIRST-CLASS LOUNGE (aka ADAM AND JOE'S VERY GOOD TIME)

PITCH: Adam and Joe travel in luxury to exciting and beautiful locations and make funny comments.

No one liked the idea of comedians being filmed making funny comments on luxury away breaks until Michael Winterbottom did it with Rob Brydon and Steve Coogan in *The Trip*, which came out at least two years *after* we first pitched *Adam and Joe's First-Class Lounge*. These days, you can't move for buddy-based travel shows on TV. Would Joe and I have had the same great chemistry as Brydon and Coogan? Of course! And like Brydon and Coogan, Joe and I were both gifted impressionists. As well as Bowie, I could do Roger Moore ('A woman?'), John Lydon ('That's just their tough shit') and my biggest crowd-pleaser: the Northern Irish poet and *Late Review* pundit Tom Paulin ('I thought it was absolutely … appalling'). Joe could do Yoda, E.T. and the entire cast of the first series of *Big Brother*. They would have been throwing awards at us.

RESPONSE FROM TV EXECUTIVES: None.

DIRECTOR'S COMMENTARY

PITCH: Adam and Joe talk over old films and TV shows in the style of the directors' commentaries that came with nearly every DVD released in the early 2000s, regardless of whether the film in question in any way deserved that level of analysis. Directors' commentaries were a little like the podcasts of their day, and I was so obsessed with them that I ended up spending several weeks recording a fake director's commentary as my character Ken Korda, for an episode of an early evening Channel 4 entertainment show called *The Priory*, which ran from 1999 to 2002 and was hosted by Jamie Theakston and Zoe Ball. When I'd finished the commentary, I flushed away several more weeks making fake DVD menu graphics, fake ads for the commercial breaks and packaging for the VHS copies that I gave to friends and a couple of TV executives.

RESPONSE FROM TV EXECUTIVES: Some enthusiasm, but ultimately nothing.

In 2004, a couple of years after we pitched this idea, Rob Brydon (again!) made a show called *Directors Commentary* for ITV. I like Rob Brydon and thought his show was fine, but it wasn't as good as the show Joe and I would have made. Mind you, things that *don't* get made are *always* better than things that do.

POP SPANK

PITCH: A sitcom set in the offices of a celebrity gossip magazine, a bit like *Heat*. When we pitched this idea, *Heat* magazine was only a few years old and was still, well, hot.

RESPONSE FROM TV EXECUTIVES: There was actually a bit of interest in this idea, but the furthest we got with developing it was writing a scene in which a couple of journalists have a snarky conversation about the still relatively new *Harry Potter* phenomenon. Joe used to do an impression of Dumbledore, which amounted to him saying 'Harry Potter!' in a booming voice. Whatever happened to *Harry Potter*? They should bring him back.

ADAM AND JOE'S TV WARS

PITCH: Adam, Joe and a small audience break into a TV studio at night and stage a 'Fight Club' for TV stars, in which celebrity guests battle to be the best at dealing with the most challenging situations TV has to offer. Can they fill in the missing facts from a faulty autocue while a producer screams abuse at them through an earpiece? How do they deal with an obsessive fan who's broken in to their dressing room? Who can improvise the best voiceover for footage that cuts randomly between a state funeral, curling and animals having sex? Who makes the best tea?

RESPONSE FROM TV EXECUTIVES: Positive.

We were so sure this was about to get the green light that when the commissioner at Channel 4 eventually knocked it back, I took it as a sign that TV was perhaps not the best place for us and maybe it was time to be less snooty about radio.

CHAPTER 14

THE COMING STORM

One evening in mid-March 2020, I was watching *News at Ten* with Sarah and dunking my fifth Belvita biscuit into my tea when the BBC's home editor, Mark Easton, did a piece about the new coronavirus. His report concluded with a stirring speech: 'A storm is coming, and we must build our defences for winds which will buffet and blow for many long months. It will be the test of a generation: to find the Great in Britain and stay united in our island kingdom.'

'Easton's going for the BAFTA!' I said, and looked over at Sarah. She looked worried. She hadn't touched her Belvita. I was worried, too, but Easton was definitely going for the BAFTA.

The next day I listened to a serious American podcast with a doom-laden intro theme in which the host said he thought people were being too blasé, especially Trump supporters. In fact, said the host, people should be taking their kids out of school. He spoke to an infectious disease specialist who said the worst thing would be for people to panic. Ah, said the host, so you think the situation is worth panicking about? Not really, said the infectious disease specialist; it's a bad situation, but it's not cataclysmic. Ah, said the host, so maybe it's a *dress rehearsal* for something cataclysmic? I suppose it might be, said the infectious disease specialist. Hmmm, said the host, sounding sort of pleased. Later, he used a phrase I hadn't heard before: 'social distancing'.

I was due to travel to London for a gig at a comedy club that night, and I wondered if it might be cancelled, but there was no word from the promoter, so I got the train and did the show, joking with the small audience about resisting the urge to sanitise the mic after the MC had introduced me. After the show, I was making my way out through the noisy bar when a tall man in smart clothes came over to tell me he listened to the podcast. He was drunk and leaned in to make himself heard. I could feel his breath on my face, and I wanted to ask him to back off, but it felt too precious and he seemed like the kind of person who might get weird, so I did my best to angle my face away and not breathe. The only thing I wanted to catch was the last train back to Norwich. As it turned out it was the last train I would take for several months.

A week later, with my laptop on the kitchen table during family supper, we watched Boris Johnson announce the lockdown.

You know the rest. No pasta or toilet paper in the supermarkets. Clapping for the NHS. Gal Gadot's 'Imagine' video. Donald Trump declaring it would all be over by Easter. Weird dreams. Homemade sourdough. Zoom. Terrible-quality video links on TV programmes that made *Takeover TV* look slick by comparison. Duolingo. Joe Wicks. Obscure items from the booze cupboard. Conspiracy theories. Mask tension. Lockdown scepticism. Educational chaos. Government incompetence and corruption. Deepening mental-health crisis. Death. Podcasts.

In England, the weather in those first lockdown weeks was beautiful, and at Castle Buckles we made the most of being together in our fortunate countryside bubble. I recorded the audio version of *Ramble Book* and did a few Zoom interviews to promote it, always regretting that my book had the word 'Book' in the title, which made it hard not to say 'book' too often in sentences like 'I've just finished recording the audiobook of my book *Ramble Book*,' But, unbelievably, there were even worse problems in the world at that moment.

Not least for me was the fact that my mum, who had been receiving treatment for a tumour on her skull that may or may not have been responsible for her rapidly deteriorating memory, was 150 miles away, alone in her little house in Sonning on Thames. I wondered if the tumour was also affecting her language skills when, during one phone call, she told me about a visiting friend's boisterous dog who had humped a sofa cushion in Mum's front room. 'I don't want to use the wrong phrase,' said Mum, 'but the dog was *raping* the cushion.' Actually, she'd always been like that.

Waitrose

On another balmy evening in mid-May, I went out to the garden and called Mum to see how she was doing. She sounded stressed. One of the builders who had done some work on her patio the year before had turned up at her front door saying she owed him more money. Mum, flustered and unable to remember exactly what had been paid and what hadn't, said she'd write him a cheque, but the builder wanted cash. He proposed walking Mum to the cashpoint to get the money. She refused. The builder said he'd be back.

I asked Mum if she knew the builder's name or could recall the name of the company, but when I pressed her she got agitated and suddenly barked down the phone, 'You're *spoiling* my evening! Please stop talking about this because it's getting me upset, and I don't want to get upset. I just want to enjoy my evening and have a glass of wine.'

After the call, I gazed out over the fields in front of the house. The combination of impotence and outrage at the builder made me lightheaded. I wanted to go and pick Mum up, bring her back and get her installed in the flat. But the lockdown rules were clear. No mixing of households. No travel except in emergencies. The next day, I called back, and again Mum insisted this was not an emergency. 'I get the impression you think I'm doing rather badly, but I'm not,' she said. 'I've got lots of friends, and my life is very nice, so you shouldn't worry.' But I *was* worried, and I had been for a while.

A few months before, I'd received a letter from Mum's solicitor saying she had repeated herself in a couple of meetings. I'd also spoken to one of her neighbours who said they'd noticed Mum's garden, which she usually kept pristine, had started to look messy and overgrown. I had done my best to shove it to the back of my mind, but I knew that, despite her protestations, 2020 would be the year Mum either went into care or came to live with us in Norfolk.

Having Dad here in his last months had been difficult, and my hopes that we would forge a new closer relationship had largely come to nothing, unless you count the cosy familiarity of emptying his pee-pee bowls, but I told myself it would be different with Mum. She'd always been great with the children, loved to potter about and prune rose bushes in the garden, and enjoyed watching a movie with a drink and some snacks. As long as we could avoid talking about politics, she'd fit right in.

A week later, I got a call from an unfamiliar number: 'I found your mother in Waitrose. She couldn't remember where she'd parked her car, so I brought her home.' People can be so kind. I felt as grateful as I did ashamed. Ma sounded confused and exhausted, but when I told her I was coming to pick her up right away, the steel came back into her voice, and she insisted she needed time to pack a bag and that I shouldn't come until the morning.

It was a shock to see her when I arrived next day. She'd lost a lot of weight, and the spirit seemed to have gone out of her. It was as if she were on autopilot. Her little house, usually spotless, was dusty and cluttered with stacks of newspapers and bottles. I looked in the fridge and found it completely stuffed. Since at least the start of the lockdown seven weeks earlier, Mum had been doing her usual shopping and putting it in the fridge until there wasn't a centimetre of space left. Now, the food on the bottom of each compartment was black, and mould was spreading up the sides. I looked in the cupboards, and they, too, were overflowing with bottles of gin, white wine and low-calorie snacks – the building blocks of Mum.

I emptied the fridge's contents into a bin bag, cleaned it out as quickly as possible, gathered up a few essential possessions and got Mum into the car. My plan was to take her to the hospital back in Norwich to get her checked out, and then get her settled in the flat next to our house. After the lockdown, I would come back to Sonning and do a proper clean-up, pick up the rest of her things and a new chapter would begin. But it didn't work out that way.

Waiting Room Fun

'This is my husband,' Mum told the nurse, putting a bony hand on my arm, and I laughed, suddenly aware I was about to cry. It was a relief to be at the hospital in Norwich and to feel things were in hand, but it was hard to see Mum in bad shape.

A young porter in a face mask entered the waiting room and asked if we were still using the wheelchair parked by Mum's seat; then, looking at me, he said loudly, 'Hang on. You look very famous. *Are* you famous?' I laughed and said that, no, I was not famous, but the porter persisted. 'Have you seen *The Adam and Joe Show*?' he said. Ma suddenly perked up, pointing at me and announcing to the whole waiting room, 'He was in *The Adam and Joe Show*!' The mobile monitor machine connected to Mum beeped with a loud electronic tone. Ma glared at it and said, 'Shut up!' It was a call and response that she seemed to have forgotten she'd been rehearsing every few minutes for the past couple of hours. The porter held out his hand for me to shake and said, 'You do great work.'

Ma wanted to ask why we were waiting so long. She shuffled slowly over to a nurse called Florence, who explained that she was about to take a blood sample and put in a cannula for some drugs to be administered before they did a CT scan. Ma raised her hands in front of Florence's face and, without smiling, did a slow hand clap. Florence laughed. 'I want to go to the toilet,' announced Ma with a thunderous expression, and when I suggested that she wait until after Florence had taken her blood, Ma jabbed a finger at me weakly and said, 'If I don't go, I will WET – MY – PANTS.'

Five hours later, Florence told me the test results indicated that Mum needed to be admitted. 'Why do I have to stay in overnight?' she asked when I told her.

'You've got a kidney problem,' I explained.

'A kidney problem? I didn't realise I had that. Oh, well. Could be worse,' she said, and I nodded just as a very overweight young man in shorts and a T-shirt walked into the waiting room, drinking a can of Coke with another unopened can in the other hand. As he settled into a chair, Ma leant over slightly and said, without lowering her voice, 'I tell you who has got a problem ...'

'Mum!' I widened my eyes and put a finger to my lips, but there was no stopping her.

'That man has a problem. He's HUGELY FAT!'

A doctor came by to ask more questions. 'Do you live alone, Mrs Buxton?'

Ma perked up again. 'Oh, no. I live with my husband and the children. Actually, no. They're all grown up now, aren't they?'

Escapism

One evening, while Ma was in the hospital, Sarah and I watched an episode of *Better Things*, an American comedy-drama that we'd been enjoying after Joe recommended it. Unfortunately, in that night's episode, the show's protagonist, Sam, realises that her mother is beginning to lose her mental faculties to the point that she will soon need full-time care.

It was so precisely what I *didn't* want to be watching at that moment that it was sort of funny. Funnier than the episode, anyway, which was brave and unflinching but low on laughs. In one bleakly comedic scene, Sam's mother becomes confused in a car park, and then, out of frustration, she deliberately steps into a manhole and ends up in hospital. Sam goes to visit and finds her mother sullen and uncommunicative. It was a scene that powerfully evoked the disconnection I'd felt between me and my dad when he'd been ailing, and I had wished so much that I could make him feel less alone.

But then Sam's mum suddenly rallies and tells her daughter she loves her and has always been proud of her, and she's sorry she failed to express that sooner. The moment rang so false I was expecting it to turn out to be a fantasy sequence, but it wasn't.

I thought of Ma a few miles away in Norwich Hospital. I wasn't able to visit her because of Covid restrictions, but even if I had been able to, I knew she wasn't going to be serving up slices of Closure Cake. Not necessarily because she wouldn't want to, but because she was tired and confused, and frightened, and old, and she had cancer, and real life isn't like TV.

A week later, the hospital called to say Mum was being discharged, but when I collected her she didn't seem any better. Back home, we got her settled on the sofa in the living room and, with the sun streaming in, she looked through a big book about flowers while I opened the door to Sarah's adjoining study, where Nat played *Clair de lune* on the piano.

The next day, Mum said her stomach hurt. I left a message for the GP but got no reply. I wasn't too worried because I assumed that if there was something badly wrong, the hospital wouldn't have discharged her. But that night, she was worse, so I slept in the bed next to hers. 'Help!' she said a few times, but I wasn't sure how best to help. How could I be 50 and be so useless?

In the silences, my mind drifted to a day in Earl's Court when I was around 12. Dad was abroad, and while Mum was at the shops, I was induced by boredom to do a chemistry experiment in the upstairs bathroom sink. There, I poured in some cleaning fluid, followed by a few glutinous glugs of bleach. Delighted by the resulting hiss and wisps of vapour, I leaned in to observe more closely. With my next breath, I felt a sudden sharp pain in my lungs – the result of having momentarily filled them with the caustic gas I had created, ammonia, I suppose. Shocked and frightened, I pulled out the basin plug by its chain, rinsed away the noxious fluid and went to my bedroom where, feeling a little faint from gas inhalation and the stabbing pain that accompanied each deep breath, I lay down on my bed and wondered if I would survive. My lungs felt tender for a few days afterwards, but I never mentioned the incident to Mum. I didn't want to get into trouble for playing with chemical products that were clearly marked as dangerous if misused, but I also didn't want Mum to be sad about having such a chronically stupid, Frank Spencer-type son.

In Norfolk, Mum lay quietly for a while and I'd think she was falling asleep when she'd cry out again. It was a relief when she said she needed the loo because, at last, I felt I could be of use, but when I tried to help her out of bed, her legs buckled and she sank to the carpet. Once down, it was impossible to move her on my own. There seemed hardly anything of her. How could she be so heavy? With the lights on, I saw how pale she was and how shallow her breathing had become, so I woke Sarah and asked her to call an ambulance.

And then it was one of those times. All the lights on at 3 a.m. Trying to be calm. Uniformed strangers in the bedroom. 'Now, I have to tell you that if we move your mother to the ambulance, there is a chance she'll go into cardiac arrest,' said the paramedic, 'and if she does, I think she's too weak to be resuscitated.'

'OK,' I nodded, not understanding the point of this information. It was obvious Mum needed to go to the hospital, so what was the alternative?

'I think it's more so you're aware of the risk,' said Sarah from the doorway.

'Right. Well, OK, I understand.'

'So you want us to move her?'

'Yes, please,' I said.

Then, as the two paramedics lifted Mum onto the yellow transfer chair, I thought about what I should take with me to the hospital. Phone, laptop, clean T-shirt, pants and socks. If I needed anything else, Sarah could bring it over tomorrow. I grabbed my stuff then went out to the ambulance, where Mum was still waiting to be lifted in. But as it happened, her heart did stop on the way downstairs, and now Mum was dead. I felt terrible about that.

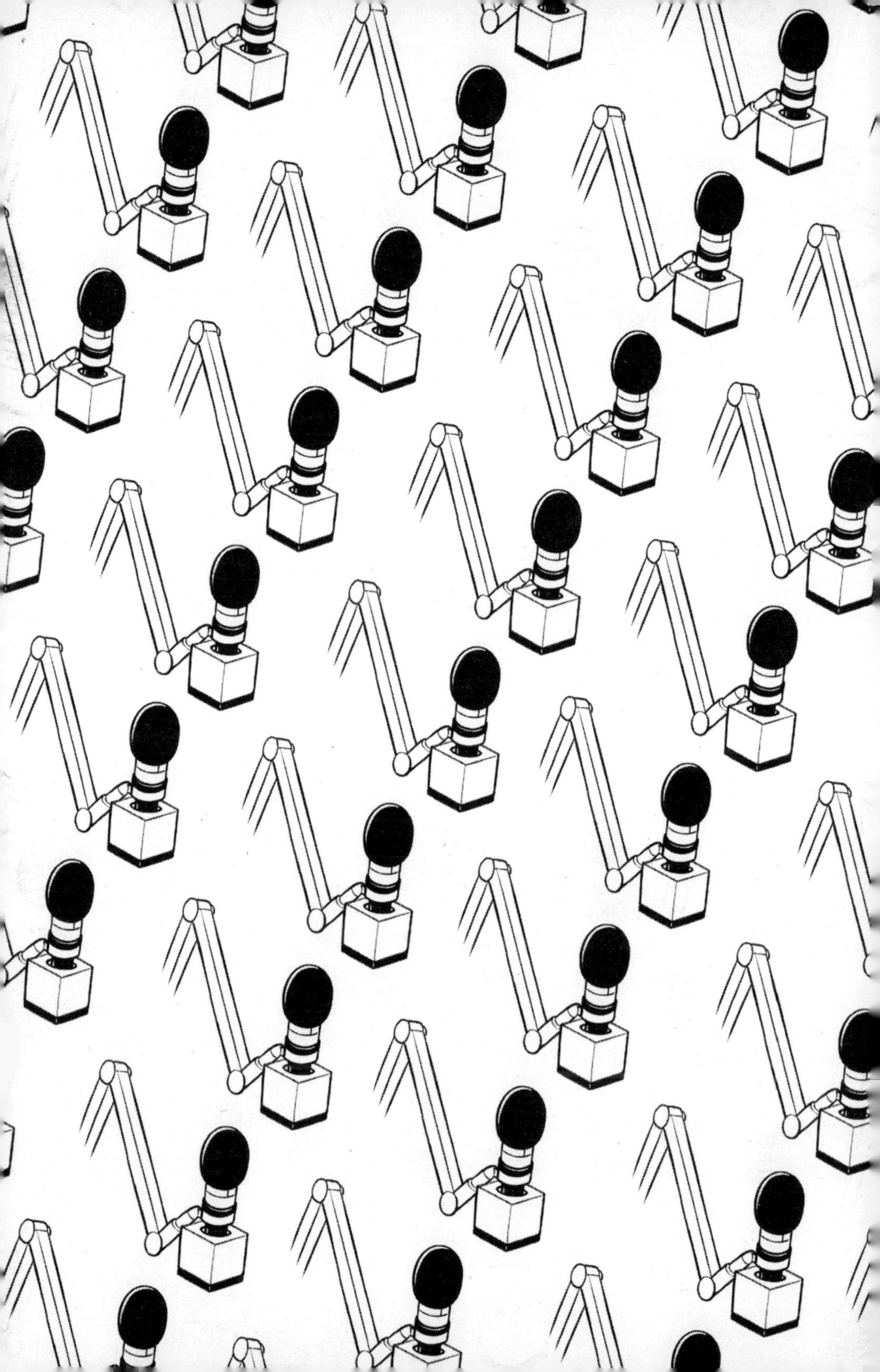

CHAPTER 15

RADIO DAYS

Although Joe and I made many timeless and important television programmes, I still look back on our radio shows and podcasts as some of the best things we did together. And yet, at the beginning of the 2000s, I wasn't excited about being on the radio again. In my mental Mainstream Media hierarchy, feature films were at the top, TV in the middle and radio very much at the bottom. Internet 'content' (at that point still accessed by dial-up modems that sounded like R2-D2 on ketamine) didn't even feature.

In 2001, Ricky Gervais, a former producer on London radio station Xfm who had just made the first series of his sitcom *The Office*, returned to Xfm to present a show along with co-writer and director of *The Office* Stephen Merchant and Xfm producer Karl Pilkington. In 2005, *The Ricky Gervais Show* on Xfm spawned what was, for many people, the first podcast they had ever heard (downloadable via Guardian Unlimited for £1).

Despite seeing how successful Ricky, Stephen and Karl's radio and podcast shows had become, when Joe and I were asked to fill in for them on Xfm in 2003, while the second series of *The Office* was being filmed, it felt to me like a step backwards. Radio was where I'd got my start in the entertainment world; going back after I'd been on TV seemed like checking into a retirement home for the hopelessly irrelevant. My agent encouraged me not to be too sniffy. After all, Joe and I weren't having much success getting our ideas on TV anymore, so it couldn't hurt to give radio a shot.

Ricky and Stephen's Xfm show was a mix of music and funny, freeform conversation, but I didn't feel confident doing three hours of live radio without having prepared something first. Though Karl Pilkington would not be producing our show, he sat down with us a couple of weeks before we were due to start and listened to the ideas we had for comedy quizzes, jingles, songs and sketches, many in the style we'd been doing on our E4 show *Shock Video*.

RAMBLE

SHOCK VIDEO

Of all the shows we did in our post-*Adam and Joe Show* wilderness years – *50 Greatest Magic Tricks, Adam and Joe's American Animation Adventure, Takeover TV* series three, *Adam and Joe Go Tokyo* – it was *Shock Video* that was probably seen the most and ended up pointing the way forward to the next chapter in our professional lives together.

A series of half-hour programmes originally made for American television, *Shock Video* featured odd clips from mildly pornographic international TV shows, and when Channel 4's newly launched digital station E4 bought it in 2001, Joe and I were given the job of providing a new voiceover. We were fairly sure viewers would be too distracted by the nudity to care what was being said, so we ended up providing a sarcastic commentary that was occasionally funny but often a bit lame and mean-spirited.

It taught me a valuable lesson, which I remind my children of every day: if you think it's beneath you to provide a voiceover for soft-porn clips, don't do it. But don't agree to do it, then be all sniffy about it; that's twattish.

Shock Video rated far better than anyone was expecting (which was definitely thanks to us and our snarky voiceover and nothing to do with all the bare breasts and penises), and in 2002 we found ourselves back in the voice booth for a second series. This time, rather than being negative about the porn, we concentrated on entertaining each other by doing silly voices and improvising some songs. It felt good to be making each other laugh again with stuff we hadn't spent ages preparing, and, of course, it was wonderful to see so many genitals.

I thought the ideas we presented to Karl at Xfm were entertainingly stupid in the same way *Shock Video* was, but Karl was nonplussed. 'Don't try too hard,' he said. 'People can hear it when you've spent ages preparing something. They can hear you want them to like it, and that makes them uncomfortable.'

Karl's advice made sense; I just didn't think it applied to me. If I didn't prepare for the shows, I'd have to go in and just be 'Myself', and at that time in my life, caught between the happy anxiety of starting a family and the unhappy anxiety that my career was on a downward trajectory, 'Myself' was frequently swirling in a deadening vortex of self-doubt. I decided that given the choice between some overproduced segments and a deadening vortex of self-doubt, most listeners would prefer the segments, especially on a Saturday.

So, each week, I spent several hours making notes on possible conversation topics and working on new audio bits for the next show with the Pro Tools software we got from making our Radio 1 pilot.

The Vortex

Inevitably, there were weeks when I ran out of time to prepare anything, and like it or not, we just had to wing it live on air. Joe was good at winging it, but it made me nervous, and when I was nervous, I got tongue-tied and made poor waffle choices.

On one occasion, our producer, Lila, pointed out a memo from the Xfm lawyer requesting that DJs refrain from commenting on the Michael Jackson molestation trial that was about to start in America. 'Don't read the memo out, though, obviously,' said Lila. During the next link, I immediately got tongue-tied and, desperate for something to say, reached for the Jacko legal memo, which I read out in its entirety live on air while Lila held her hands aloft as if to say, 'What exactly the fuck is your problem?' The problem was the Vortex of Self-Doubt.

Someone claiming to be a fan once sent us a MiniDisc on which they'd taken one of our Xfm shows and edited together every single 'umm', 'ah', 'er' and lazy rejoinder that me and Cornballs had come out with on air. It was a long montage.

> *'er, umm, sure, um, exactly, umm, err, yeah, uh huh, erm, exactly, um …'*

I should have been able to laugh off the MiniDisc or ignore it, but I had already worried idly that I did too much 'umming' and 'aahing' on the Xfm show. I had tried to reassure myself that listeners wouldn't notice, but the MiniDisc proved otherwise. It didn't so much hit a nerve as drill into it and connect it to the National Grid.

Meltdown

Joe and I hosted a Saturday show on Xfm semi-regularly from 2003 to 2007, and though we grew more confident and relaxed as the years passed, my insecurity buttons remained big and easily pushed. On one occasion, I went into full passive-aggressive meltdown.

It was coming up to noon one Saturday in early 2005. Joe was looking at the big boxy computer monitor on the other side of the desk from me in the smoky studio above Leicester Square when he gave a mirthless chuckle. We had just finished chatting on air about crisp flavours, and now we were playing a song by Pete Doherty's band Babyshambles, after which we were planning to chat about *Brat Camp*, a TV show Joe was fond of at the time. Cornballs had been scanning texts from listeners, and now he looked over at Lila and said: 'Here's one from a guy who says: *Why don't you two infantile cunts shut up and play some music?*'

We gave out the number for texts on the Xfm show constantly. Most of the responses we got were friendly, but there were always a few from people who wanted to hear less from us and more of the Kaiser Chiefs, Maxïmo Park, Hard-Fi and Stereophonics. Joe claimed not to be bothered by the negative messages, but they got into my head, and I preferred not to hear about them.

This particular Saturday morning, I must have been feeling more sensitive than usual because when Joe read out the 'infantile cunts' comment, I found myself suddenly enraged, barking at J-Corn that I thought I'd been clear about reading out abuse from Text Monkeys (in 2005 the term 'troll' was still a few years away from becoming standard terminology for offensive commentators, though I don't think anyone else called them 'Text Monkeys').

From there, the conversation went like this (I wrote down what I could remember when I got home that day):

JOE – I just think we should listen to what people have to say and make an effort to make the listeners feel more included because sometimes we have a tendency to talk amongst ourselves in quite an exclusive way.

AD – I don't think we do at all. I think these texts are being sent by fucking morons who haven't put any thought into them whatsoever, and responding to them just gets in the way of us doing the show.

JOE – I'm not saying we should respond to them on air – in fact, I think we should never mention them on air – but I don't see why you're getting so angry about me saying we should try to make people feel included by asking them what they think.

AD – I'm just saying I don't think texts saying 'why don't you infantile cunts shut up' are constructive, and we should just ignore them.

JOE – Sure, but I don't care about what they're saying in the text.

AD – Well, you obviously do, or you wouldn't be suggesting we change the way we do the show.

JOE – I'm not suggesting we change the way we do the show, man, I'm just saying that we should be careful not to make people feel excluded.

AD – I think we do that perfectly well already. We're always asking people to call in with their suggestions and opinions.

JOE – Fine, let's carry on doing that, that's all I'm saying.

AD – But what are you saying? That we are doing it or we're not? I don't understand what you're saying!

JOE – This is just stupid. I just made a very simple point, and now it's turned into this.

AD – Well, that's what happens when we don't talk at all during the week, and the first words we say to each other are when we're on air.

JOE – That's a totally separate conversation, which is not appropriate to have here.

AD – Sure, well, let's talk about it later because we need to sort this out; it's fucking ludicrous.

Lila cued up a few more songs to play because it didn't look as if we'd be chatting about Brat Camp just yet. Joe gave a heavy sigh.

JOE – Well, I think I'm going to leave actually, because I don't want to do the rest of the show in this atmosphere. This is just horrible.

AD – Fine, then! Go!

LILA – I don't think that's a good idea. Let's all just calm down a bit, get through the rest of the show, play some records, have a chat about some TV, give away these DVDs for the competitions and we can sort this out later.

I knew I had massively overreacted, so after several minutes of self-reproach and the latest single from the Darkness, I took a breath and apologised for losing my rag. By that time, we'd played three songs back to back, and Lila felt we needed to remind listeners we were still there, but Joe and I still had a case of Wobbly Confrontation Voice. Cornballs had been planning to unveil a new jingle he'd made for 'Crap Commentary Corner', a segment in which he played clips from DVD directors' commentaries, but I'd spoiled the mood.

For the rest of the show, we kept our headphones on between brief, functional links, and as soon as the final track had been played, we said our regular goodbye to the listeners and Joe left, saying thanks only to Lila.

Happily, we were able to avoid similar confrontations from that point on. I calmed down a bit, Joe carried on being funny, and we started to attract an enthusiastic gang of listeners. But as far as I was concerned, the thing that helped most with the Vortex was podcasting.

Casting the Pod

At first, I didn't see the point of having a podcast, but when I realised we could edit down portions of the live show and supplement them with specially recorded segments in which we could talk more freely than we did on live radio, the idea made a lot more sense. It was also safe to assume that most people listening to a podcast liked us enough to have bothered downloading it, and in that more sympathetic podcast environment I was able to have more chill cake.

We only put out a handful of Xfm podcasts, but with important content that included our improvised football chants, a thoughtful discussion about why Colin Farrell had (at that point in his career) never been in a good film, and an overview of R. Kelly's musical soap-opera series *Trapped in the Closet*, our first foray into podcasting was regularly featured in magazines and supplements that had begun taking notice of the emerging medium. It also put us on the radar of the Big British Castle.

Adam & Joe on BBC 6 Music 2007-11

In August 2007, we were invited to fill in on the 6 Music breakfast show while regular host Shaun Keaveny was away for a couple of weeks. 'Depping' for a well-loved host like Shaun is always a tough gig, as we knew from having filled in for Ricky and Stephen at Xfm, but the modest popularity of our Xfm podcast had made us more confident, and we accepted.

We arrived armed with Big British Castle jingles, a segment called 'Band Aid' (later rechristened 'Song Wars') in which we played a song each of us had made specially and asked the listeners to vote for their favourite, and an innovative twist on a segment we'd had at Xfm called 'Anecdotties', for which listeners were invited to email (or text) stories on a given theme. At 6 Music, we also invited listeners to email (or text) stories on a given theme, but Joe's gamechanging idea was to call the segment 'Text the Nation' (that's the other story I'm going to tell on *The Graham Norton Show*).

Soon after our breakfast-show depping stint, 6 Music asked if we wanted to do a regular show on Saturday mornings from 9 to 12. Feeling that, for the first time since the early days of *The Adam and Joe Show*, we were on a bit of a roll, we said, 'Yes, please.'

At 6 Music, the more offensive listener messages were filtered before Joe (once again manning the computer) got to read them, so as far as we were aware, everyone loved us. Or at least they didn't detest us. For me and my fragile ego, that meant I could relax and enjoy myself a bit more for the live shows, and that helped to soften my sharper edges. At Xfm, I would regularly talk on air about how terrible I thought this or that TV show, advert or film was. I may not have been unrelentingly positive at 6 Music, but I was a little sunnier.

Still reluctant to rely solely on our freeform waffling abilities, Joe and I once again created several segments and recurring features to give the three-hour live shows a bit of structure and 'content'.

BLACK SQUADRON

We referred to those listeners who tuned in from the very start of the show as Black Squadron. Joe would issue gnomic instructions to test the loyalty of Black Squadron members and ask them to send in photographic proof that they had complied. Some of the instructions included:

Leaning Tower of Stuff
Felt Pen Tattoo Face
Sit in Bin
Alien
Catalogue Pose
Surgery
Tinsel Undies
Bacon Bracelet

STEPHEN!

One weekend in May 2008, the theme for 'Text the Nation' was childhood creative projects/juvenilia. A listener called Stephen Curran told us about an action comic he had created as a youngster called *STEPHEN!* Joe and I imagined dialogue for a *STEPHEN!* film adaptation:

PERSON – *Stephen!*

STEPHEN – *Yes?*

PERSON – *I'm in trouble!*

STEPHEN – *Just coming!*

STEPHEN! became a minor meme for the next few months, and we received reports of people shouting *STEPHEN!* at gigs and other gatherings of switched-on groovers. Fleet Foxes lead singer Robin Pecknold asked the audience at a London show, 'Who is this Stephen guy?', and Natasha Khan of Bat for Lashes suggested to her Cambridge audience that the *STEPHEN!* shouting on her 2009 tour was getting out of hand, and penalties might have to be introduced (lashes, presumably).

Incidents like these became known as 'Stephenage', and to this day, when I'm out and about, Black Squadron veterans will sometimes catch my eye and call out a bashful, '*Stephen?!*'

My standard reply is, 'Get a life!' Only kidding! I always try to call back, 'Just coming!', and I hope I would do so even if I was in the middle of a huge argument with my wife or had just been run over by a bus but was still conscious. I just think it's important for someone in my position to give something back to the community.

A Couple of Tunes from a Couple of Prongs

Shortly before we filled in for Shaun Keaveney on 6 Music in late 2007, I got a new laptop that came with Apple's music-making application GarageBand. The software included hundreds of short musical loops that could be dragged onto a blank audio canvas or 'timeline' and snapped together to create a song, as well as generic ready-made jingles that, unlike expensive library music, could be used without a licence. The first thing I did with GarageBand was to drag in a jingle called 'Island Long', 30 seconds of spicy salsa over which I improvised a song about sausages.

Delighted with the results, I suggested to Joe that he should play around with GarageBand too, and we could play the songs we came up with when we filled in for Shaun. When we got a regular show, we asked listeners to propose a theme, and we'd play our songs the following Saturday.

I'd imagined we'd toss off our songs with the same low level of effort (but high level of genius) with which I'd produced 'Sausages', but the more we played with GarageBand, the more ambitious we got, and before long, I started to become over-invested in the competition again.

The first signs that I was losing perspective came one weekend early in 2008. The theme for that week's 'Song Wars' was 'ringtones', and I'd struggled. Joe had claimed twice as many 'Song Wars' victories as I had at that point, and it was beginning to annoy me. I'd imagined that the segment was going to be an opportunity for me to prove my worth, and now Cornballs was wiping the floor with me, so when he arrived at the 6 Music studio and told our producer Jude that he wanted to play THREE short ringtone songs he'd made, I sulked, like an actual toddler. I tried to play the sulking for laughs on the show, but anyone paying attention would have been able to hear that I was entering the undulating environs of Wobbly Voice Valley.

As a result, to my shame, the listeners took pity on me, and I won that week's battle, but Joe beat me again the next couple of weeks. So when listeners put forward the theme of 'Internet piracy', I spent the entire week working on my song. It was called 'The Mind of a Pirate', and I was smug about the fact that it featured an (unlicensed) sample of music from the anti-piracy ads you'd get on DVDs in those days that equated illegal downloads with stealing a handbag, a television or a car.

Every night that week, I sat up, smoking cigarettes, drinking red wine, adding sections, tweaking effects and changing lyrics. When I went to bed, the song would play on a loop in my head, and when I woke, I went straight back to tweaking it. It was, I told myself, my masterpiece, and if it didn't win, I was going to quit, not just 'Song Wars', but maybe the whole show. Maybe my life.

Luckily, 'Mind of a Pirate' did win, although I think by then the listeners realised they were dealing with someone who needed careful handling.

Thereafter, I took a little perspective bath and, when I calmed down a bit, my songs improved. 'Festival Time', 'Nutty Room', 'Special Bath' and 'Party Pom Pom' followed, and Joe countered with classics including 'Dr Sexy', 'The Sontum of Quolace', 'The Right and Wrong Song' and 'Antiques Roadshow'. 'Song Wars' on 6 Music was an invaluable exercise in creativity that certainly helped with my ongoing mission to get over myself, but it was also, I think, a very special time for music.

Bronhomme

One evening early in 2011, I was on the bill at a charity show at London's Almeida Theatre, and in the green room I got talking to my fellow comedians Dave Armand and Justin Edwards about my fondness for weird line deliveries in films. 'Well, then, you must have seen Pierce Brosnan in *Taffin*,' said Justin.

There's a scene in *Taffin*, a crime thriller released in 1988, in which Brosnan's character, a tough-guy debt-collector called Mark Taffin, is having an argument with his love interest, Charlotte, who's warning him not to tangle with a local crime boss. 'What goes on in this town is none of your business,' barks Taffin from a sofa where he sits wearing shades and holding a glass of Scotch.

'While I'm living here, it is,' replies Charlotte, provoking the explosive and winningly crazed delivery of the line, '*Then maybe you shouldn't be living heeeere!*'

This excellent piece of dialogue work from former Bond actor Brosnan (or 'Bronhomme', as Joe and I knew him) already had fans on YouTube, but during our final 2011 run on 6 Music, Joe included the *Taffin* clip as part of a compilation he'd put together of Pierce Brosnan's greatest movie grunts and odd noises, and thereafter listeners responded with a stream of *Taffin* remixes and homemade Bronhomme merch.

One of the few guests we'd had in the studio previously was another former Bond, Roger Moore, whom Joe revered so deeply that he became completely tongue-tied when Roger visited us after doing an interview elsewhere in the building. But despite all attempts to connect with Bronhomme, he was having none of it. Very wise.

Controversy

The popularity of the 6 Music show and the open channels of communication with our listeners via text, email and early incarnations of social media meant that Joe and I were more aware than ever of how passionate our audience could be. Most of the time, it felt great to know the listeners were so invested, and their frequently witty and heartfelt responses to our nonsense encouraged us to keep striving to fill the show with bigger, bolder, more ambitious nonsense.

However, as well as the support, listeners were never shy of letting us know when they felt our standards were slipping.

These were a few of the controversies that swirled around life-or-death issues in our four years at 6 Music:

MADE-UP JOKE THEFT

When we asked listeners to send in jokes they'd made up themselves, I read one out that proved to have been stolen from master chucklesmith Tim Vine ('My dog Minton ate a shuttlecock. Bad Minton'). The avalanche of fury that followed from listeners outraged on Vine's behalf ensured that only jokes with tortured and obviously homemade setups got through subsequently. Some personal favourites:

What does any aspiring person working in journalism or the arts want to get in their Christmas cracker?

A pull-it surprise. *(by Ivor Haton)*

Have you heard about the new BBC sitcom in which a young man advises his stepmother about the British weather?

It's called 'It Ain't Hot Half Mum'. *(by Kevin Core)*

What do you call a Fifties skiffle singer who keeps going missing?

Lonnie Don-e-gone-again. *(by Kate Finney's mum)*

A man received an invitation to join a competition, the purpose of which was to find out which American comedy actor owned the heaviest collection of objects made from elephant tusks. He accepted because he was keen on ivory weigh-ins.

(by Mike Singleton)

NOTE – Keenen Ivory Wayans does not, as far as I'm aware, collect elephant tusks.

BRUSHGATE

My admission during one show that Sarah and I sometimes shared the same toothbrush provoked such an outpouring of dismay and revulsion from listeners that I had to issue an apology for all the pain I'd caused and invest in an electric toothbrush with multiple heads. I still don't really understand the outrage. We would rinse the toothbrush head thoroughly each time it was used, and it really wasn't the most unhygienic thing we'd ever done as a couple. Imagine if I'd told the listeners how we came to have children! They'd really have lost it.

BOGGINS

Towards the end of 2009, I started doing an impression of my sister-in-law's dog on the show that involved me making the sounds of panting, slobbering, licking and farting, close to the microphone. Joe christened the fictional dog Boggins. Listener response to Boggins was strongly polarised (see *Ramble Book*, Chapter 16, DOGFUN), and after a few weeks, two warring camps formed: SAVE BOGGINS and KILL BOGGINS.

In those days, I wasn't familiar with the concept of misophonia, which has become better known in an age in which so many people listen to podcasts on headphones. People affected by misophonia experience strong negative emotional responses to certain everyday sounds that most people would find relatively easy to ignore. Mouth sounds are often a trigger, particularly the noise of people eating close to a microphone.

One of the most complained-about episodes of *The Adam Buxton Podcast* was not one in which I got embroiled with discussions of the Culture Wars, but one that featured an American academic whose busy schedule meant she had to eat her lunchtime chicken salad while we were recording. The apoplectic response from listeners took me back to Boggins times, when all that panting, slobbering, licking and farting close to the mic must have sent a few misophonia sufferers into a dogatonic state. Pffft.

Attack the Buck

In 2010, we took a break from the Saturday morning show while Joe was making his first film, *Attack the Block*. The idea for his sci-fi horror comedy in which kids from a south London housing estate do battle with invading alien monsters had come to Joe when he was carjacked by local youths outside his Stockwell home in 2003. The experience of working with Edgar Wright on a script for *Ant-Man* a couple of years later gave Joe the confidence to get *Attack the Block* written and then to bring it to Edgar's producer, Nira Park at Big Talk, who took it to Film4.

While Joe was filming, James at 6 Music suggested I do a solo interview show. This ended up being called *Adam Buxton's Big Mixtape*, in which guests talked me through their music choices for an imaginary mixtape. The title of the show, *Adam Buxton's Big Mixtape*, was a pun based on my paranoia that listeners would think my doing a show without Joe was *a Big Mistake*. In fact, it turned out fine and was fun to do. Nevertheless, the worry nagged often that my creative partnership with Joe was ending, and he was out there realising the filmmaking dreams we'd both shared at school, but which only he had the talent to bring to life.

Joe and I returned to 6 Music for one final run of our Saturday show in 2011, during which *Attack the Block* was released and met with a rapturous response. A couple of months later, when it was clear that Joe was going to need to commit full-time to labouring at the Dream Factory, we called it a day.

Cornballs had made good on the filmmaking ambitions he'd had all his life, and *Attack the Block* was the kind of funny, exciting and stylish movie we'd have loved as teenage filmgoers in the 1980s. Yes, it would have been even better if Buckles had been in it ('You were in it!' says J-Corn, but I'm sorry, a voiceover on a TV in the background of a scene does not count as being in anything, other than a state of indignation), but with a cast that included Jodie Whittaker, Nick Frost, and the film debut of John Boyega, not even my absence could prevent *Attack the Block* from becoming a hit.

Towards the end of 2011, I returned to the Saturday morning slot on 6 Music with Edith Bowman, who might just be one of the kindest and coolest people I've ever worked with. I was stuck in the heart of the Vortex – grieving what felt like the end of a friendship that had defined my life for over 25 years – but even on days when I was frying in a lake of self-absorbed turmoil, Edith was funny and positive. Meanwhile, I had no real idea what I was going to do next. With me in that frame of mind, the Saturday show wasn't a sustainable arrangement, and after 12 weeks I said goodbye to radio for good.

Podding On

For the next few years, I focused on other things. We had recently moved out to Norfolk and the children were little, so there were many happy moments as we renovated the old farmhouse we'd moved into and adjusted to life in the country. I also spent more time doing *BUG*, the live show about music videos that I occasionally hosted at the BFI Southbank. In 2012, Sky Atlantic commissioned *Adam Buxton's BUG*, a TV version of the live show that featured some favourite music videos as well as a few that had been specially made for the series. One of my favourites was directed by Garth Jennings for a cover of 'Summertime Blues'. It was filmed on West Wittering beach on the Sussex coast and I spent a beautiful summery day striding around in a stripey onesie as ice creams, a tent and random sections of the beach exploded. It was Benny Hill meets *Saving Private Ryan*. My dad even had a cameo, his last, as it turned out. All the while, I missed the 6 Music show with Joe, especially the podcast.

A few times, I'd got together with Cornballs when he had a free moment between Hollywood commitments and tried recording some stuff to put on my SoundCloud page, but it felt weird. There were funny bits, but we weren't relaxed, and I couldn't help feeling that Joe was throwing me a bone.

By 2014, I was spending more time listening to podcasts than listening to music. My love of Jon Ronson's Radio 4 show *Jon Ronson On* led me to the NPR podcast *This American Life*, to which Jon was an occasional contributor. It was exciting to discover a vast archive of beautifully produced stories waiting for me to munch through as I drove or walked with Rosie.

Another podcast I liked, which had been recommended to me by Louis, was *WTF*, in which American comedian Marc Maron chatted with other comedians and interesting creative types. Maron, a recovering addict who would begin episodes by delivering monologues that sometimes examined his neuroses with self-lacerating frankness, was a strong flavour as a host. If I listened to several episodes on the trot, I would find myself *over-Maronated*, but his podcast introduced me to the joys of long, free-ranging, often emotional conversations where the host contributes as much as the guest. It made me think that it might be time to give podcasting another go.

I decided the way forward was to record with other friends and anyone else interesting that I came across. The only person I didn't want to talk to was Joe. It wasn't that we'd fallen out. We hadn't, but I was determined to make something that wouldn't be compared with the old 6 Music show.

In late 2014, I was doing a *BUG* show in Los Angeles and asked Louis, who was living there with his family at the time, if he'd be up for recording a conversation as an experiment. As ever, Louis said he'd be happy to help out, and when I put together the first episode of *The Adam Buxton Podcast* in 2015, it contained the chat we'd recorded in Louis's Los Feliz garage about the ethics of loading up on food from hotel buffets for later consumption. The episode ended with me discussing the subject with my dad, whom I had always believed encouraged the practice of buffet burglary. He insisted I was mistaken.

I made a few jingles, including an intro theme in which I sang over some library music, recorded a non-self-lacerating intro while I was out for a walk with Rosie, watched a YouTube video about how to upload a podcast using SoundCloud, and I was all set.

Making the new podcast provided some welcome distraction from looking after Dad during his last months, and when he died at the end of November, the little funeral we had for him at a local church was attended by, among others, Dougie from Travis, our Channel 4 commissioner Peter Grimsdale and Joe, along with Joe's mum and dad. It was so good to have Joe there. After the funeral, he and his partner Annabel stayed over, and we watched some old BaaadDad bits from *The Adam and Joe Show* and reminisced. Joe said he'd been enjoying the podcast, and we agreed it was weird that Christmas was coming and someone else was going to be the guest on the Christmas episode after all the years at 6 Music when we'd record festive podcasts together.

So, I changed my 'No Cornballs' policy, and we've done a Christmas podcast together every year since, with the last couple in front of an audience of thousands at the Royal Festival Hall in London. The live shows are fun for us, but I know some listeners don't like live episodes because they feel you don't get the same intimacy and connection that you do when it's just two friends talking nonsense on their own. People really care about this stuff, you know. It's not some TV show or film. This is important.

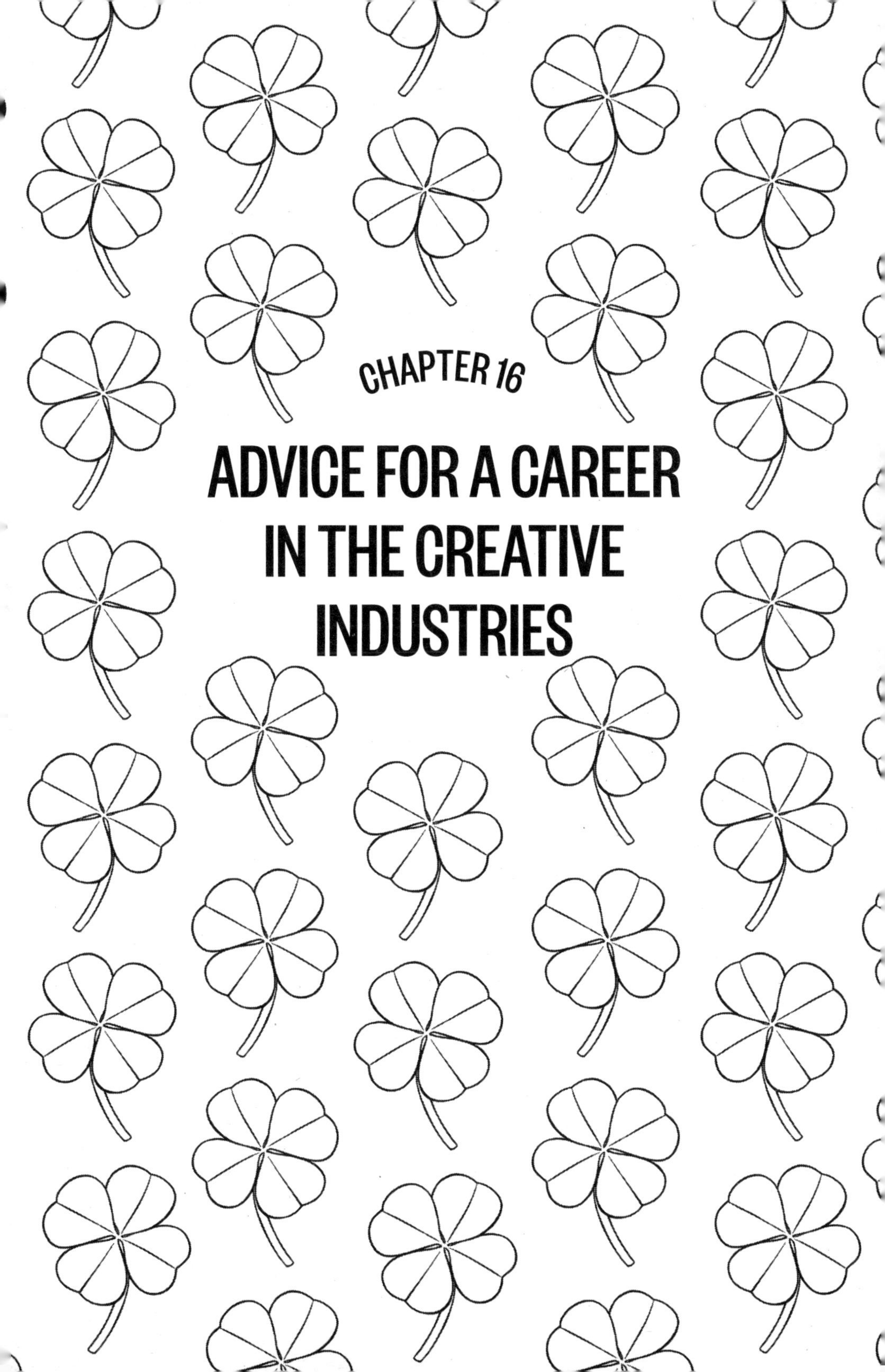

CHAPTER 16

ADVICE FOR A CAREER IN THE CREATIVE INDUSTRIES

Occasionally, people hoping to make a living from being 'creative' ask me for advice. When they do, it makes me feel a bit of a fraud because, as I've established in earlier chapters, I've never been much good at taking advice myself, and for the time being, my career continues despite not knowing what I'm doing, stumbling along and making things up as I go. But for what it's worth, these are some of the things that have helped me over the years.

Be Lucky

Luck has played a large part in helping me do most of the things I've been happiest with in my career. I appreciate that saying it's important to be lucky sounds about as helpful as suggesting people should try being talented, but there are ways to increase your access to luck, and chief among those is to be persistent.

Be Persistent

One of my dad's favourite quotes was from the thirtieth US president, Calvin Coolidge. Coolidge was strong on the economy, not so good on social justice, but he smashed it with words of wisdom and said in one of his biggest quote bangers:

Nothing in this world can take the place of persistence. Talent will not; nothing is more common than unsuccessful people with talent.

Genius will not; unrewarded genius is almost a proverb. Education will not; the world is full of educated derelicts.

Persistence and determination alone are omnipotent.

It's easy to be persistent when you're starting out and your enthusiasm is high, but it's when nothing seems to be happening and you're feeling discouraged that persistence becomes most valuable. Sometimes, when people hit a wall with their creative efforts, they feel the universe is telling them something, and they should switch course or give up entirely. That's when you have to stay Coolidge.

You can find another version of the same message in *The Secret of Succeeding at Success* by Yandrew, who sometimes does ads for Squarespace on my podcast:

Failure is the most important ingredient in the cake of success (you can find the full recipe behind a paywall on my website). No matter how many times you fail, YOU MUST NOT STOP. *Even if you fail so hard that your partner leaves you and your friends turn their back on you because what you're doing is so bad and they're embarrassed,* YOU MUST NOT STOP. *Even if you have failed so many times that it's obvious to everyone that you should be doing something else,* YOU MUST NOT STOP. *Even if you are training to be a surgeon and you fail the exams, keep going and do some surgery anyway. Even if you fail to stay alive,* YOU MUST NOT STOP.

If you carry on, your luck will change. OK, maybe it won't change so much that all your dreams immediately come true, but it will change. So hang in there.

The Big Questions

* *Would I like this if someone else was making it?*
* *Is what you're doing a worse version of something that already exists? If 'yes', find a way to make it your own, to improve it without being cynical and lazy. Or do something else.*
* *What is the thing I do best? That's a hard question to answer. Ask the friend you admire most.*

Make a Lot of Work

* *Think of ideas for pieces of work you can repeat in various forms that will evolve and improve.*
* *Figure out what works and what doesn't.*
* *Show your work to friends and notice what they respond best to.*
* *Work with other people if you can. You'll get more done, and another perspective will improve what you're doing, as long as you're not threatened by it and sulk like a baby when someone comes up with ideas that are better than yours.*
* *Find people with skills you don't have and harness them without exploiting them. Don't forget to give them proper credit, or they'll tell everyone what a dick you are on podcasts.*
* *Organise everything you make and file it properly so you can look back through it easily. The process of going through old ideas and finishing or repurposing them is central to staying productive, as long as you don't find yourself producing the same old shit over and over again.*

Stay in Your Comfort Zone

Speaking in Michael Apted's 1997 documentary *Inspirations*, David Bowie said that an artist should always feel a little bit out of their depth, 'And when you don't feel that your feet are quite touching the bottom, you're just about in the right place to do something exciting.' It's a quote that gets passed around social media as a brilliant insight into creativity, but whenever I see it, I feel it needs qualifying.

Getting out of your depth is all very well if you're David Bowie, aged 50, and you have vast reservoirs of innate talent, but for most ordinary mortals, the reverse is true. If you're lucky enough to find a comfort zone at all, I would advise staying there and getting as comfy as possible while hammering away at whatever you do for years and years until you're amazing at it. Then, by all means, shuffle over to the deep end.

Perhaps Bowie was trying to drown the competition.

Get a Useful Job

The best way to get a good job in the creative industry is to be related to someone already working there. If nepotism isn't an option and you have no luck applying for your ideal positions, try to get a job that will be at least tangentially useful for what you want to do.

Look for somewhere you could get some experiences that might feed into what you want to do, even if only as funny stories. If your colleagues include a diverse selection of idiosyncratic-but-likeable people who won't mind being turned into characters in a sitcom, so much the better.

Don't Be a Dick

Politeness, enthusiasm and initiative go a long way. When Garth Jennings was established in the pop-promo industry, he received a CV from someone applying for a position as a runner who had also included a colour chart, like a paint swatch, with circles of brown in every shade to demonstrate all the different strengths of tea and coffee he could make. Garth hired him immediately. 'Is there anything I can do?' is a phrase that always impresses unless you use it too much. There's a line between being proactive and being annoying. My advice is to stay on the not-annoying side of the line.

Don't Waste Time Writing Letters

Conventional wisdom is that writing a good cover letter can make or break your chances of getting hired in the media, film and TV industries because it allows you to show your personality, passion and potential to the employer. By all means, send examples of your work with a note including your contact details, but if you're spending ages writing letters you hope will impress someone so much that they'll find you a job, I think your time would be better spent having a wank.

When I was working on *Takeover TV* in 1994 and wondering what I would do next, I wrote to people I respected in television to see if I could get any job, paid or unpaid, on one of their productions. I sent letters to people including Chris Morris, Vic Reeves and Bob Mortimer, Harry Enfield, Janet Street-Porter and the producers of my favourite TV shows. Here's the one I wrote to Armando Iannucci:

28th October 1994

Dear Mr Iannucci,

I am writing to ask you to consider me for a position on any current or forthcoming production. The tape I have included contains examples of the kind of videos I make and have made for several years, some of which are due to be shown on Channel 4's 'Take Over TV' in the New Year. I have also been asked by the show's executive producer Fenton Bailey, to present an edition, so impressed was he by my overwhelming camera friendly talent.

I don't know if you're in a position to take people on for work experience, I suspect not, suffice to say that any opportunity you could afford me, writing researching or whatever, would be ideal. I will contribute in such an inspired and innovative yet obsequious and obedient way it may well frighten you.

However, please do not let this put you off. Perhaps I could just talk to you at some stage. Any advice you may have for me about pursuing a career in light entertainment would be greatly appreciated. I think you are the hooty mac.

Thankyou very much for your time

Yours sincerely,

Adam Buxton

I didn't get a single reply to any of the letters I sent. If I were writing something similar now, I'd probably keep it shorter and more specific and trim some of the attempts at wordy humour. I recall being very pleased with the 'hooty mac' line. It was a phrase implying that someone was smooth and suave that I'd heard Joe or Louis using after they heard it in a song by New Jack Swing innovators Bell Biv Devoe (who actually spelt it 'Hootie Mack'). I used the phrase a lot in the mid-Nineties and thought Armando would enjoy it, too. I pictured him asking someone what it meant and being flattered when he found out. Exactly ten years after I sent that letter,

I got to work with Armando on his show *Time Trumpet*. He didn't mention my letter or refer to himself as the 'Hootie Mack', though it was still what I considered him to be.

Commit

In 2009 my agent told me I'd been asked to audition for the main role in an ITV drama about a divorced alcoholic police detective. In one of the scenes I was sent to read, the surly DCI was at the bedside of a young woman who'd been hospitalised after being beaten up and sexually assaulted. 'I think this part might lie *outside* my specialised range as an actor,' I said to my agent, but she encouraged me to go along anyway. 'The producer really wants to see you,' she said. 'And you never know, something else might come of it.'

The following Monday, I went into ITV Studios on London's Southbank and met the casting agent and the show's producer, a big cheese at ITV who said he liked my work and was interested to see what I would make of a more serious role. I admitted to being surprised they thought I'd be a good fit, but I was ready to give it my best gritty policeman shot.

Over the weekend, I had decided to use an accent for the part. When we actors are trying to find our way into a role, an accent can sometimes help, but we need to be careful that the accent doesn't end up being a shield. The danger of choosing to do an accent is that it can lead to an actor doing an *impression* of a character rather than truly inhabiting the part using 'Acting'. On this occasion, I was going full 'shield' and using an accent that sounded like a cross between David Bowie and Keith Richards to deliver lines like, 'Did you get a good look at him? We're gonna catch this bastard.' Given that this was a serious drama, my accent choice wasn't so much a shield as a reinforced concrete wall with 'DON'T HIRE THIS GUY' painted on it in giant letters.

The first read-through was bad, and I was embarrassed. The idea that anyone thought I might have been right for this kind of part was so absurd, it crossed my mind that the audition might be a prank, although, with my accent choice, the producer may have wondered if I was the one doing the pranking. 'Shall we try another one and maybe just use your own accent?' he asked after my first attempt. The more naturalistic read was better, but it was obvious that I was still a long way from what they were looking for, so I said my goodbyes and went back to not being a divorced, alcoholic police detective.

Out in the corridor, the casting agent caught up with me. I was expecting her to thank me for coming in, but instead she said, 'You just talked yourself out of a part in there. If you don't want to do the audition, don't come in. You made us both look like idiots.' Still jangling from the humiliation of pretending to be a hard-bitten detective chief inspector in front of two other human beings, this dressing-down caught me off guard and I was defensive, but as I trudged out of the building into the sunlight, vowing never to audition for anything ever again, I knew the casting agent was right.

Acting, much as I love it and admire the people who do it well, is fundamentally fucking stupid and ridiculous, and the only way it stands a chance of being anything more than embarrassing and shit is if you commit 100 per cent, as you'd be told by the many jobbing actors who would have been delighted to get an audition like the one I'd just taken a giant crap over.

Take Advice with a Pinch of Salt

No one has the answer. The ones that say they do DEFINITELY don't.

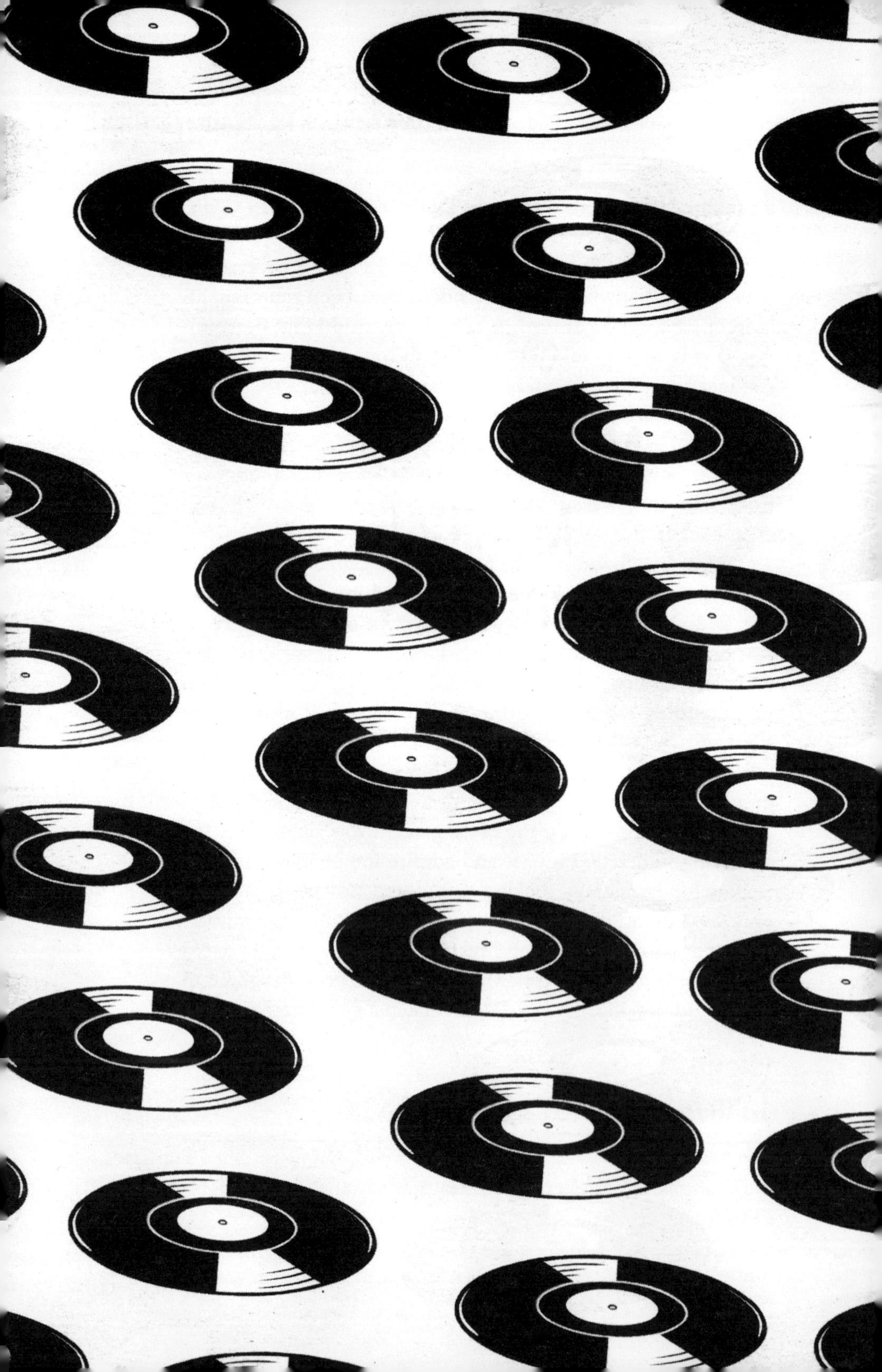

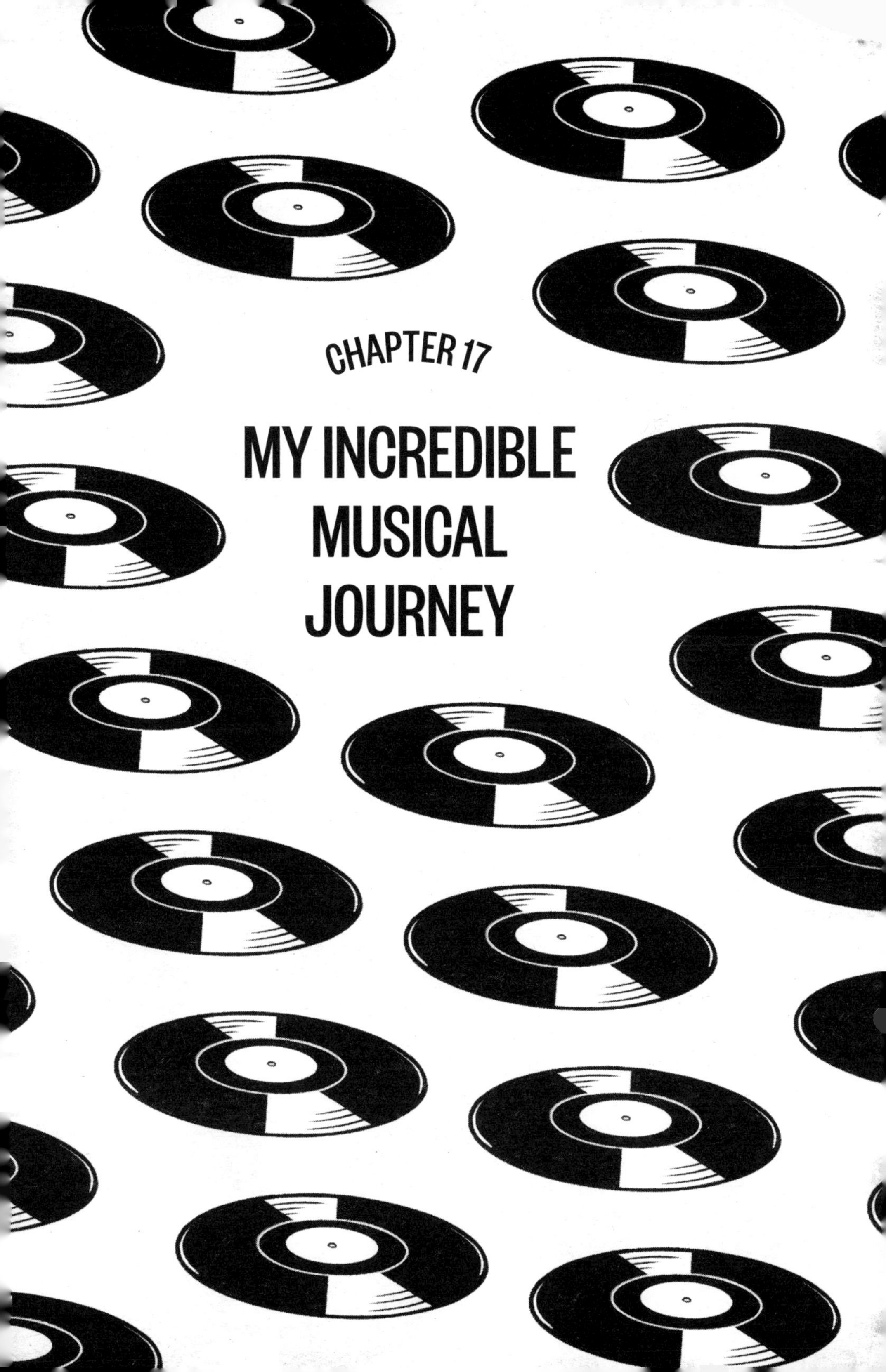

CHAPTER 17

MY INCREDIBLE MUSICAL JOURNEY

I'd love to write a song
That didn't sound wrong
I wish I knew
How the geniuses do it
I've tried to pick up tips
From songwriting guys
But when I tries
I always screw it
The problem often is I'm trying to be deep
Instead, I come off sounding like a mediocre creep
And I don't know where the music should go
I'm always hoping for surprises, but no
I go around in circles on the same old chords
Round and round and round and round I go
If it's a nice bit, then it's got to happen again
Is that true or not? I just don't know
Weird harmonies
And left-hand turns
Attempts at variety
Come off sounding forced and twee
I'd love to write a song
Well-structured and strong
That nerdy internet guys
Would cover and analyse
I know that it would be better
If this wasn't so meta

And came straight from the heart
The part I wish I could access
But I haven't the key

One of the many ways in which my wonderful wife is also a wonderful mother is that she forced all three of our children to have music lessons. They didn't like it, and relations between mother and child were frequently strained by angry protests at the extra work, but for two of them at least, the lessons were an important part of feeling that making music was an option, should they choose to do so. The other one was so bad that everyone was relieved when they stopped.

I don't remember being given the option to learn an instrument when I was young, but if I had been, I know that I too would have baulked at the increased workload. Instead, I grew up assuming music was something only naturally gifted people made. If only my potential had been tapped in its prime, just imagine how many more annoying songs I could have brought into the world.

My route into music was that of the non-musician. In my early twenties I made jingles and musical snippets for sketches on my Cheltenham radio show by singing over other people's music and layering up my voice on a 4-track tape recorder. For the musical numbers on *The Adam and Joe Show*, we relied mainly on the musical skills of our school friend Zac Sandler. Zac wrote and played the music for the original versions of 'The Footie Song', 'Roscoe' and 'What Do You Do?' He and Joe came up with most of the lyrics, I would contribute the odd brilliant line, the three of us would sing, and I was the producer.

When I got married in 2001, I wanted to put on a show for Sarah and our guests at the wedding reception. The members of Travis were there that day and Fran, the only person in the room with a bright pink mohawk, played 'Sing', and everyone sang, even Mum and Dad. Then, I surprised Sarah by also performing a couple of songs on the guitar, an instrument I'd never been able to play before. I had secretly bought one a few months earlier (a Godin A6 semi-acoustic) and, with the help of a friend (hello, lovely Graham Rawle!), I learned to play a rudimentary version of 'Kooks' by David Bowie and 'Take the Skinheads Bowling' by Camper Van Beethoven specially for the big day.

After the wedding, I was determined to carry on practising the guitar and start writing some of my own songs. Some of my first attempts were performed at live comedy shows in the early 2000s. I had a character called Famous Guy, inspired by rich, hell-raising actors who join bands, dress like leathery roustabouts, play earnest rock and get angry if journalists ask about the actor's forthcoming movie project instead of asking the rest of the band about their hobbies. One of my first original guitar compositions was for Famous Guy's band, Those Bastard People from the Town Over. It was a jaunty three-chord number called 'I Like to Rock', about all the things that Guy liked to do, including *rock*, *drink*, *fight* and, it was revealed in the final verse, *ski*.

Writing silly songs was all very well, but more than anything I yearned to write a 'proper song': something you'd want to listen to more than once, with a decent tune and lyrics that weren't simply amusing, but stirred the *deeper* emotions. I tried strumming some minor chords and intoning a few phrases about my hang-ups, but that didn't work at all. I needed to find a more circuitous route into my tortured psyche. So, for the sake of experimentation, I challenged myself to write about a subject I knew nothing about, hoping that in so doing, I might avoid my more introspective tendencies.

I set myself the task of recording a heartfelt song called 'We're the Jimi Hendrix Experience' after seeing the band's famous performance in D. A. Pennebaker's 1968 documentary

Monterey Pop, even though I knew almost nothing about Hendrix beyond the kind of information you'd find in the first few lines of a Wikipedia page. I wrote:

I'm Jimi Hendrix
I play in a band
There's just me on guitar
And there's Noel, the bassist
And Mitch, who's the drummer
We're the hard rocking sound
Of the Summer of Love, my friend
Check my technique
It's completely unique!
I use distortion and feedback
At maximum volume
And I laugh at convention
My guitar's an extension
Of my body and my soul

The music was lo-fi indie. Three chords on the guitar, a Neanderthal chorus riff and a beatbox, all drenched in effects, and deliberately unlike anything Jimi Hendrix ever recorded, mainly because I could barely play the guitar.

Twenty years later, digging out the Pro Tools session for the unfinished 'We're the Jimi Hendrix Experience', it was immediately clear what the project was: an exercise in overthinking and bet-hedging, doomed to fail from the moment I wrote the first verse. Was it supposed to be funny or serious? Sincere or ironic? It was like a suit of armour with 'Don't Judge Me!' scrawled all over it.

In 2007 I got the music-making software GarageBand and suddenly I had the tools to sound, if not sophisticated, at least musically competent. So I put my guitar away and set out on my digital jingle journey. For the next few years my 'Song Wars' entries and podcast jingles for the 6 Music show and then for my podcast were created with GarageBand, and its more professional cousin Logic Pro. I also relied on music-making gadgets equipped with buttons for every chord you could want and automatic accompaniment in a selection of styles, which varied from pleasingly kitsch to maddeningly grating (the part of the musical spectrum I always tend to drift back to).

In this period, the song that turned out the best, while not perhaps being particularly 'proper', was one that took the form of a plinky-plonky piece of educational children's music about counting, which I wrote in 2012 when I was starting to feel overwhelmed by the world as I approached middle age. Over the song's 100-second running time, we go from counting cakes, hats and fluffy cats to counting pennies, calories and non-stop problems until the inevitable zero-sum conclusion.

I recorded 'The Counting Song' for the TV version of *BUG*, where it was accompanied by an animated video by Cyriak Harris and Sarah Brown that perfectly realised the idea of a cheery kids' song that has made the obnoxious decision to tell toddlers the truth about what the world is *really* like..

RAMBLE

PARENTING WITH STAR WARS

There may have been a few kids who stumbled across 'The Counting Song' on YouTube and were left profoundly confused, which I don't feel good about. I'm probably also guilty of having supplied my own children with too much information about the adult world when they were little.

In 2014 my daughter Hope, then aged five, was going through a phase of being particularly chatty and enthusiastic, and she liked it when I would record some of our conversations for posterity. At the time, she was obsessed with the original *Star Wars* films, which she had begged to be allowed to watch after hearing about them from her older brothers, one of whom was so little when we watched the first film together that he later said his favourite parts were 'the scary dog and the Troom Storpers'. Perhaps I should have insisted Hope wait another couple of years before seeing the original *Star Wars* trilogy, but I gave in and she adored them.

One of the conversations we recorded was about the skimpy outfit Princess Leia is forced to wear by Jabba the Hutt in *Return of the Jedi*. Hope thought the monstrous bounty hunter had put together an excellent look for Leia and that the ensemble was very chic. I had tried gently to introduce the idea that for a woman to be forced to wear a sexy slave outfit was perhaps not in the best interests of the woman. Hope said she understood, but insisted it was still a great look, and if she were Leia she would escape from Jabba's clutches but keep the outfit.

An animation was made to go with the Slave Leia outfit conversation by the Brothers McLeod, and it was shown in a programme I presented for Sky Arts at the end of 2014 called *Adam Buxton's Shed of Christmas*. When the 'Five-Year-Old Girl Discusses Princess Leia's Slave Outfit' animation was uploaded to my YouTube channel in early 2015, it became a modest viral hit. George Takei, aka Mr Sulu in the original *Star Trek*, was one of the people who said how much they liked it on Twitter. But not everyone was a fan. What we now think of as the Culture Wars had begun heating up, and there were fierce disagreements in the comments section about the extent to which Hope was being indoctrinated by her *woke beta cuck* dad.

Ten years on, I feel OK about discussing the potential problems with Leia's slave dress with my five-year-old daughter, but I'm less confident about another *Star Wars* conversation we recorded around then.

Hope wanted to tell me how much she loved Han Solo and how she had admired the casual way he'd dispatched another bounty hunter, Greedo, in the Tatooine cantina at the beginning of the first film. Once again, wearing my *woke beta cuck* dad hat, I mentioned that she had seen the version of *Star Wars* that had been altered to make Han look as though he shot Greedo in self-defence, and that in the original Han had shot first. Hope said she didn't care because Greedo was a baddie. 'But what if Greedo had a family?' I said. Hope was silent for a little while, and I felt an icy flutter in my chest. I knew I'd been a jerk. It's all very well to encourage empathy in your children, but why complicate an innocent enjoyment of *Star Wars* in a child? Hope said on reflection that she felt sorry for Greedo and that maybe if things had been different, he could have been a good Jedi.

Watching *Star Wars* at five and my ham-fisted attempts at sensitive parenting don't seem to have done any serious damage so far. But if society crumbles, we get captured by bounty hunters and need to shoot our way out, I don't think Hope's going to be much help.

HAVE U SEEN MY PHONE CHARGER?

Many of my attempts at writing proper songs have ended up as jingles for my podcast. One of my favourites started life in 2017, when I was sorting through some of Dad's old books, and I found several by the British philosopher Roger Scruton, including his 1980 grumble banger *The Meaning of Conservatism*. Leafing through (how could you not?), I was struck by how similar many of Scruton's opinions on modern culture were to those of my dad. I googled Roger Scruton and came across a series of conservative grumbles he'd recorded for Radio 4 in 2015, just weeks before Dad died. One of them, *The Tyranny of Pop*, reminded me so much of my dad whanging on when I was first getting into pop music in the 1980s that I got quite nostalgic for the sententious cobblers he used to come out with. This passage from the Scrute could be a transcript of one of my dad's anti-pop stem-winders from those days:

> *I don't think we should underestimate the tyranny exerted over the human brain by pop. The constant repetition of musical platitudes, at every moment of the day and night, leads to addiction. It also has a dampening effect on conversation. I suspect that the increasing inarticulateness of the young, their*

> *inability to complete their sentences, to find telling phrases or images, or to say anything at all without calling upon the word 'like' to help them out, has something to do with the fact that their ears are constantly stuffed with cotton wool. Round and round in their heads go the chord progressions, the empty lyrics and the impoverished fragments of tune, and boom goes the brain box at the start of every bar.*
>
> *Roger Scruton,* The Tyranny of Pop, *2015*

The day I listened to *The Tyranny of Pop,* I'd been working on a new jingle for my podcast, which was an attempt to sound like a song that my son Frank had played me the night before. I'd said to Frank, 'What's a recent song that sounds modern?', and he played me 'Magnolia' by American rapper Playboi Carti. I wasn't sure if it was intentionally funny or not, but it made me laugh, especially at Carti randomly saying, 'What?' to punctuate the flow, so I stole that and added some lines based on a long phone conversation I'd overheard on a train about trying to locate a lost charger. I was channelling Dad for the voice of the charger hunter, but in the instrumental section I dropped in a few lines from the Scruton piece, and they fitted nicely.

I didn't agree with my dad or with Roger Scruton about the corrosive effects of pop music. In fact, Scruton also concedes that there is some worthwhile pop music, but curiously cites Metallica as an example because his son likes them. The part of Scruton's piece I did agree with was another of my dad's favourite grumbles: the inescapability of pop music in restaurants and pubs where it would be nice just to be able to talk without accompaniment from Ed Sheeran.

On several occasions I've gone for a meal with Sarah and the children and been sitting at a table right next to a speaker pumping out chart hits at builders' radio volume. In these moments I become my dad and ask our server whether the music might be turned down. If that isn't possible, but the speaker is within reach, I'll wait until we're alone again and surreptitiously disconnect the cable. I reconnect it when we leave, but my children cringe. They think disconnecting a speaker in a public place because you don't like the music is supremely dickish, something not even my dad or Scruton would have done. Part of me agrees with them, but the other part is congratulating myself for no longer having to strain to hear what's being said over the sound of hits. I feel the same way about music as I do about swearing: I love it, and it's great fun, but as far as possible I want to choose when to hear it, not have it forced on me.

Anyway, the result of all that was one of the best jingles I've ever made and maybe one of the best jingles of all time, though until they introduce a Jingle category at the GRAMMYs, you'll just have to take my word for it.

Buckle Up

'Have U Seen My Phone Charger?' is the only podcast jingle on my debut solo album, *Buckle Up* (2025). Rachel Holmberg, an executive from Decca who liked my podcast, first got in touch about the idea of putting out an album in 2019. I think she imagined me knocking together some slightly longer jingles and putting the resulting collection out that Christmas. Evidently, Rachel didn't realise she was dealing with a master of self-deluded over-complication. The album I wanted to make was more along the lines of Berlin-period Bowie and Eno going for lunch with Radiohead at Nina Simone and Brian Wilson's beach brasserie, where they'd be served delicious and innovative cuisine by Frank Ocean and Flight of the Conchords. It was as if I'd learned nothing from the 'We're the Jimi Hendrix Experience' experience.

Having agreed to make an album and with renewed resolve to finally write some 'proper songs', the months that followed were notably free of music making. I finished *Ramble Book*, the Covid-19 pandemic took hold, Mum died, society shifted in many profound ways and I made a few podcast jingles, but I was no closer to starting the album. Then Frank learned to play the guitar with lockdown lessons on Zoom from our friend Danny. Hearing Frank strumming away in his room eventually inspired me to rescue my Godin wedding guitar from the shed. I still couldn't really play it, but I loved cradling it as I sat at my desk, and when I needed a break I would pick out simple riffs. Trying to come up with music for a podcast, one day I recorded one of those guitar riffs on Logic and then started adding some jangly picking in layers to see where it went. The result, consisting of three chords and my riff, was beyond amateurish but it had a warm, analogue feel that was a refreshing contrast to the usual pristine, perfect pitch of my software instruments and Logic loops.

The music was too rough to work for the advert, but I thought maybe it could become a 'proper song'. After all, it wasn't *that* much more basic than some early tracks by bands like the Go-Betweens or Guided by Voices. But what to sing about? The news was dominated by Russia's invasion of Ukraine and Will Smith slapping Chris Rock at the Oscars. I didn't think I had anything the world needed to hear about either of those situations. Instead, as I often do, I looked closer to home.

Pizza Time

My son Nat was 18 at the time and had finished school a few months earlier. It was a relief that he no longer acted as though his family were the stupidest, most boring people in the world, and in our gratitude we'd agreed to let him enjoy a few months of doing more or less what he wanted before getting a job and figuring out what was next. For Sarah and me, this presented the constant challenge of picking the right moment to nag when he spent whole days watching box sets, playing *Fortnite*, drinking beer and eating only pizza. Actually, that isn't entirely fair. Sometimes he drove to McDonald's too.

On a couple of occasions when I found Nat standing by the oven in a bathrobe waiting for a pizza to cook at 11 in the morning, I failed to resist the impulse to remind him that this way of life couldn't last much longer. Robotically, I recited the same script my dad had recited to me when I was Nat's age. In those days, I, too, was happy to let weeks evaporate in clouds of spaghetti Bolognese, Pepsi and VHS rentals from the corner shop. That was the guy who made *The Adam and Joe Show*. Now that I was in my fifties, could I say for certain that the way I spent my days was so much more worthwhile than the way Nat spent his? Well, yes, I could, but it was hard to ignore the hypocrisy in my lectures.

Back in my study, I wrote:

My teenage son comes down the stair
Makes his way to the frigidaire
He's looking for pizza
He's pleased to find there's a pizza there
Slides it in the oven and ten minutes later,
It's pizza time

The rest of the lyrics came to me over the next day or two. Fairly literal stuff about trying to prevent your teenage child from making the same mistakes you've made while keeping in mind that your admonitions will only influence the person they eventually become up to a very limited point. It would be a shame to burn down that last carefree outpost of indolent joy before the adult world takes hold and life threatens to turn into 'The Counting Song'.

Recording that first demo of 'Pizza Time' was pure happiness, and when it was finished I went back over to my studio after supper and spent an hour listening to it over and over. There's a thin line between post-creation euphoria and smelling your own farts, but by the time I closed my laptop and headed up to bed, not only was I thinking about my speech for the GRAMMYs, I had emailed my 'Pizza Time' demo to Radiohead's guitarist and instrumental genius Jonny Greenwood.

I had seen Jonny in January 2022 after a performance by the other band he's in with Thom Yorke, the Smile, and when I told him I'd been working on music for an album, he said that I should feel free to send him anything if I ever wanted a second opinion. In the haze of the creative afterglow, I had fantasised that within ten minutes of receiving 'Pizza Time', Jonny would write back something like, 'Wow! This is great, Buckles. A proper song! Don't think you need to do anything else to it.' When two days had passed without a reply from Jonny, I started to feel a tickle of regret at having sent over the song so impulsively.

Then I listened to 'Pizza Time' again. I wondered if there was something wrong with my speakers. It didn't sound like the song I'd played on a loop just a couple of nights before. That song had been so jaunty and tuneful, so charmingly simple, so movingly direct. This one was stodgy and embarrassingly inept. No wonder Jonny hadn't replied. What had I been thinking? He didn't mean I should actually send him my demos; he was just being polite.

I tried to get some perspective. What did it matter what Jonny thought, anyway? Just because I like him personally, I respect his opinion, and I love the music he makes; why should that change how I feel about 'Pizza Time'? It shouldn't. But it did.

After a week had passed with no reply from Jonny, I never wanted to hear 'Pizza Time' again and wondered if it wasn't too late to return my advance from the record company. Then Jonny replied:

> Adam! Musically – harmonies/bass line all very nice. Quite 1988-like. I didn't ever listen to much Monochrome Set, but in my memory, they sounded like this. I think you're double-tracking the main vocal. I'm not sure that helps. Feels like you're trying to hide one voice behind the other same voice. No need. Lyrically feels a bit like you're in the uncanny valley between funny and sincere. I'm not sure anyone's ever made that work ... Wild card opinion though: you should make electronic music – all your jingles in the world have been really strong: I know they are often apple-based/library loops etc. but still. I think you'd free up your imagination being liberated from guitar chords. Hope this is more motivational than not. I don't doubt your musical ability, but it's sounding a bit hemmed in by the instrumentation at the moment. You did ask. Can we still be uneasy friends?

Jonny clearly hadn't loved 'Pizza Time', and I was still embarrassed to have put him in an awkward spot to service my craving for validation, but these were good notes and I was glad he'd replied. I wrote an email to say thanks, waited a week and then sent it.

'*The uncanny valley between funny and sincere*'. That was the note that stood out. I changed some of the lyrics to nudge 'Pizza Time' somewhere a tiny bit funnier and less cloying, and I recorded a new vocal. Jonny had correctly identified that the original had been double-tracked, i.e. two versions of the same vocal layered together, a trick I often use to beef up my voice. But he was right; even with the limitations laid bare, the single vocal is usually better and more direct.

I kept thinking about the '*uncanny valley*'. Was my album doomed to turn out like 'We're the Jimi Hendrix Experience' because I didn't have the skill to be sincere and wasn't content with trying to be funny? At supper that night, I outlined my quandary. 'Dad, I think you need to get a grip,' said Hope. 'Anyway, no offence, but who's actually going to listen to this album?'

It's now three years since I recorded my 'Pizza Time' demo. The album is finished thanks to my musical collaborators Pete Robertson, ex-Vaccines drummer turned producer who helped me re-record *Pizza Time*, and Joe Mount, the multi-instrumentalist mastermind behind one of my favourite bands, Metronomy. Joe agreed to be the overall producer on *Buckle Up*, and every few months, when he was back from tour, we'd spend two or three days at his home studio in Kent, sprucing up and re-recording some of my other attempts at 'proper songs'.

Joe Mount works fast and doesn't get bogged down, which is good for me because, left to my own devices, I tend to become Peter Bog-down-ovitch. Though Joe didn't dismiss my grand ambitions for the album out of hand, he showed me it was more practical and more fun to make the best of what was already in my musical locker rather than torturing myself trying to be what I wasn't. He was encouraging me to 'find my voice', I guess.

As for a song that gets closest to me being myself, it's probably the one that's barely a song at all: 'Standing Still', written on a sad morning after Mum died.

Every single morning
I make myself a tea
I pour it in the cup
And then I pour it into me
When the tea is finished

I make myself another
The tea is helping me
With all the thoughts I have to smother

I'm not sure I completely escaped the uncanny valley, or, for that matter, wrote anything that could be called a proper song, but it's only album number one. You won't be able to move for self-assured authenticity on my second album, which, given my work rate so far, should be out some time around 2040 or shortly before my death, whichever comes first.

CHAPTER 18

I LOVE YOU, BYE

They say you face death the same way you face life.

I'm hoping that means there'll be wine and snacks (maybe some sweet-chilli-flavoured morphine), and overall I'll be feeling OK about death as long as I haven't been on the internet that day. Or maybe facing death the same way I face life means that in my final months, I'll be doing a podcast about dying. Imagine how poignant that final 'I love you, byeee!' will be. Although what will probably happen is that when I'm a few weeks from death, Louis will also get terminally ill and do a much more successful terminal-illness podcast in which famous philosophers, spiritual leaders and musicians visit his deathbed to read poetry, share deep thoughts and perform heart-rending versions of their best-known songs (plus one from their new album). Louis will live long enough to record two series and a Christmas special and collect an armful of awards. Meanwhile, I'll end up dying as I'm struggling to sort out audio problems with my last guest on Zoom.

* * *

I didn't say 'I love you, bye' to my mum before she died because I didn't think she was going to go when she did. If someone at the hospital had said, 'There's nothing more we can do, so get those final words and podcast catchphrases ready,' I'd like to think I'd have come up with something worthwhile. But that isn't the way things work.

The night after she died, I sat under the stars in my favourite camping chair and listened to one of Mum's favourite songs, 'One Day I'll Fly Away' by Randy Crawford. With its lush arrangement and wistful lyrics, it could be a classic Bond theme in the mould of 'You Only Live Twice' or 'We Have All the Time in the World', another two tracks Mum loved that also made my heart soar many times over the years.

Listening to 'One Day I'll Fly Away' and looking up at the stars on a warm, clear night would usually have made me smile with a sense of goofy universal oneness. But that night, the song's wistful lyrics – 'I follow the night, Can't stand the light, When will I begin, My life again?' – suddenly seemed ghoulish. Before I knew it, I was gripped by fear and loneliness as one of the most beautiful songs ever written mutated into a supernatural lament for a cold cosmos. I resisted the urge to take out my headphones and told myself to get a grip, but for a while, there was no grip.

A few weeks later, my phone pinged. 'You have a new memory,' it said, and up popped a slide show featuring photos of Mum accompanied by some cheesy guitar music. Included in the short slide show were pictures I'd taken at the hospital when I still thought we'd be going home and that Ma was going to live with us for at least a few more years. Other than being another example of the arseholiness of AI, this felt like the universe telling me something. 'You take too many photos', perhaps.

Negative Creep

If your idea of a good time is to listen to a middle-aged man howling from a pit of despair while trying to sound upbeat on a podcast, look up my second appearance on Cariad Lloyd's *Griefcast*. I recorded it just after I'd spent most of the day looking through Mum's haunted boxes and staring at photographs of us all when everyone was alive and happy. I got emotional telling Cariad about the feeling I'd had while I was looking at those photos. The feeling that it was all over.

Of course, I understood the part of my life in the photographs was over; much as I may resent Time, I do understand how it works. Instead, the thing that intensified the grief was the feeling that the *fun* was over. It seemed to me that Mum's death marked the end of the largely carefree playground part of my life, and all that remained was the bumpy slide towards the final sandpit.

I don't feel that way anymore. Not all the time. Fun creeps back. I've realised I need to stop thinking of the past as a place where things are better, and instead think of it as a place where something wonderful hasn't yet happened. I might get that printed on some mugs and T-shirts and sell them on Etsy.

A few weeks after I'd recorded *Griefcast*, I was in my study catching up on some procrastinating, and I looked over at a pile of negatives waiting to be scanned. Come on, Buckles, I told myself. You've really got to move on. So I took a deep breath, gathered an armful of negatives and dumped them all in the waste basket.

It felt so wrong. Quite apart from the worry that I was denying myself the chance to glimpse one more unfamiliar moment of my mum's life, everyone knows you shouldn't put all your negs in one basket.

Dear Mummy,

How are you? I am fine.

I wrote a letter to Dad at the end of Ramble Book, so I thought I should write you one too, especially as you were the one who believed in heaven.

Firstly, I wanted to check if you were OK with the stuff about you in this book. I did ask a few times while I was writing it, but I didn't hear anything back. I wonder if you think I talk about you and Dad too much in general and that airing my hang-ups and insecurities so freely is a bit 'wet'. I suspect you'd have agreed with the American director John Waters, who said during an interview I saw on YouTube:

> *If you haven't gotten over some things, you can blame your parents until you're 30. But after 40s, forget whining about anything. Everybody's dealt a hand. Everybody has ups and downs. You can't order your kids. You can't order up your parents. You just popped here. And you're cast with whatever's in you. And you have to make the best you can with that character.*

I don't think you ever saw any films by John Waters. In one of his most famous early movies, Pink Flamingos, a big drag queen called Divine picked up some real dog shit and ate it. That's even worse than Long Shot with Seth Rogen, isn't it? And yet, at the risk of alienating therapists everywhere, I do think John Waters has a point when it comes to resisting the urge to whine about your parents.

You would never have done it, would you, Mum? But you were always more stoical than I. Instead of dwelling on misfortune, you preferred to pour another glass of wine and appreciate what made you happy about the world: the people you loved, books, music, TV and films, walks by the river in Sonning, going to church, tending to the flowers in your garden and working on your embroidery. Thanks to Sarah, we still have that embroidery, reminding us of you around the house, with some pieces in frames and others on the covers of comfortable cushions that Rosie only seldom violates.

I also think about you whenever I see the Bollox to Brexit sticker on the door of the fridge. We argued about Brexit a few times, remember? I thought it was a mistake to turn our back on the ideals of cooperation symbolised by the European Union, whereas you were looking forward to taking back control of our destiny and making Britain great again. Nowadays, everyone's making things great again. You would have loved it.

Anyway, a few weeks after the referendum, you visited for the weekend and gave me the Bollox to Brexit sticker. I knew it wasn't meant as a taunt or a patronising gesture of consolation. You knew how I felt and thought I would appreciate the sticker. You may also have known that I always liked spelling 'bollocks' with an 'x'.

I will also think of you laughing whenever I see Monty Python's Life of Brian. Remember how much you loved 'Always Look on the Bright Side of Life'? I thought of playing that song at your memorial, but it gets played a lot at funerals, so we went for another of your favourites instead. The vicar said, 'Now, I think Nathaniel Buxton is going to play something by the Beatles on the piano?' There were a few chuckles when Nat started to play 'Something' by the Beatles. OK, maybe it was just one chuckle from our friend Danny. Nat played the song so beautifully that the combination of parental pride, the loveliness of the music and the sadness that you weren't there to hear it left me struggling with an 'Emoverload'.

At the end of the service, we walked out to another song that you loved: 'One Day I'll Fly Away' by Randy Crawford. In the order of service, I put a picture of you as a young flight attendant beneath the title, which is cheesy, but I thought you'd forgive me.

Do you get full access to BBC Sounds up there, or are certain programmes blocked for rights reasons? I ask because I was interviewed by Kirsty Young the other day, and I thought you'd be impressed. No, I'm afraid it wasn't for Desert Island Discs. It was her show Young Again, the one where guests give advice to their younger selves.

Actually, I don't know how much you would have enjoyed it. I talked about you and Dad again, and I came away feeling I'd overshared even more than usual, perhaps because I was nervous. It's Kirsty Young, after all! Towards the end of the interview, when she asked what I'd learned about myself, I completely dried up, as if I'd forgotten the premise of the show.

I did actually write down a few bits of advice for my younger self after I was invited to be on Young Again, but it was mainly the sensible but boring stuff I tell the boys now that they're in their twenties: Read more. Drink less. Eat better. Get up earlier. All the things Dad advised me to do when I was a young man. When I say to the boys that I wish I'd appreciated how important those things were when I was their age, they nod and then totally ignore me. Exactly as I did with Dad.

Other advice for my younger self: Try to be more positive. Have more adventures. Don't lick the back of a metal ice tray. Learn to play an instrument. Start a band, and don't worry if it's shit. Don't mix cleaning fluid and bleach. Ask Mum more questions about her life.

I really wish I'd done that last one. While we're on the subject of regrets, apart from being sorry that I wrote so seldom and that I didn't take your side more when you were arguing with Dad, I hope you know how sorry I am that I didn't do more to prevent you from dying. I really feel I let you down there. People keep telling me there wasn't anything more I could have done, but I don't know. Anyway, I really am so sorry. Can I send you something by way of apology? A nice bottle of wine or a Fortnum's hamper? Do let me know the address when you get a moment.

But I also wanted to say thanks. I wasn't ungrateful while you were alive, I hope, but it won't hurt to set a few down for the record:

Thanks for all the driving to and from school, to parties miles away in the country, to college, to the airport … so much driving! Getting into the car with you at the end of term at boarding school in the early Eighties and munching the raisin and biscuit Yorkie you'd brought me as we drove home along the A24 listening to Kenny Everett on Radio 2 – now that was a good feeling.

Thanks for taking me to see Star Wars, buying me all those Star Wars toys and keeping them safe in the loft all those years. It was a headache for the Channel 4 legal department when we used them in The Adam and Joe Show, but it was great for us. And thanks for all the other trips to the cinema and all the Fruit Pastilles once we were there.

Thanks for lending me your make-up and showing me how to apply it, not only when I was afflicted by volcanic outbreaks of bad skin as a teenager but also when I just wanted to look more intense and interesting.

'Are you wearing eye liner?' friends would ask.

'No, I just have very dark lashes,' I would reply. 'I get it from my mum; she's South American.'

Thanks for those amazing birthday cakes. The children still talk about how delicious they were. Speaking of the children, thanks for looking after them whenever we asked and for insisting each time that they were unusually gifted and special. Come to think of it, you always did the same with me.

I need to finish this book now. I've been stuck in the past too long. Not that I have a problem with the past anymore – I like to think of it as a place where something wonderful hasn't yet happened. No, not Brexit.

I love you, Mum. Bye.

ACKNOWLEDGEMENTS

AUDIOBOOK

The audiobook version of *I Love You, Byeee* features a specially recorded conversation with Joe about this book as well as jingles, music clips, and a bonus chapter about David Bowie in the mid-Nineties.

For playlists containing music mentioned in this book, visit Spotify and search for therealadambuxton

My website: adam-buxton.co.uk

Joe Cornish's Instagram: mrjoecornish

THANKS

Everyone who worked on *The Adam and Joe Show*, especially Debbie Searle, Rob Baker, Toby Welfare, Ruth Phillips, John Gannon, Grainne Jordan, Anna Pocock, Matt Reid, Louise Holmes, Paul Young, Jo Chiles, Michelle Kinsler, Annabel Raftery, Annette Gordon, Martin Phipps, Jon Willis, Mark Lambert, Loretta De Souza, Cheryl Taylor, Andrew Newman and Peter Grimsdale.

Paul, Glynn, Bill Bruno and Tonya Shaw at CD603.

Andy Ashton, Matt Everitt and our Xfm producers Lila Dowie, Brian Murphy and Xanthe Fuller.

James Stirling, Lucy Winter, Ben Appleyard, Charlotte Guzzan, Jude Adam, Claire Slevin, Leslie Douglas, Shaun Keaveny, Edith Bowman and all at the Big British Castle.

Fran Healy, Dougie Payne and Travis, Ed O'Brien, Jonny and Colin Greenwood, Nigel Godrich and Radiohead, M.E.S, Frank Black, Brian Eno, Zavid (obvs), Spoon, Daudi Matsiko, Laura Marling and Richard Dawson.

Joe Mount, Pete Robertson and all at Decca, especially Rachel, Fiona, Emma and Jude.

Caroline Chignell, Peter Bennet-Jones, Becca Ptaszynski, Magda Bird, Jennifer Rhodes, and all at PBJ.

Séamus Murphy Mitchell, and all at Acast.

Louise Stephens, David Knight, Phil Tidy, Miland Suman, Stuart Brown, Clive Tulloh, Nicky Waltham and the *BUG* team.

Fenton Bailey, Randy Barbato and all at World of Wonder.

Liam Miller, Langdon Page, Maria Victoria Birrell and Heather Inglis.

Sue Terry Voices.

Jack Fogg, Joel Simons, Fionnuala Barrett, Terence Caven, Simeon Greenaway, Simon Gerratt, Gaurika Kumar, Sarah Burke, Orlando Mowbray, Alex Layt, Tom Dunstan, Dean Russell, Steve Burdett, Wilf Dickie and all at HarperCollins.

Helen Green.

Janice, Christine, Jonathan, Trevor and Ross.

Woz, Garth, Suzi, Ed, Tilda, Sandro, Annabel, Nancy, Steph, Jo, Chris, Lydia, Richard, Mark, Ziv, Ben, Patrick, Julia, Julian, Miriam, Johnni and Karen.

Clare and David.

Joe, Louis and Zac.

My wife, children and Rosie.

You.

I love you, byeeeee!

Adam Buxton, April 2025

To Johnny,

with best wishes,

Elaine Pearson